84942

E
185.93
Sterkx   **WITHDRAWN**   L6
S7

The free Negro in ante-bellum
Louisiana

Date Due

OCT 25 '78			
OCT 18 '89			
MAY 3 0 2002			

The Free Negro
in Ante-Bellum Louisiana

Mr. Sterkx is also the author of

Partners in Rebellion: Alabama Women in the Civil War

The Free Negro in Ante-Bellum Louisiana

H. E. Sterkx

Rutherford • Madison • Teaneck
FAIRLEIGH DICKINSON UNIVERSITY PRESS

© 1972 by Associated University Presses, Inc.
Library of Congress Catalogue Card Number: 76-146165

Associated University Presses, Inc.
Cranbury, New Jersey 08512

ISBN: 0-8386-7837-8
Printed in the United States of America

Contents

Tables

Preface

To revive a doctoral dissertation almost two decades old requires the courage of youth and the ego of a gamecock. The author readily declares himself as being neither one nor the other, but one who is still possessed with that compelling drive to produce something that might merit the attention of both scholars and general readers. In pursuit of this goal, a considerable amount of the original material has been revised and new archival sources consulted in a premeditated effort to upgrade the new product.

It was surprising how little of the material on this subject has been added to libraries and archives of the Southern region and indeed of the nation. There still seems to linger the atmosphere that it is something which should be "kept under wraps": a 19th-Century "no-no," which is none of the 20th Century's business. Perhaps the descendants of articulate free Negroes want it that way. However, such reticence is groundless, for the survivors can be proud of many of their ancestors' accomplishments.

During the long period from 1724 to 1860, there were free Negroes (or free persons of color, or free colored persons—as they were variously called by their contemporaries) in every walk of life. They were planter-aristocrats, members of the professions, skilled artisans, unskilled laborers, ladies, gentlemen, soldiers, whores, and just plain folk struggling to survive in a social environment geared in law and tradition to tolerate only Whites and slaves. Yet it would be an exaggeration to say that the free Negro had a perfectly horrid time, just as it would be an understatement to say that he had an easy life. The overwhelming majority were an admixture of Negro and White in various color combinations, commonly designated as mulatto, quadroon, octoroon. A considerable number could claim blood relationship with some of the "best families" of White Louisiana. For this reason more than any other, they fared much better than their "half cousins"—the Black slaves.

In truth, this group was an anomalous class: too proud to identify with the slave and stigmatized by Whites for being Negro; they were indeed "neither fish, nor fowl, nor red herring." They originated during the French and Spanish colonial period, and much of their status as quasi-citizens—which included certain civil and economic rights—carried over into the American period. They could own property, bear witness in court, make wills, and in rare cases cast votes through the sufferance of conniving politicians. Their numbers grew during the opening years of the 19th Century, because of immigration from the war-torn island of Haiti. There were, to be sure, efforts to stop such immigrants, and even more stringent measures were effected against those coming into Louisiana from other states of the United States. Private emancipations and the inevitable consequence of natural increase accounted for further enlargement of this population until by 1860 it numbered over 18,000.

By in large, most lived out their lives as ordinary persons as did their White neighbors, but there were those whose "high living" evoked much interest in the South and notoriety in the free states. Leading the list were the famed quadroon beauties whose balls attracted white lovers and where extra-legal liaisons came into being. Such was the unusual: the majority engaged in more acceptable forms of social outlets. More than a few became devout members of the various Christian denominations of Louisiana. Some excelled in the fine arts, mechanical skills, as farmers, as planters, and in the field of literature. Others sought satisfaction in education in Louisiana or Europe.

Even with all these apparent advantages the knowledge that they could not be equal to Whites hovered over them; astonishingly enough, no campaign was ever launched by the free Negroes to acquire the privileges that belong to all Americans. Undoubtedly, the timid as well as the bold knew that stepping out of caste would have brought about punitive action. A deferential, but not cringing posture toward the White majority was thus adopted by free Negroes in order to survive, but they lived in constant fear of mounting anti-free Negro forces as the race question grew more and more heated during the 1850s. In fact, as the ante-bellum period drew to a close, a small but especially vocal White minority passionately dedicated themselves to ridding the state of this class. They were accused of violating almost every code of decent behavior, but were especially singled out as suspect agents of the dreaded Northern abolitionists. Fortunately, the extremists failed in their original purpose. There was still that something which Louisianians of calmer dispositions could not effect: the forcible expulsion of the entire free Negro population. Perhaps there was also the knowledge that the state could not function without free Negroes in their respective fields of endeavor, nor could any White relish the idea of expelling kinsmen even though such persons had become in their estimation dangerous persons.

A studied effort has been made to treat the subject objectively. If any prejudices show through it is in favor of the oppressed minority. Such, however, should not be construed as an indictment of the mass of White Louisianians of the period, but only against those few who would have inflicted serious harm against a defenseless and sophisticated race.

In the main it is not a happy history, though as usual life went on as it always has in the past. It is also a microscopic account of only one of the many byproducts of slavery in a deep South state before the Civil War. Some of it is dull, some silly and stupid if equated with 20th-Century standards, but at no time is the subject insignificant. The drive towards social democracy never is.

There are many former mentors and friends to whom I must express deep gratitude for helping make this study possible. At the head of a long list are the late Professors Frank L. Owsley and James B. Sellers. In particular I am in debt to Professor Hugh C. Bailey of Sanford University whose encouragement during graduate days was a source of strength. Librarians and archivists mentioned in the bibliography are due thanks for not only donating their time, but actually went out of their way in making piles of manuscript materials available to me.

The Free Negro
in Ante-Bellum Louisiana

1

Origin and Status of the Free Negro during the French Colonial Period

O VER the years Louisiana has won the reputation of being vastly different from all of the fifty United States. Whether it deserves such a reputation or not, few of the other commonwealths experienced a more hectic and rapid change of colonial masters and fewer still retained a colonial culture for a longer period of time as has the well-named Creole state. The rule of France, Spain, and Anglo-America bequeathed colorful legacies in languages and law, but none has been so colorful as the ethnic make-up of its people.

Louisiana[1] came into existence under French domina-

---

1. During the French colonial period Louisiana extended from the Appalachian Mountains on the east to the Rocky Mountains on the west. On the south from the Gulf of Mexico to the Great Lakes on the north. For the purposes of this book, the present boundaries of the state will be followed. As such, Louisiana lies roughly between the 33° Parallel of north latitude and the Gulf of Mexico; and between the Sabine River on the west and Mississippi and Pearl Rivers on the east.

tion during the second decade of the 18th Century. After failing to discover fabled mineral resources, the Gallic colonists turned to agricultural pursuits and promptly introduced Negro slave labor to help work the soil. These two innovations not only insured the permanence of the colonial experiment, but also ushered in centuries of economic affluence as well as grinding poverty.

The privilege of sending Negro slaves was at first given to Antoine Crozat. In 1712, the canny French capitalist was awarded the exclusive right to send "a ship to Africa for Negroes" once a year, during a fifteen-year period.[2] In addition he was granted the power to establish a governing body, which soon became known as the Superior Council.[3]

Crozat's company failed to supply the colony with sufficient slaves, for, by 1716, only a few of them were found in the vicinity of Mobile and Dauphine Island.[4] In 1717 the Crozat company was forced to surrender its

2. Charles E. Gayarré, *History of Louisiana,* I, 102.

3. Henry P. Dart, "A Criminal Trial Before the Superior Council of Louisiana, May, 1747," *Louisiana Historical Quarterly,* XIII (1930), 367. The Superior Council, 1712–1769, was the center of civic activity in the French colony. It was the place of registry of deeds and mortgages, and slave emancipations. It was not only the place where the vital statistics of the colony were recorded and preserved but it was also the repository of all documents, papers and agreements needed to establish rights and protect property. It was set up by the king and he appointed members who served at his pleasure. It had jurisdiction over all cases, civil and criminal. The Council, as a court, held weekly sessions. The personnel of the court consisted of three principal officers: a Governor, Ordonnateur, and the Lieutenant in command of the military forces, with two residents of the colony chosen from those best fitted to exercise judgment and common sense in the determination of the business of the court. It had a Procureur General (attorney general) sent by the king. A particular feature of this court was its rule by majority. It interpreted and applied the Custom of Paris, the General Law of France, and the contemporaneous French law of Civil and Criminal Procedure.

4. Gayarré, *History of Louisiana,* I, 161.

concessions to the King.⁵ In the same year, the Mississippi Company was given commercial and governmental privileges in Louisiana for a 25-year period. In addition to searching for precious minerals, the company was to concern itself with the development of agriculture, and obligated itself to transport to the colony six thousand White inhabitants and three thousand Negroes.⁶ In the following years, serious efforts were made to comply with this provision and the company sent a number of Negro slaves to the infant colony. With these actions the Negro became a fixed and essential element in the population of Louisiana.

Almost coincident with slavery was the appearance of free Negroes. During the ancient regime in Louisiana such persons were designated as *nègre libre, négresse libre* and collectively called *gens de coleur libre.* These terms were used in the records of the French authorities and the Roman Catholic Church to identify those still in bondage and to distinguish them from those persons of African extraction who were no longer slaves.

It is not possible to date the first appearance of free Negroes in the Louisiana colony. No doubt there were people of this class by 1724, as attested to by the marriage of the free Negroes Jean Baptiste Raphael and Marie Gaspar in the St. Louis Church of New Orleans. Raphael was a native of Martinque, and his bride was an emancipated slave of the province of Louisiana. Little else is known about the early arrivals except that a few came to Louisiana from the English colonies of North America and the French possessions in the West Indies. Jean Mingo, a free Negro from the English colony of

5. *Ibid.,* I, 184.
6. *Ibid.,* I, 204.

Carolina, for instance, celebrated the "sacrament of mat-
rimony" with the slave Thérèse in 1727. Two years later
one named Babé, a free Negress from St. Domingo, married a slave belonging to the Mississippi Company.[7]
Apart from outside sources substantial numbers of free
Negroes came into being through the emancipation
clauses of the *Code Noir*.

In 1724, the Superior Council adopted the Royal regulations pertaining to the governing of slaves known as
the Black Code of Louisiana. In this body of laws there
also were provisions allowing slave owners to free slaves.
This right fell to owners over 25 years old. The permitted methods were either by last will and testament
or by the execution of a deed between the slave and
master. In emancipating slaves the owner was required
to secure permission from the Superior Council before
such an action was declared legal. "This permission will
be granted," read the law, "without cost when the motives of the master have been shown to be legitimate."
Any "enfranchisement" without the required permission
was automatically deemed null and void.[8] This provision
was purposely made stringent to prevent private emancipations from proliferating without governmental supervision and control.

The Black Code also provided ways for effecting automatic emancipations. For example, a slave appointed as
a teacher of the master's children was held to be auto-

---

7. MS. Marriage Register of St. Louis Church, New Orleans, July 1,
1720 to December 4, 1730.

8. *La Code Noir, ou Recueil des Reglemens rendus jusqu'à présent.
Concernant le Gouvernement, l'Administration de la Justice, la police,
la Discipline & le Commerce des Negres dans les Colonies Francoises.
Et les Conseils Compagnies etablie à ce Suject*, 310–311. Hereinafter
this work will be cited as *The Black Code*.

matically free.[9] Free Negroes were allowed one method of manumission of slaves denied to white persons; if a free Negro were "married during his concubinate with his slave and shall marry her according to the prescribed rules of the Church, then by this act she will be [automatically] enfranchised and the children made free and legitimate."[10]

Once freed Negroes were released from all responsibilities, services and rights their former master had assumed "regarding their persons, possessions and successions, as owners."[11] Moreover, emancipated persons were entitled to the same rights, privileges, and immunities enjoyed by free born subjects.[12] The Code provided that "the merits of an acquired liberty might produce in them the same feeling which the happiness of natural liberty gives to our other subjects."[13] The Black Code followed the ancient practice of sanctioning the perpetuation of the free Negro by allowing the status of the child to follow that of the mother.[14] Such a rule tended naturally to enlarge the number of free Negroes.

The manumission of slaves by deed and will, was well under way by the first half of the 18th century. Many achieved free status solely for charitable or humanitarian reasons, while emancipation by legislative act accounted for the freedom of a number of others. Slaves freed by the latter method usually earned their liberty by some meritorious act or action in behalf of the colony in times of danger or serious crisis.

---

9. *Ibid.*, 311.
10. *Ibid.*, 286–287.
11. *Ibid.*, 312.
12. *Ibid.*, 313.
13. *Ibid.*
14. *Ibid.*, 288–289.

Among the first owners in the colony to emancipate a slave was no less a person than its governor. On October 1, 1733, Jean Baptiste le Moyne, Sieur de Bienville, by deed, emancipated his two slaves—Jorge and his wife, Marie—in recognition of faithful service during twenty-six years.[15] Among ordinary folk, Adrienne Houmard of Point Coupee district, emancipated her sixty-year-old Negress slave, Françoise, for faithful service to the family.[16]

A considerable number of colonists on manumitting their slaves revealed a genuine affection for the Negro, and at the same time disclosed additional motives for emancipation. Joseph Meunier, on March 28, 1736, freed his twelve-year-old slave, Marie, because she had served him well and was affectionate toward him. Meunier desired her emancipation at this particular time because he was leaving for the Chickasaw war and did not know whether he would ever return.[17] Two years later, on September 5, 1738, Meunier was again called into service to fight Indians. Before departing he filed a nuncupative will granting freedom to several other Negroes belonging to his household. In a will Meunier gave specific instructions directing his executor to protect the former slaves and "raise their children in the fear of God."[18] Later, Meunier and his wife petitioned the Governor for permission to manumit the slave, Françoise, and her son. This act of emancipation was to take effect on the death of Meunier. Françoise and her son were given their free-

15. Heloise H. Cruzat (trans.), "Records of the Superior Council of Louisiana," *Louisiana Historical Quarterly,* V (1922), 250. This work will be hereinafter cited as Cruzat (trans.), "Records of the Superior Council of Louisiana."

16. *Ibid.,* XXIII (1940), 603.

17. *Ibid.,* VII (1925), 287.

18. *Ibid.,* X (1927), 121.

dom because she had faithfully cared for her master during his long illness. Governor Vaudreuil and the Attorney General, d'Auberville, approved and confirmed these manumissions on July 14, 1744.[19]

Another soldier, Sieur Jacques de Coustilhas, on August 26, 1736, before departing for the Indian wars, left a will granting freedom to his Negro slave Conrad, Catherine, his wife, and their four children.[20]

In some cases a slave was granted freedom on condition that he remain in service until the death of the owner. For example, François Trudeau, a member of the Superior Council, emancipated his slave, Jeanneton, "for her zeal and fidelity in his service," provided she continue to serve him the rest of her life.[21] In 1743, Governor Bienville, on the eve of his departure for France, manumitted one of his slaves, Jacob, with the condition that the latter serve his former master, or his representative, for a period of five years. It was further stipulated that Jacob was to be supported "in health as well as treated during illness, by those who will employ him in M. de Bienville's name." After the termination of the five year period the black man would be "perfectly free" to enjoy the privileges of all free men.[22] Another case of deferred emancipation occurred when a Dr. Antoine Meuillion of Point Coupee, granted freedom to Charlotte and her son, Louis, to take effect on his return to France or in case of his death. Until that event, Charlotte and her son were to continue to serve Meuillion as his slaves.[23]

---

19. *Ibid.*, XIII (1930), 141.
20. *Ibid.*, VI (1923), 303–304.
21. *Ibid.*, V (1922), 403.
22. *Ibid.*, VII (1924), 637.
23. *Ibid.*, XV (1932), 133–134.

It was not uncommon for slaves to be rewarded with emancipation after performing some public service to the community. Such a condition was imposed on the slave of a Sieur Bertrant Joffré, alias La Liberté, in 1747, who directed the following in his will that he did not know:

> a better way of rewarding the service that was rendered, and is being daily rendered to him, by one Jenneton, his negress slave . . . and little daughter about six years old; and intending to set her and her child free . . . begs the Governor . . . for permission to grant said freedom upon condition . . . that after his death she be placed in the hospital for the Poor in this city [New Orleans] to assist the sick for the term of two years in succession, her own and her child's maintenance to be provided during such time.[24]

Jenneton complied with these conditions, and was consequently granted the highly prized freedom.

Freed Negroes had the right to petition the Superior Council for a copy of a will if the executors of an estate refused to abide by its terms. Such a case occurred on March 4, 1739, when two slaves, Louis and Catherine, acting for themselves and other slaves of the late Captain de Coustilhas, petitioned for a copy of his will, which they averred promised them liberty provided such action approved by Governor Bienville. The Superior Council honored their petition and granted them a copy of de Coustilhas' will and perhaps their freedom as well.[25]

As would be expected, executors often resorted to trickery to prevent the freeing of slaves. The case of the

---

24. G. Lugano (trans.), "Records of the Superior Council of Louisiana," *Louisiana Historical Quarterly*, XXIV (1941), 557–558.

25. Cruzat (trans.), "Records of the Superior Council of Louisiana," *loc. cit.*, VI (1923), 303.

slave Marie Charlotte is an excellent example of this type of chicanery. Marie Charlotte's master, a Monsieur St. Julien, had, on October 9, 1735, provided in his will that she should be given her freedom at his death. However, Dausserville, the executor of the estate, declared the provision for Marie Charlotte's manumission invalid on the grounds that the total assets of the estate were not sufficient to cover St. Julien's indebtedness to the Company of the Indies. Dausserville then took it upon himself to place the Negress on sale and bought her himself for the sum of 1300 livres.

After Dausserville's death the intrepid Marie Charlotte petitioned the Superior Council on February 6, 1745, through the Attorney General for her freedom, citing Article XX of the Black Code.[26] Her petition also included a suit against Dausserville's heirs for the payment of wages for the time she had served in slavery after the demise of her original owner. The petition, ended with the statement that a free woman should not be kept in slavery through trickery and she therefore asked for the cash amount of 20 livres for the period dating from the day Dausserville bought her until the day of his death.[27] It is not known whether Marie Charlotte's charges were upheld, for the records of the decision of

26. *The Black Code,* Article XX, 294–295, "Slaves who shall not be properly fed, clad, and provided for by their masters, may give information thereof to the attorney general of the Superior Council, or to all other officers of justice of an inferior jurisdiction, and may put the written exposition of their wrongs into their hands: upon which information, and even *ex-officio,* should the information come from another quarter, the attorney general shall prosecute said masters without charging any costs to complainants. It is our will that this regulation be observed in all accusations for crimes or barbarous and inhuman treatment brought by slaves against their masters."

27. Cruzat (trans.), "Records of the Superior Council of Louisiana," *loc. cit.,* XII (1929), 485; XII (1930), 517.

the court in this case are lost. Nevertheless, the action clearly illustrates that the right of petition and suit by Negroes was honored by the colonial officials of French Louisiana.

Although free Negroes were allowed to marry slaves, marriages were seldom celebrated between the two castes. The records of the St. Louis Cathedral in New Orleans list only three such unions between 1720 and 1730.[28] A possible deterrent may have been the fact that these marriages required the approval of the owner of the slave concerned. There were, however, some cases in which free Negro men married slave women with the intention of purchasing the freedom of their wives. In 1727, for example, Jean Mingo, described as an English free Negro from Carolina, was granted a license to wed Thérèse, a slave on the plantation of a certain White man named Darby. The contract specified that Mingo was to pay as much each year as he "clearly could" for the redemption of his wife, whose value was set at 1500 francs. Darby, meanwhile, was to provide a specified amount of rice, corn, beans and sweet potatoes for Thérèse, and also supply her with suitable clothing. When the terms of this agreement were met, the slave in question would be free. Furthermore, it was stipulated that any children born to this union were to be considered free.[29]

Two years later, Mingo was allowed to take his wife with him to his place of work. On October 21, 1729, he contracted to work as an overseer on the plantation of a certain DeClavannes for a period of three years. His

28. MS. Marriage Register of St. Louis Church, New Orleans, July 1, 1720 to December 4, 1730.
29. Cruzat (trans.), "Records of the Superior Council of Louisiana," *loc. cit.*, IV (1921), 236.

duties consisted of supervising slaves in the cultivation of tobacco, cotton and other crops. Thérèse's duties consisted of domestic work for an annual wage of 200 francs which amount was to be paid Darby until Mingo's debt to him was discharged. The annual amount awarded to Mingo was 300 francs together with a jug of brandy each month, when in stock. Besides this remuneration, the Negro overseer was also to receive eight percent of everything produced on the plantation, except the increase of slaves and cattle. The eight percent was to be paid promptly after each harvest, provided Mingo and his wife continued to serve for the full three years stated in the contract.[30]

By 1730, difficulties between Mingo and Darby broke out over the annual payments for Thérèse. When the White seized Thérèse, Mingo entered suit for the return of his wife, together with a plea for a general adjustment of the agreement. In the suit, Jean Mingo charged Darby with causing difficulties of "a haggling skinflint on the score of allowing for supplies furnished by Mingo and some building operations that ought to be credited to the settlement of the agreement." Darby entered a counter suit and suggested that since Mingo spoke only English, the trouble between them was undoubtedly due to "a malevolent and incompetent interpreter." He further stated that it had always been his intention to treat Mingo fairly and he now considered him a "meritorious loser." The court ordered Thérèse restored to her husband, but decreed that Darby should receive the annual payments which Mingo had agreed to pay in the original contract.[31]

---

30. *Ibid.*, 355.
31. *Ibid.*, V (1922), 102–103.

A piteous example of a free Negro purchasing his wife's freedom was that of François Tiocou. This free man was so attached to his slave wife, Marie Aram by name, that he agreed with the director of the Charity Hospital of New Orleans to work for seven years without pay with the understanding that at the end of the stipulated period Marie would be emancipated. At the end of the seventh year, the labors of Tiocou were rewarded with the freedom of his wife. He had served so well that it was decreed that freedom was due to the free Negro's wife.[32] Such was not an isolated case since free Negroes took all sorts of jobs to earn money to free their spouses. For example, Jean Baptiste Marby agreed to serve Lieutenant Delfaut de Pontalba for three years as a cook in return for the freedom of his wife, Venus. The terms of the contract also called for the maintenance and medical attention for the two persons in question.[33]

In French Colonial Louisiana free Negroes could be reduced to slavery by action of the Superior Council. The grounds for such drastic action were theft, non-payment of debt and immoral conduct. Although cases in which free persons were reduced to slavery were rare, there were a sufficient number to serve as a warning and a disciplinary measure. Among the list was the case of Jeanette, who was cited to appear before the Superior Council for holding nightly assemblies of slaves and servants in violation of the law. On September 4, 1746, the governing body reprimanded the free Negress, and admonished her not to repeat this offense.[34] Six months

---

32. Henry P. Dart (trans.), "Cabildo Archives, French Period," *Louisiana Historical Quarterly*, III and IV (1920–1921), 366, 55.

33. Cruzat (trans.), "Records of the Superior Council of Louisiana," *loc. cit.*, IV (1921), 594.

34. *Ibid.*, XVII (1934), 187.

later, however, the recalcitrant Jeanette was arrested and tried before the Superior Council for theft and failure to pay her debts. Following a hearing she was convicted of these charges and sentenced to be reduced to slavery. In addition the proceeds of her sale were to be applied to the payment of her debts and court costs. A certain colonist named Layssard purchased Jeanette for the sum of 1900 livres.[35]

In still another case, Jean Baptiste was reduced to slavery for having stolen some shirts and other clothing from the home of his employer.[36] Several years later Jean Baptiste petitioned the Superior Council through a White friend, M. Jean Trudeau, asking the governing authorities to permit the former free Negro, "who had been condemned to slavery and exile," to be allowed to remain in Louisiana as his slave. The petition further stated that Jean Baptiste had repented his licentious behavior and concluded that his desire was to remain in the Louisiana colony. This petition was allowed and Trudeau purchased the slave for the sum of 100 livres.[37]

Emancipation by legislative action had its origin in the colonial era. The vast majority of such manumissions were awarded for services rendered to the commonwealth in periods of emergency. Many also represented an award for military services in the Indian wars. In December of 1724 the very existence of the infant colony was threatened when two ragged, hungry and frightened Frenchmen from Natchez arrived in New Orleans with the news that the Indians had massacred the French garrison. Details of the tragedy were such as to increase

---

35. *Ibid.*, XVIII (1935), 168.
36. *Ibid.*, XI (1933), 145–146.
37. Lugano (trans.), "Records of the Superior Council of Louisiana," *loc. cit.*, XXV (1942), 1135.

the fears of the inhabitants, who were already all too conscious of inadequate defense installations. Matters took on graver proportions as rumors spread that the Indians intended to attack New Orleans in the very near future. The fear was so pervasive that Governor Périer, in one of his dispatches, sorrowfully reported:

> I am extremely sorry to see, from the manifestations of such universal alarm, that there is less of French courage in Louisiana than anywhere else. Fear [so] . . . uncontrollable . . . that the insignificant nation of the Chouachas . . . became a subject of terror. . . . This induced me to have them destroyed by our negroes, who executed this mission with as much promptitude as secrecy. This example given by our negroes, kept in check all the small nations up the river. . . . I have ordered that a certain number of negroes be sent to make intrenchments around the city of New Orleans.[38]

This was the first recorded use of Negro troops in Louisiana.

In the summer of 1730 the French speedily sent an expedition against the Natchez Indians. The forces of the colonial armies contained not only white troops, but also slaves and free Negro military elements. These Negro troops performed the tasks of war so efficiently and bravely that Governor Périer commended them for having "performed prodigies of valor."[39]

After the successful termination of the Natchean war, the Superior Council took under consideration the emancipation of those slaves who had sided with the colony in its struggle against the Indian menace. The attorney general was so moved by the loyalty and affection these

38. Gayarré, *History of Louisiana*, I, 422–423.
39. *Ibid.*, I, 435.

Blacks displayed for the French nation that he declared "we cannot regard them otherwise than by granting them freedom."[40] The grateful official further urged defensive measures to prevent a recurrence of the Natchez massacre, by organizing a company of free Negroes to be ready for instant call against any future attacks.[41] That the governing council emancipated some of these Negroes is evidenced by the petition of the free Negro Diocou who on June 28, 1737, asked that he be freed for his service in the Natchez war, and for permission to buy the freedom of his wife. His request was probably granted.[42]

Frequent use was made of free Negro troops during the French period. In 1736, when a war broke out between the French and the Chickasaw Indian nation, Governor Bienville's army consisted of 544 white men, excluding officers, and 45 Negroes, commanded by a free Black named Simon. The Chickasaw stronghold of Ackia was located near the Tombigbee River. In the first engagement there, the Indians easily routed the French forces. Shortly afterwards, a group of French officers were seated around a campfire discussing the tragic events of the day. With them was Simon, the free Negro commander of the company of Negroes who had thrown down the mantelets they were carrying to protect the French attempts to storm the Indian village. Although his men had fled the scene of battle, Simon had remained with the French officers until retreat was sounded. The free Negro commander became so vexed by the cowardly action of his men and the jeering he was receiving from

---

40. William Price (trans.), "Sidelights of Louisiana History," *Louisiana Historical Quarterly*, I (1918), 132.

41. Cruzat (trans.), "Records of the Superior Council of Louisiana," *loc. cit.*, IV (1921), 524.

42. *Ibid.*, V (1922), 401.

the white officers that he retorted: "A Negro is as brave as anybody, and I will prove it to you." Simon succeeded in capturing one of the Indians' horses and riding it back from their fort, under fire, to the French officers. Such bold action won Simon the acclamation of the French.[43]

Whenever necessary Negro troops were employed on frontier posts to prevent the intrusion of English explorers. John Peter Salley of Augusta County, Virginia, at the head of an exploring party on the Mississippi River in 1742, tells of being taken captive by a company of ninety French soldiers, "consisting of Frenchmen, Negroes and Indians." "We were taken prisoners," wrote Salley, "and carried to New Orleans where we were examined under oath before the Governor [Bienville] and then committed to prison."[44]

The free Negroes played a significant role in the economic and legal affairs of the French colony. There are many instances to show that they contracted debts, effected partnership agreements with Whites, and engaged in a great variety of business enterprises for themselves. One free Negro named Raphael even expanded his business interests to include the lending of money. On May 10, 1724, he entered suit against a White colonist named Paulin Cadot for the repayment of 200 francs copper for non-payment of mortgage due. The court awarded this amount to the colored man and also ordered Cadot to pay the court costs.[45]

Another incident which illustrates the high economic

---

43. Gayarré, *History of Louisiana*, I, 480–481.

44. Fairfax Harrison (ed.), "The Virginians on the Ohio and the Mississippi, 1742," *Louisiana Historical Quarterly*, V (1922), 327–328.

45. William Price (trans.), "Abstracts of French and Spanish Documents Concerning the Early History of Louisiana," *Louisiana Historical Quarterly*, I (1918), 238.

and legal status of the free Negro was the agreement made by Raphael Bernard with a White man. In this case Bernard tells of hiring himself in France, to a Jean Baptiste Dumanoir in 1719 for an annual salary of 200 silver francs together with a complete outfit of clothing. Bernard had served Dumanoir "with fidelity and affection, but lately his boss had treated him roughly and stinted him his clothing and hire." He wanted all that was justly due him under his agreement, and when this was obtained, he would return to France. Although the outcome is unknown at least the court ordered Dumanoir to appear in court to answer the charges.[46] Another enterprise in which free Negroes were engaged was the manufacture of tar in almost every section of Louisiana. A free Negro named Diocou successfully recovered 150 francs from the estate of a certain St. Julien for the sale of this product to the deceased planter.[47]

Some emancipated Negroes even engaged in the shipping business. In this lucrative occupation one Scipion attained the rank of barge master. In reaching this rank he entered agreement with a merchant named Rene Petit to take charge of the latter's barge to carry produce from New Orleans to the Illinois country. Scipion's wage was set at 200 livres for each trip which amount was to be paid as long as he complied with the conditions of "seeing to it that the cargo was on board in New Orleans and properly discharged in Illinois."[48]

Another example of business connection was the contract between a Dr. Prat and a free Negro named Pierre Almanzar. The latter was suffering with a venereal dis-

---

46. *Ibid.*, 242.
47. Cruzat (trans.), "Records of the Superior Council of Louisiana," *loc. cit.*, V (1922), 418.
48. *Ibid.*, VI (1923), 306.

ease which necessitated his being treated with "extreme remedies," and since the Negro could not afford the doctor's fee, he obligated himself to serve Dr. Prat as a cook in exchange for the necessary treatment. The contract, however, stipulated that Almanzar would not be required to "wield an ax or work the ground." Furthermore, Prat agreed to provide medicines, necessary utensils and nourishment until the Negro was cured of the disease.[49]

Toward the end of the French regime in Louisiana, the dairy business attracted the free Negro. A case in point in 1762 was that of a free Mulatto named Louis who made a favorable contract with two White men of the Pointe Coupee to care for their dairy stock in the Opelousas district. In order to insure good treatment of the cattle, Louis was to receive as payment for his services one-tenth of the proceeds from the offspring. The contract was to be in effect for as long as Louis remained as keeper and caretaker of the cattle.[50]

A fairly constant source of wealth and income came from White relatives and even friends. Whites often left small legacies to free Negroes who rendered satisfactory service or out of a sense of duty and affection. One White named Vignon LaCombe, for example, left 100 piastres to Mariane, and 100 piastres to each of her two children.[51] At no time during the French period did any free Negroes attain great wealth, but many did engage in occupations that gave them a comfortable and secure economic position in the colony.

Colonial Louisianians lived in an atmosphere hardly

---

49. *Ibid.*, IX (1926), 115.

50. Lugano (trans.), "Records of the Superior Council of Louisiana," *loc. cit.*, XXIV (1941), 565.

51. Dart (trans.), "Cabildo Archives, French Period," *loc. cit.*, III (1920), 567.

conducive to high moral standards. Even for the tolerant 18th Century, personal conduct often reached new lows in personal behavior. Such is of no wonder with a population consisting of a heterogeneous mass of garrison soldiers, convicts, loose women, planters, Indians, slaves and free Negroes—all of whom seemed bent on getting the most out of a dreary colonial existence. To escape boredom many resorted to the immoderate use of rum, which one observer claimed stupefied most of the population.[52] If all the bad things said were true it is no wonder that the last French governor, D'Abbadie, described Louisiana and its inhabitants as "a chaos of iniquity and discord."[53]

In this environment tempers flared, crime flourished, and quarrels erupted into violence. Sharing part of the blame were the free Negroes. Among a long list of law violators from this class was one Thomas, who shot and wounded a slave in the left eye when the latter tried to separate his master's cattle from those of his assailant.[54] Marital difficulties were created for Gros when he charged Martha with "always seeking a quarrel with him, with the result that he could not live with his wife, who took Martha's side in the quarrels." When Martha killed one of his turkeys and even threatened physical harm to Gros himself, he appealed to the Superior Council for a peace bond.[55]

Although not so common as alarmists thought, free Negroes did attack Whites verbally and physically. Charles Lemoine, a Caucasian cabinet-maker, had the free Negro Raphael, and his wife, Franchon, arrested for insulting

52. Gayarré, *History of Louisiana,* II, 106.
53. *Ibid.,* 165.
54. Cruzat (trans.), "Records of the Superior Council of Louisiana," *loc. cit.,* V (1922), 249.
55. *Ibid.,* XIV (1931), 43.

and attacking him without provocation. Lemoine alleged
that they had him "followed and pelted by their children
with stones, the eldest of them sixteen years old, and as
he often had to work near them on a conveyance," he
requested that such action be stopped for his peace of
mind and body.[56]

In 1747, a levee fracas near New Orleans involving a
free Negro was provoked by the levity of three convales-
cent soldiers who were leaving the hospital late one afternoon. Upon meeting a free Mulatto named Stephen
LaRue, they called to him "Bonsoir Seigneur Negritte."
[Good Evening, Mr. Little Negro] LaRue, a free Negro
from Saint Domingue responded promptly, "Bon Soir
Seigneur Jean Foutre [fool]." The soldiers took offense,
seized the Mulatto by the throat, and a street brawl
broke out. Even though the soldiers outnumbered the
colored man three to one, they deemed it necessary to
call for help. One White named Tixerant came to their
aid by beating the Mulatto with his cane. The cane-
swinging White then called the police to take the unfortunate LaRue to jail. En route, the badly mauled
Mulatto managed to fire a pistol and the minor fracas
took on the aspects of a serious crime. LaRue was brutally beaten and thrown into the dungeon with shackles
on his hands and feet. He was fined 110 livres and his
weapon confiscated.[57]

The records of the French colonial period do not show
accurate information concerning the number of free
Negroes in Louisiana or their location in the colony. In
some cases it is not certain whether they were included

---

56. *Ibid.*, XIII (1930), 506.
57. *Ibid.*, 367–390.

in the categories of hired persons or Negro slaves.[58] The Spaniards, who were to take control of the territory in 1769, were the first to conduct a trustworthy census of the inhabitants of their new possession. This counting gives as accurate a picture of the number and distribution of free Negroes as can be found at the close of the French regime in Louisiana.

The methodical Spanish found a total of 165 free Negroes in the Louisiana colony in 1769. Among this number, 73 were listed as free Blacks and 92 as free Mulattoes. The city of New Orleans contained 99 free Negroes, while 66 free Negro inhabitants lived in the rural areas. In both instances the free Mulattoes outnumbered the free Blacks and the number of free Black and Mulatto females exceeded the males by almost two to one.[59] Although these numbers indicated a tendency on the part of free Negroes to concentrate in the city, there were a sizeable number of them who remained in rural areas of the colony. Both rural and urban free Negroes were destined to play a prominent role in the Spanish and national periods of Louisiana history.

The official policy of the French authorities may be called liberal in many respects. For instance, the governing officers, with few exceptions, enforced those provisions of the Black Code guaranteeing Negro freemen

---

58. Jay K. Ditchy (trans. and ed.), "Early Census Tables of Louisiana," *Louisiana Historical Quarterly*, XIII (1930), 220. The census of 1721 lists 293 men; 140 women; 96 children; 155 French servants; 514 Negro slaves; 51 Indian slaves. Alcée Fortier, *A History of Louisiana*, I, 102. The census of the colony in 1727 indicated that there were 1329 masters, 138 hired persons; 1561 Negroes; 73 savages.

59. Lawrence Kinnaird (ed.), "Spain in the Mississippi Valley, 1765–1794," 3 vols., *Annual Report of the American Historical Association, 1945*, II, 196.

economic and legal rights. Few restrictions were placed on slaveowners wanting to free their slaves, and the absence of a complicated manumission procedure clearly indicates that in the beginning there was no fear of an increase in the free Negro class. Furthermore, there is no evidence that either the government or private individuals feared this class; consequently no serious attempts to exile the free Negro population were made during France's control of Louisiana. In fact as long as such persons complied with the rather mild regulations governing their conduct, they enjoyed the same economic and legal privileges as White persons.

In other respects, French colonial laws considered free Negroes as inferior to Whites. This was especially true in social matters, or in the stringent regulations governing intermarriage. Any persons found guilty of violating this regulation were subject to "a severe and arbitrary fine." In an effort towards the better enforcement of this law, all clergymen and lay officials were prohibited from officiating at weddings involving a free Negro and a White person.[60] Social discrimination also was evident in personal relationships between two races. For example, an emancipated Negro was required to show "special respect" at all times toward his former master and his family. Failure to do so could place the free Negro in danger of severe punishment.[61]

It is significant, in terms of discriminatory legislation, that White colonists could not be reduced to slavery for any offense whatsoever, while this severe penalty was possible in the case of free Negroes. Such discrimination was due in the main to fear of a possible collusion be-

---

60. *The Black Code,* 286–287.
61. *Ibid.,* 312–313.

tween the free Negroes and the slave population. Apprehension of the Whites on this matter was expressed in many laws, especially in the one that provided a maximum penalty of reenslavement for any free Negro found guilty of giving aid to or hiding runaway slaves. On the other hand, White colonists found guilty of the same offense were merely fined the sum of 10 livres.[62]

It was the operation of a double standard that produced an anomalous class—a class that found only partial security while France exercised sovereignty over Louisiana.

62. *Ibid.,* 301–302.

2

The Free Negro during the Spanish Domination

IN many ways the coming of the Spanish regime in 1769 had only a small effect upon the inhabitants of Louisiana. Upon taking command of the province, General Alexandro O'Reilly and his successors did change the existing French governmental structure for that of Spain, and the Spanish language, customs, and laws gradually replaced those of the French government. These changes, however, were not so great as appeared on the surface, since both French and Spanish laws were largely taken from the Roman Code and bore a remarkable resemblance to each other.[1] The Black Code of 1724 was kept in force for the governing of slaves and free Negroes,[2] but those provisions of the French regulations that were deemed impractical were either ignored or over

---

1. John R. Ficklen, *History and Civil Government of Louisiana,* 69. O'Reilly replaced the French Superior Council with the Spanish Cabildo. The officials of this governing body enacted those laws necessary for the colony and also served as a Supreme Court of Louisiana.

2. Gayarré, *History of Louisiana,* III, 69.

the passage of years entirely replaced with equivalent sections of Spain's *Las Siete Partidas*.[3]

Under Spanish law, slaves were provided with more opportunities to obtain freedom than they had under French rule. For example, by a procedure known as prescription, any slave was permitted to claim freedom if he had enjoyed liberty for ten years in the country where his master lived or twenty years in a foreign country. In order to avail himself of prescriptive rights, the slave must have thought himself free for the stipulated number of years. On the other hand, if the Negro had not acted in good faith, he was presumed to be a fugitive and subject to reduction to the status of a slave. On the other hand, if a slave had been deserted by his owner for a period of thirty years, the master lost all rights "whatever over him."[4]

According to Spanish law, a slave could become free because of some "good action" even though the owner opposed the emancipation. Freedom was possible if a slave denounced to a royal official anyone who had forced or carried away a virgin against her will. Another occasion for emancipation was provided for any slave discovering anyone making counterfeit money. Furthermore, liberty was granted to any slave who had avenged the death of his master. In all these cases the government was required to pay the slaveowner a "suitable price" for the slave.[5]

Automatic manumissions were also provided for in a number of other ways under the Spanish law. Any female

3. Henry P. Dart (ed.), "A Murder Case Tried in New Orleans in 1773," *Louisiana Historical Quarterly*, XXII (1939), 823.

4. Moreau L. Lislet and Henry Carleton (trans.), *The Laws of Las Siete Partidas Which are Still in Force in the State of Louisiana*, I, 591.

5. *Ibid.*, 589.

slave who had been placed in a brothel so that her master could "profit by her" was considered as immediately free. Emancipation was also awarded to slaves who had become clergymen.[6] In the case of a slave owned by two masters, that owner wishing to free the slave bought out the interest of the partner. Failure to fulfill this regulation would result in the immediate emancipation of the slave.[7]

Slaveowners wishing to manumit their slaves were permitted to do so by will or deed. In order to legally free a slave by deed, the owner had to be at least twenty years of age and have five witnesses present to the act of emancipation. Persons bequeathing freedom had to be at least fourteen years old, but this condition could be set aside if the owner was related to the slave in question. Other dispensations included the master's wet nurse, teacher, or a slave who had saved his owner from death or "infamy."[8]

Spanish law followed the same rule as the French by allowing children born of free mothers to be considered free-born persons.[9] This feature of the code carried such an iron bound guarantee that the offspring of a free mother could never be reduced to slavery. Under Spanish law slavery was deemed "the basest and most despicable thing on earth, except sin, and liberty as the most dear state known to man." Consequently, freemen and their children were required to honor and respect former owners in every possible way. As evidence of respect a manumitted Negro was expected to greet his former master

---

6. *Ibid.*, 590.
7. *Ibid.*, 589.
8. *Ibid.*, 587–588.
9. *Ibid.*, 582–583.

and his children in a humble way every time they met in public. If the freedman chanced to be sitting when his former master approached, he was expected to rise and greet him in a respectful manner. Freed Negroes were not allowed to sue former masters unless permission for such action was given by a competent judge. Moreover, a free Negro could not accuse or defame his former master unless the latter had done him great personal injury. A manumitted slave was also required by law to assist his former master in event the latter had become impoverished. In this case, the freedman had to supply the White man with food, drink, and clothing to the best of his financial ability.[10] Failure to comply with these obligations entitled the former master to claim the Negro in question as a slave.[11]

A slave under the Spanish law could petition for his liberty. This privilege was allowed if the master, in the exercise of his authority, had exceeded the bounds prescribed by law, in which case the slave was entitled either to require his liberty or be sold to another master.[12] Slaves could also acquire their liberty by self-purchase from their owners. In this case the same legal procedure was followed as when White masters freed them by deed.

During the Spanish regime emancipations account for the growth of the free Negro element in Louisiana. Many slaves took advantage of the law allowing them to purchase their liberty. This group usually bought freedom through overtime work or extra labor performed for the master. By March 1772, the eighty-year-old slave named

---

10. *Ibid.*, 591–593.

11. *Ibid.*, 594.

12. *Appendix to An Account of Louisiana, Being an Abstract of Documents in the Office of the Department of State, and of the Treasury* (1803), xxix.

Angelica had accumulated the sum of 12 pesos, which amount she offered for her liberty. When no objection was made by her owner, the governor ordered an act of sale made out with the "greatest clearness" in favor of Angelica.[13] The free Negress then possessed a deed to herself. Father Barnabe, the Capuchin missionary in the German Coast district [later St. Charles Parish], allowed his Negress slave, Maria, to buy her freedom for the sum of 300 pesos. The clergyman also indicated the desire to reward Maria for the "services and benefits" she had given to him for many years.[14]

An example of the procedure followed under Spanish law when a slave sued for freedom and his master was unwilling to agree to the emancipation can be found in the case of the slave Nicholas. In a suit filed in 1780, the Negro claimed that he belonged to a Madam Prévost, whose property was under the administration of a planter named Mercier. He further contended that for four years his owner had intended to sell him for 400 pesos, but that no one offered that amount for a slave without a trade or any kind of skill and who was known to be sick with a stomach ailment. Nicholas offered to pay the 400 pesos and requested that his owner or someone authorized to act for him come to an agreement of a fair evaluation of his worth.

Acting Governor Piernas sent the petition to the Auditor of War for adjudication. Madame Prévost was also notified of the proceedings so that she could appoint an appraiser to help in fixing the value of the slave in question. At this juncture, Nicholas presented a second peti-

---

13. Laura L. Porteous (trans.), "Index to the Spanish Judicial Records of Louisiana," *Louisiana Historical Quarterly*, XI (1928), 37–38.
14. *Ibid.*, VIII (1925), 778.

tion, declaring his owner was on his upriver plantation and unaware of the decree rendered in his favor. The slave therefore asked that official notification be sent to inform his White owner. Such a writ was served, and a Francisco Cheval was named by the White woman as her representative. The slave, in turn, named an Antonio Picout to serve in his behalf. The two appraisers, however, differed in estimating the value of the slave; Cheval fixed the price at 1200 pesos, while Picout insisted that 800 pesos was fair. Nicholas then asked for a third appraiser to break the deadlock. The Governor appointed a Francisco Blanche, who set a value of 800 pesos for the slave. When the two original appraisers agreed on this amount the Governor ordered a deed of emancipation issued in favor of the slave, but Nicholas was required to pay court costs.[15]

It was not uncommon for slaves to buy their freedom with money advanced by friends. One such case occurred in 1776, when a slave named Maria Juana, appeared personally before the Governor's court demanding her freedom with money advanced by a White friend. She told the Governor that her master, a planter namer Suriray, had treated her with great cruelty after having married a prominent White woman of the province. According to the slave, this cruel treatment was meted out to her because Suriray wished to atone for his sin of concubinage. The jilted Negress also accused the White man of denying her the recourse that "charity concedes to all slaves, namely, to look for a master more to their liking," and that he had also refused to accept 250 pesos for her liberation.

The White master appeared in court in his own de-

15. *Ibid.*, XV (1932), 164–165.

fense, and, while he did not deny having lived with the Negro woman, refused the slave's request to purchase her freedom. In addition, Suriray, accused Maria Juana of wishing to enter the possession of an Englishman. Governor Unzaga ruled that according to the laws of Spain, there was no obligation for a master to free a slave if he did not desire to, and therefore Maria Juana was denied the right to purchase her freedom.[16]

On the same day that Maria Juana instituted proceedings for her freedom, Suriray entered suit against Jenkins, the Englishman, who had furnished the money for the slave's emancipation. The plaintiff testified that his slave had confessed to him that Jenkins had furnished the money and that a free Mulattress named Maria Deslattes acting in the Englishman's behalf was to complete the transaction. Suriray asked the court to summon the free Mulatress and Jenkins. The former obeyed the summons, but Jenkins fled to his ship and filed testimony through a lawyer. The latter alleged that the Negress on one occasion came to him "full of tears saying, 'you see me so unhappy with my master, because a cat had carried off a turkey that had died [sic] he wished to give me 100 lashes each day. I have come to see if you will have the charity to buy me.'" Feeling compassion for the slave, the Englishman commissioned the Mulattress to attend to the transaction.

When Suriray demanded the sum of 600 pesos, Jenkins countered with an offer of 450 pesos for the slave. It was without his knowledge that the mulattress and the slave went to Governor Unzaga's court to petition for freedom. At this point, the Governor interrupted the proceedings, remarking that the case demonstrated the "lowest dregs

16. *Ibid.*, XI, (1928), 338–343.

of the passions of two white men over a worthless colored woman . . . evidence that the Negress was her master's concubine before his marriage when he dressed her well and took the best care of her. . . ." When she "refused to further consort with him out of respect to his wife he . . . abused her . . . even to deprive her of her shoes and stockings and to force her to wear dirty rags." The governor was so incensed that he refused to render a decision in the case and sent the proceedings to Havana for a ruling.

A year later, Governor Galvez cited the parties to appear in court for judgment in the case. Veranes [Attorney of the Royal Audencia of Mexico and Santo Domingo] advised the Governor of Louisiana to declare Jenkins innocent and grant "letters of Liberty" to Maria Juana. This ruling was based on the Royal Cedule granted in Aranjuez, Spain, in 1768. Galvez exonerated Jenkins but refused to honor the ruling regarding the slave because he interpreted the royal order of 1768 as intended only for Cuba and as such "cannot influence the rest of His Majesty's Dominions." "This province," Galvez ruled, "must be governed by the general laws of the kingdom."[17]

A large number of slaves were freed as a reward for faithful, good, or heroic service rendered to masters or other White persons. This honorably earned freedom was a highly prized privilege and was most frequently rewarded for lifelong devotion to duty. Jean Bautista Lebreton, before leaving for France in 1771, manumitted his slave Liceta because she had served as his wet nurse and had merited his confidence for many years.[18] Another

---

17. *Ibid.*, XI (1928), 343–347.
18. Laura L. Porteous (trans.), "Torture in Spanish Criminal Procedure in Louisiana, 1771," *Louisiana Historical Quarterly*, VIII (1925), 14.

Louisianian who wished to reward slaves for valuable services was Juan Bautista Blaquet, who petitioned the Governor for permission to buy the Negress Cataline, and her son, Francisco, slaves of a certain Francisco Many. The White man, who was a resident of Pointe Coupee, wished to free these two slaves belonging to his neighbor for saving his life.[19]

Concubinage with a slave and the children of such unions often furnished reasons for emancipating slave children as well as the Negro concubine. In December of 1782, for example, Antonio Guichard informed the Cabildo that a Mulatto boy had been born to a slave belonging to a planter named Francisco Daniel Dupain. Guichard admitted that the child was his son. When the owner had refused an offer of 100 pesos for the child, the White father instituted suit to force the owner to accept a reasonable price. Governor Galvez, doubtlessly impressed with the White father's frankness, instituted the usual motion of having the interested parties appoint appraisers for determining the value of the slave. Both parties complied, and January 15, 1783, was set aside as the day of appraisal. The first named appraisers could not agree on the value of the slave and a third party in discord was appointed to resolve the question. Finally, the child was valued at the sum of 60 pesos, which Guichard promptly paid to realize the freedom of his natural son.[20] Another White father, Garret Rapalje of Baton Rouge, freed his 22-year-old Mulatto son in 1802 because he thought it unnatural for his child to remain in a state of slavery. In order to guarantee future security

---

19. Porteous (trans.), "Index to the Spanish Judicial Records of Louisiana," *loc. cit.*, IX (1926), 149–150.

20. *Ibid.*, XIX (1936), 1124–1125.

for his son, Rapalje specifically denied his heirs any right to claim his Mulatto son as a slave after his death.[21]

In addition to good and faithful service, personal affection for certain slaves by masters accounted for numerous emancipations during the Spanish colonial period. Father Antonio Barnabé was quite typical when he manumitted Francisco, because of "the love he bears for him."[22] In 1801 Raymond Boisclair, a free Negro resident of Baton Rouge, gave a power of attorney to Hypolite Chavois to execute an act of emancipation in favor of his slave Rose. The emancipation was awarded in consideration of "the love and affection" which Boisclair felt towards this slave.[23]

A remarkable case of affection was expressed by the Baron de Pontalba, a member of the minor Spanish nobility living in New Orleans. In a letter to his wife in 1790, this nobleman referred to "little Julian," his son's favorite slave, as being in "robust and good health," and informed the Baroness that a friend of the family had become so attached to the slave boy that he wanted to buy him in order to give him freedom. Pontalba thought he would sell the slave at a "bargain price," provided the purchaser would agree to the freeing as soon as it was convenient.[24]

---

21. *Archives of The Spanish Government of West Florida, 1783–1812,* V, 152.

22. Porteous (trans.), "Index to the Spanish Judicial Records of Louisiana," *loc. cit.,* VI (1923), 530.

23. *Archives of the Spanish Government and West Florida, 1783–1812,* XVIII, 322.

24. Joseph Xavier Delfau de Pontalba to his wife Jeanne Françoise le Breton des Charmeaux, June 10, 1796; *id.* to *id.* July 16, 1796, Henri Deville de Sinclair (trans.), *Journal Letters of Joseph Xavier Delfau de Pontalba to his Wife Jeanne Françoise le Breton des Charmeaux, Works Progress Administration, Survey of the Federal Archives in Louisiana,* 166, 241.

Quite understandably there were some objections to freeing slaves in situations other than financial controversies. Most of these were not based on any individual anti-emancipation sentiment nor upon the demands of a group opposed to freeing slaves. For the most part, these objections disclosed a desire of particular slave owners to recover an alleged fugitive slave or cancel the emancipation of a former slave. One Claudio Gullorie alleged that for more than six years he had been unable to locate his slave Margarita. In 1781 Gullorie had seen her near the levee in New Orleans in a pirogue belonging to a fruit merchant named Miguel Barre. Gullorie asked that civil and criminal proceedings be brought against Barre and Margarita, their property seized and "their declarations taken."

In the ensuing trial, the fruit merchant admitted having hired Margarita to help him sell fruit, but at the time he had employed the Negress, she was a free person having been emancipated by Gregorio Gullorie, the father of the plaintiff. Margarita testified she had been legitimately freed by an act of her former master in 1770 and to prove her free status submitted her emancipation papers. This act of emancipation is an example of what was done in the country parishes to accomplish an end when the services of neither judge or notary could be obtained. It stated that Gregorio Gullorie, who was then in the city but a resident of Opelousas, freed Margarita on April 13, 1770. Previous to that time he was on his plantation without a notary or judge to authorize such an act. So in order to legalize the document, he got a notary to copy it literally; the terms of which were as follows: "I Gregoire Gullorie, over my ordinary mark, of my own free will and that of my children . . ." for the good services, "rendered me by Margarita, my slave, not only to me, but to my children, before and after the death of my wife, I free her and declare that she serve me up to my death."[25] On the strength of this document, Margarita was exonerated from the charges of being a fugitive slave and declared a free person.

The case of Maria, alias Mariquina, was an example of an attempt to revoke an act of emancipation. This Negress alleged she was free on the basis of a written declaration of her master allowing her to travel to any part of the province. The written statement also contained an act of emancipation for Maria and her son, Charles. When her former owner attempted to sell her, Maria threw herself on the mercy of the court. She asked that the White man be ordered not to molest her and to declare under oath his previous act of emancipation. Pierre Methodé denied ever having emancipated any slaves; he claimed it had merely been his intention to give them license to travel in the province without being bothered by the officers of the law. Methodé also stated that he could not legally free any of his slaves because his creditors would not allow it. Despite the testimony of the slaveowner, the Governor ruled Maria and her son free on the basis of the document in the Negress's possession. Furthermore, Methodé was required to grant his former slaves new emancipation papers. Maria was required to pay the court cost, which amounted to 8 pesos 6 reales.[26]

An appreciable number of emancipations were effected by free Negroes who purchased the freedom of members of their family with the idea of making their lot easier.

25. Porteous (trans.), "Index to the Spanish Judicial Records of Louisiana," *loc. cit.*, XV (1932), 546.

26. *Ibid.*, XV (1932), 165–166.

A case in point was Margaret, a free Mulattress, who made arrangements before sailing for Havana to sell her property on Royal Street in New Orleans, in case of her death while abroad. The proceeds of the sale were to purchase the freedom of her mother and brother.[27] A free Negro named Valentino brought suit against the estate of Andrews Juen to sell him his brother, Silvestre. In this case, a physician was called to examine the slave to reduce the price from 1000 to 800 pesos. It was discovered that the slave's infirmity consisted of a dislocated knee which fact was held as justification for the selling price of 800 pesos.[28]

Still another case to effect the freedom of a slave relative was the petition of Maria Theresa, to free her mother, Francisca, from slavery.[29] The appraisers unanimously agreed upon the price of the slave at 300 pesos, which sum the free Negress immediately paid. The free Negress Angelica, who had bought her freedom in 1772, begged alms in the streets of New Orleans to earn what she thought was enough money to purchase her grandson's freedom. When appraisers fixed the value of the slave child at 200 pesos Angelica almost hopelessly had to return to begging.[30]

A free person of color named Joseph Casenave, on learning that there would be a public sale of the slaves of the late Marie Eva LaBranche, petitioned the executors to sell him the Negress slave Magdalena, who was his wife, and her Mulatto son. Since the child of Magdalena's was his son "his soul was moved to desire their freedom."

27. *Ibid.*, VI (1923), 316.
28. *Ibid.*, XXIV (1941), 1279–1280.
29. *Ibid.*, XXVI (1943), 1197–1198.
30. *Ibid.*, XIII (1930), 701.

Casenave offered to pay cash for the slaves at the price which they had been estimated in the inventory of the estate. Casenave also requested that the Negress and her son not be put up for sale at public auction. After no objections were made to these conditions, the free Negro was allowed to buy his wife and child.[31]

Not all cases resulted in such good fortune. For example, in August of 1780, Elena attempted to buy her son, Maylois, from his master, Henrique Deprez. The free Negro, Jasson, the slave's father, had supplied 600 pesos to buy his freedom. With this amount available, the mother asked that appraisers be named to fix a price for her son. When the officials set 800 pesos as the value of the slave Elena became so outdone she accused Deprez of claiming all sorts of impossible talents for the child, a Negro without a trade and a thief and drunkard. Elena went on to cite several precedents of slaves who had a trade selling for less than was asked for her poor miserable slave son. "After all," pleaded the woman, "Luis a master carpenter of the Capuchins was freed for 800 pesos, as was Andres, an expert blacksmith belonging to Mrs. Bienvenue."[32] She begged the Governor to consider 600 pesos as sufficient, but the petition of the hapless Elena was denied.

Many free Negroes received generous financial aid from White friends so that they might purchase slaves in order to free them. Armand Duplantier, a White planter of Baton Rouge, sold to a free Negro named Julien Bienville three slaves for the reasonable price of 100 pesos. The White philanthropist stipulated in the bill of sale in 1803 that the vendee set these slaves free as soon as possible.

31. *Ibid.*, XIV (1931), 119–123.
32. *Ibid.*, XIV (1931), 619–621.

In the same year Duplantier sold a slave to Louis Du-
bordeau, a free Mulatto, on condition that the latter free
the slave within a matter of days following the sale. At
the same time, Duplantier disposed of three slaves to a
free Negro named Jean Massey on the condition that they
too be free within a short period of time.[33]

One of the most dramatic and pathetic instances of an
attempt to buy a slave relative by a free Negro was the
case of Marie Montreuil. In 1810, this Mulattress, who
was not a resident of the Territory of Orleans, made a
trip to Baton Rouge, then under Spanish control, to buy
the freedom of her niece, Delphina, from a certain Chris-
tobal de Armas. This slaveowner, who had previously
agreed to sell the slave in question for a reasonable price,
changed his mind when the travel weary Mulattress arrived
in Baton Rouge to complete the final phases of the sale.
Failing at a compromise price, the free Mulattress instituted suit against de Armas to compel him to sell her the
slave. In the trial that followed, the colored woman
charged de Armas with making impossible demands. She
testified that he had told her in a rage that it was "first
necessary to make a sack into which the Mulatto girl
can get, and after the . . . sack be filled to the top with
pesos then he will give freedom to the . . . girl." "This
attitude," Marie Montreuil continued, "seems to me improper in the heart and character of a Spaniard, generally
the most magnanimous of all the races, and as I have
understood Spanish laws are serious and accredited with
permitting any slave to buy his freedom or permitting
someone else to buy his freedom."[34]

---

33. *Archives of the Spanish Government of West Florida, 1783–
1812,* VI, 208, 224, 226.
34. *Ibid.,* XVIII, 14–15.

During the Spanish period, free Negroes reached a comfortable level of economic affluence which was at once secure and in some cases even rivaled the security enjoyed by prominent White persons. In the main, most derived a livelihood from agricultural pursuits. Some even owned plantations of considerable size which afforded them not only a comfortable income but also a respectable status in society. Jean Baptiste Bienville appeared to play a more important role as a free Negro planter in Spanish West Florida than any other settler of his race. Of obvious French extraction, bearing an illustrious name, and a resident of Point Coupee district, Bienville apparently was held in highest esteem by both his fellow planters and Spanish officials. This free man first appeared in the succession of Pierre Avarre, an Arcadia bachelor who appointed his trusted Mulatto friend, Bienville, as testimentary executor of a large estate. Antonio Ricard de Rieuterd, a neighbor who wrote this will, was requested to give legal advice to the illiterate Mulatto.[35]

Jean Baptiste Bienville was married to Marie Ricard, who brought a considerable dowry to an already expanding estate.[36] The couple had three children: Basile, Julian and Françoise. A plantation on the Mississippi River served as dowry on the occasion of Françoise's marriage to Paul Huban.

The succession of Bienville appears to prove that he was not only a good citizen but also an able businessman. Upon his death the estate was valued at almost 14,000 pesos and free from debt. His three children inherited the estate.

---

35. *Ibid.,* I, 252.
36. *Ibid.,* V, 796.

The inventory and estimate of the property holdings in the Baton Rouge district held on October 7, 1802, disclosed that the free Mulatto left an estate composed of the following:

Cattle

2 broken oxen	30 pesos
1 pair of old oxen	25 pesos
3 cows and calves	45 pesos
1 heifer and cow	15 pesos
1 heifer	5 pesos
3 cows and 1 calf	45 pesos
1 cow and 1 young bull	15 pesos
1 ox	5 pesos

Horses

2 old horses for plowing	65 pesos
1 white horse	40 pesos
1 mare with 2 fold	25 pesos
2 old plow horses	35 pesos
1 riding horse named Tapajon	50 pesos
1 pair broken horses	30 pesos
1 pair broken horses named Taupain and Moret	30 pesos

Slaves

1 Negro named Augustin of Voye nationality, 32 years, ruptured and one eyed	350 pesos
1 Negress named Thérèse of Fond nationality, 55 years	400 pesos
1 Negro named Nöel, Creole, 38 years	800 pesos
1 Negro named Antonia, Creole, 19 years	800 pesos
1 Negress named Henriette, Creole, 19 years	850 pesos
1 Negro named Mercury of Hibou nationality, 40 years	400 pesos
1 Negro named Estevan, Creole, 35 years	700 pesos
1 Negress named Geneviève, Creole, 22 years	750 pesos
1 Negro named Joseph, Creole, 17 years	800 pesos
1 Mulatto girl, Creole, 6 years	300 pesos
1 Mulatto girl, Creole, 3 years	200 pesos
1 Negro named Cupidon of Hibou nationality, 55 years	500 pesos

1 Negro girl named Froisine, 12 years	500 pesos
1 Negro named Caesar of Congo nationality, 50 years	600 pesos
1 Negro named Francois, Creole, 18 years	800 pesos
1 Negress named Iris of Hibou nationality, 45 years	400 pesos
1 Negress girl named Ermie, Creole, 6 years	250 pesos
1 Negress girl named Magdalene, Creole, 2 years	200 pesos
1 Negress girl Marie, Creole, 2 years	400 pesos

Plantation Implements

2 plows	24 pesos
1 rake	12 pesos
1 grind stone	10 pesos
1 set scales	1 peso
1 grind stone	10 pesos

Real Estate

A plantation where the said deceased died located on the west side of the Mississippi River being bounded on the upper side by the lands of Joseph de Favrot and below by those of Mr. Beranger, the said land measuring twelve arpents in front with the usual depth of forty, all the timber in front being felled having all the necessary fences and wells a medium sized house a warehouse a kitchen and negro cabins and some other small buildings, all of these inventoried and estimated by the appraisers at . . . 2900 pesos. A plantation where Françoise resides and where her deceased father purchased and paid for when she married the said Paul Huban . . . . 180 pesos.[37]

Other free Negroes were classified as well-to-do property owners in Spanish Louisiana. Among them was Henry Collin, who owned 5½ arpents front and 40 arpents deep, in the Pointe Coupee district across the Mississippi River from the town of Baton Rouge. This land, which the colored man had purchased from Felix Dumontier on the installment plan, was valued at 1200 Mexican silver pesos. According to the terms, Collin obligated himself to pay 550 pesos down in March 1802, and the balance

---

37. *Ibid.*, V, 268–271.

the following year.[38] Another, Bacus, ranked high in property, and it was said that he owned more land than he could cultivate.[39]

Few free Negroes could be classified among the large planter class, but few of their White countrymen ever achieved this status. Both Blacks and Whites engaged in agricultural occupations which afforded a plain but adequate living. Among the majority in this category was Luis, a free Mulatto who entered suit against the estate of Carlos Favre Deunoy for claims amounting to 488 pesos for services as overseer on the plantation of his late White employer. All total Luis's claims amounted to 519 pesos, 6½ reales. This amount was granted to the colored claimant by the estate's executors.[40] A free Negro overseer named Jacob was employed on the plantation of the Ursuline nuns from 1796 to the date of his death in 1811. This colored man had been emancipated by the nuns in 1796 so that he could serve as an overseer.[41]

Just as were their White neighbors, free Negroes of Spanish Louisiana were engaged in the slave business. In fact some found it quite a lucrative enterprise, as did Francisco Monplaisir, a free Negro, as evidenced by the suit he filed against a White planter named Carlos Leconte for the return of a Negro slave belonging to the plaintiff. According to the testimony of the Negro, he had hired a slave to a White man named Chaser to make a trip to Natchez on the condition that as soon as they

38. *Ibid.*, V, 189.

39. *Alphabetical and Chronological Digest of the Acts and Deliberations of the Cabildo, 1769–1803,* III, 189.

40. Porteous (trans.), "Index to the Spanish Judicial Records of Louisiana," *loc. cit.*, XV (1932), 534.

41. *Jacob et al. v. Ursuline Nuns,* 2 Mart. La. 269, (Fall 1812).

arrived there, the slave would be returned to his owner in New Orleans. The slave in question escaped from Chaser's service at Natchez and was employed by Leconte as a sailor on the latter's ship, which was destined for the Illinois country. When Monplaisir learned of this arrangement, he asked the court in New Orleans to order a dispatch sent to Governor Francisco Cruzat of Illinois to return his property. When questioned, Leconte declared he was under the impression that the Black was no slave, and he had so engaged him as a free laborer. Although Leconte was absolved from blame in the matter, the slave was returned to his rightful owner.[42]

It was not uncommon for free Negroes to derive their source of income from donations made by White persons. In June 1770, for example, Jean Perret not only awarded his slave, Angelica, freedom, but he also deeded her a house in New Orleans.[43] Magdalena Canella, who had been the concubine of Luis Beaurepas, was given a plantation and slaves as a recompense for her services.[44] In May 1774, Angelina, a free Negress, instituted suit against the estate of Juan Perrer for the possession of his "clothes, linen, furniture and other movables in the house" which the White man had bequeathed to her. There had been some objection to this legacy by the heirs of Perrer, but Angelina won her suit, and she was awarded all the legacy provided.[45]

Another case of donation of land was that of the free Negro Bartalome. To secure his property, which he al-

---

42. Porteous (trans.), "Index to the Spanish Judicial Records of Louisiana," *loc. cit.*, XXVI (1943), 1210–1212.

43. *Ibid.*, VI (1923), 340.

44. *Ibid.*, XII (1928), 341–348.

45. *Ibid.*, X (1927), 445.

leged was given to him by a certain White planter named Alberto Bonne in return for services rendered, the free Negro instituted suit against the White man. As the plaintiff Bartalome presented four certificates dated July 25, 1781, signed respectively by four White men, stating that they were present when Bonne made the donation. Using this instrument as proof of claim, Bartoleme also testified that about three years previously Bonne had made an agreement with him to clear six arpents of land and in payment for this work gave the free Negro four arpents. Bartolome stated that he had cleared his land, built a cabin and other small buildings, placed fences, cultivated and worked the land well.

While the colored man was absent on military duty, Bonne evicted his family and sold the land. Soon after Bartolome returned from the military expedition against the British at Mobile and Pensacola, he was obliged to buy the land from the person who had bought it during his absence. Protesting against the White man's bad faith he asked the court to condemn him to pay that sum and also the value of crops which had been raised on the land. Alberto Bonne answered these accusations in a six-page petition stating that all was false. He based his claim on the allegation that the land was sold during the Negro's absence to be untrue. The sale had been made in the free Negro's presence, and the transfer of land had been clear to the latter before he had departed for military service. When Bartolome failed to answer those charges, presumably, the suit was dropped.[46]

Free Negroes frequently engaged in financial and business dealings with White persons. In some instances they

---

46. *Ibid.*, XVII (1934), 203–204.

borrowed money from White friends and in turn it was not unknown for certain free Negroes to lend money to impecunious White neighbors. In 1778, for example, the free Mulattress Janeta sued a Marcos Darby for the payment of a note amounting to 200 pesos. The defendant in the case was a lieutenant in the local militia stationed in the Attakapas district. When summoned before the court to answer the charges, this officer admitted signing the note in question but contended that it had no validity because of certain extenuating circumstances. At the time the note was made, Darby contended, it was given for the support of Janeta's daughter, but at the child's death he claimed the note became null and of no value. In addition, he testified to having paid for the child's medical and funeral expenses. On these grounds the White man asked that the suit be dismissed. A determined Janeta pressed payment and stated in rebuttal that the amount stipulated in the note was legitimately due her for the rental of her services for five years when she lived with Darby "as his wife and servant in sickness and in health."[47]

In a torrent of words she stated that Darby was solely responsible for enticing her away from honorable employment to live in a state of concubinage. Such state had existed for four years and the two parties had acted as man and wife and had two children. When the White officer entered into a legal marriage, she continued, he did not have enough money to pay her for services she had rendered, so he made a note for 200 pesos, which Janeta maintained legally belonged to her. After much delay, the case was dropped by mutual consent of the interested parties and the situation settled out of court.

---

47. *Ibid.*, XIII (1930), 525–526.

In the professional fields a few free Negroes were represented as doctors, but for the most part such individuals appear to have been either quacks or witchdoctors. In 1801 the status of free Negro doctors was best illustrated when Governor Salcedo recommended to the Cabildo that it exclude certain persons who were not physicians but who were practicing that occupation in Louisiana. Among the number excluded from the practice of medicine was a free Negro named Derun.[48] Another listed as practicing was a free Negro who lived on the plantation of a Mrs. Dupart, but most of his patients were slaves, and it is little wonder that his services were eagerly sought, for he frequently prescribed rest and travel as a cure for physical disorders.[49]

A number of free Negroes were in businesses for themselves or in certain occupations that required some degree of skill and independence. Berquin-Duvallon, a traveler in Spanish Louisiana at the turn of the 18th century, mentioned that a number of free Negroes of both sexes "carried on small businesses, or engaged in those menial trades for which they had so much aptitude and so little liking."[50] In the city of New Orleans, where Berquin-Duvallon had visited, were located many persons of this class; they were carpenters, shoemakers or tailors. For example Juan Bougin, a free Negro carpenter, received payment from the Cabildo for work he had performed

48. *Alphabetical and Chronological Digest of the Acts and Deliberations of the Cabildo, 1769–1803,* X, 106.

49. Porteous (trans.), "Index to the Spanish Judicial Records of Louisiana," *loc. cit.,* XI (1927), 156–157.

50. Berquin-Duvallon, *Vue de la Colonie Espagnole du Mississipi ou des Provinces de Louisiane et Floride Occidentale, en l'Année 1802,* 253. Hereinafter this work will be cited as Duvallon, *Vue de la Colonie Espagnole du Mississipi.*

in the cemetery and on the Carondelet Canal. This free Negro artisan had constructed a bridge over the canal and for this work his labor amounted to the sum of 297 pesos, 5 reales.[51] Another, named Carlos Brule, also was employed by the municipality of New Orleans to make some necessary repairs on the levee near the French market.[52]

An example of a successful small-business operation was that of Juana and Pedro Viejo. These two Negroes owned and operated a small shop of dry goods in New Orleans, in which they sold such items as thread, buttons, ready-made clothes and other dry goods. Business must have been brisk, for when Juana died she left the cash sum of 800 silver pesos to her heirs.[53]

During the Spanish regime free Negresses often found employment as housekeepers on plantations operated by White persons. In 1783, Franchon, a housekeeper of a White planter named Pedro Bonne, brought legal action against her employer, to recover the sum of 1920 pesos due her for sixteen years of services in his household. The colored woman had made a contract with the planter to work for ten pesos a month, but she charged in the suit that she had never received any money as called for in the agreement. When the two parties agreed to adjust the matter outside of court, the case was dismissed.[54] A planter named Pedro Acher employed a free Negress housekeeper on his plantation in the Opelousas district whom he accused of robbing him of 700 pesos. The court,

---

51. MS. New Orleans City Records Collection 1790–1799.
52. *Alphabetical and Chronological Digest of the Acts and Deliberations of the Cabildo, 1769–1803*, II, 114..
53. Porteous (trans.), "Index to the Spanish Judicial Records of Louisiana," *loc. cit.*, XI (1928), 519–523.
54. *Ibid.*, XXI (1938), 1260–1261.

however, found the Negress innocent of these charges when the evidence presented by the White employer proved insufficient for conviction.[55]

Business partnerships with White persons were not unusual, and, in some cases, the colored partner even furnished the necessary capital for the business enterprise. For example, Nicholas Duquenay, a White blacksmith, furnished his knowledge and the tools of his occupation, while a free Negress named Marie Louise invested the sum of 500 piastres in the shop. According to an arrangement agreed upon by the two persons they divided the profits from the business, and as a result of hard work amassed a small fortune. When Duquenay died, he left his share of the business to the Negress and his Mulatto son.[56]

An example of a free Negro achieving financial security in the field of business in the rural areas was Derosier Lavesperé, who operated a tailor shop in Baton Rouge. At his death in 1808, the inventory of his shop indicated that he had enjoyed a good business. Among the items listed were, 12 shirts valued at 15 pesos, 4 shirt patterns valued at 10 pesos, 5 pantaloons of linen valued at 15 pesos, 1 pair corduroy pants valued at 5 pesos, 2 short coats valued at 6 pesos, 4 linen shirts valued at 15 pesos, 5 pairs of hose valued at 5 pesos, and 5 linen handkerchiefs valued at 2 pesos.[57]

Frequent contact between Blacks and Whites has everywhere led to some intermixture, and Louisiana was no

55. *Ibid.*, XXV (1942), 601.
56. MS. Brown (James) Papers, 1764–1811.
57. *Archives of the Spanish Government of West Florida, 1783–1812,* XIII, 148–152.

exception. Apparently, the practice of living in open concubinage with Negro women had become so widespread
by 1788 that it warranted the attention of the Spanish
authorities. In that year, Governor Estevan Miro issued
an order to restrict the practice. Article five of his *Bando
de buen gobierno* was specifically directed against Negresses. It declared that any free Negresses, Mulattresses
or Quadroons found in idleness would be considered as
prejudicial to the good order of the province. The Governor, therefore, urged them to give up idle ways and go
to work or he would have their conduct investigated, and,
"if found vicious," he would expel them from the province.
"Luxury in dress," the decree further stated, "would be
sufficient proof of their guilt and would lead to an immediate inquiry." Miro's order also declared his intention
of investigating all persons living in concubinage with
persons of color.[58]

The high officers of the Catholic church also manifested
anxiety over the growing practice of illicit unions between
White men and Negro women. In 1795, Bishop Don Luis
de Peñalvert y Cardenas, in a report on the moral and
religious conditions of Louisiana, complained that most
of the married and unmarried men lived in a state of concubinage with free women of color. According to this
prelate, White fathers even procured courtesans for the
use of their sons, "whom they thus intentionally prevented
from getting lawful wives."[59] Again in 1799 the same
bishop complained that many of the military officers and
a good many of the inhabitants lived almost openly with

---

58. Gayarré, *History of Louisiana*, III, 179.
59. *Ibid.*, III, 377.

colored women and "they do not blush at carrying the illegitimate issue they have by them to be recorded in the parochial registeries as their *natural children*."[60]

Concubinage with colored women may be attributed to a number of causes. Among these were the paucity of White women in Spanish Louisiana which frequently led provincials to take Negro women as sex partners. But none the less pertinent were the personal charms of some free Negresses who were described as not lacking in "discernment, penetration and finesse, and as superior to many white girls of the lower classes of society." Provincial White girls came out last in charm, and according to at least one observer they were "so impenetrably dull, that like Balzac's village, they were too stupid to be deceived by a man of gallantry and wit."[61] There was always a certain amount of danger in liaisons with colored women, although they were often depicted as "almost white." Furthermore, through their bearing, dress and gestures they inspired such lust that many well-to-do White persons were financially and morally ruined in pleasing them.[62] Another factor that contributed much towards increasing the practice of concubinage was the Spanish law forbidding governmental officials from marrying colonials during their term of office. Such officials were not, however, specifically prohibited from effecting relationships with women of color, or of any race, for that matter.

---

60. *Ibid.*, III, 408–409.

61. Berquin-Duvallon, *Vue de la Colonie Espagnole du Mississipi*, 254.

62. Paul Alliot, *Historical and Political Reflection on Louisiana* translated in James Alexander Robertson (ed.), *Louisiana Under the Rule of Spain, France, and the United States 1785–1807. . . .* 2 vols., I, 85. This work will hereinafter be cited as Robertson (ed.), *Louisiana Under the Rule of Spain, France and the United States, 1785–1807.*

Since this was the law of Louisiana under Spain, and as there were in the colony very few women of the White race, and hardly any of equal social status of government officers, the inevitable consequence was connection with women of color. This custom, practiced by the ruling class, soon spread throughout the colony and continued to prevail long after there ceased to be any excuse for its existence.[63]

One of the most prominent of the Spanish colonists to live in open concubinage with Negro women was Augustine Marcarty. This nobleman and Spanish army officer was reared by one of his uncles, who lived with a woman of color. During the course of his life, Augustine had several liaisons with women of that class. Finally in 1799, he took Celeste Perrault, with whom he lived for nearly fifty years until his death in 1844. To this union was born a child named Patrick, who Marcarty always addressed as "mon ami," and in all respects treated him as his legitimate son.[64] Another officer of the government who lived with a free Negress was Nicholas Vidal, the Spanish Auditor of War. In 1798, the latter made a will in which he directed that a portion of his estate be given "in equal portion," to four natural colored children whom he recognized as his own.[65]

It is abundantly apparent that Latins were very considerate of their Mulatto children and frequently provided for their education and economic well being. In some cases White men who had formed sexual liaisons with colored women became so fond of their children that they

63. *Badillo et al. v. Francisco Tio*, 6 La. An. 131–132, (February, 1851).

64. *Ibid.*

65. *Vidal's Heirs v. Duplantier*, 7 La. An., 45–46 (August 1834).

bequeathed large fortunes to them. For instance, Andres Juen in his last will and testament declared that he had three living illegitimate colored children. The first, named Roseta, aged 25 by a free Negress named Goton; the second, called Goton, aged 23 by a Negress slave named Luizon; and the third, Juan Luis, aged 22 by the free Negress Isabel. The three colored children had been fed, educated and maintained in Juen's home as members of his family.

After leaving his two brothers 2000 pesos each to prevent the possibility of their contesting a legacy to his colored offspring, Juen directed his executor to invest 2000 pesos in favor of his Mulatto son, Juan Luis, to support the latter for the remainder of his life. This was so arranged because Juen thought his son incapable of properly managing financial affairs. The White man also ordered his executor to give his Mulatto daughter, Roseta, 2000 pesos to "enable her to help herself." This amount was given in remuneration for her special care of him and "the paternal love he professes for her." For the same reasons he willed 1000 pesos to his daughter, Goton, so that she might enjoy this legacy at the proper time. Juen's free Negro family lived in luxurious surroundings as was evidenced by the inventory of the estate. At the house, for example, the inventory revealed an iron box containing the sum of 1871 pesos in cash. The house itself was described as built on brick columns with a surrounding gallery and was estimated at 4500 pesos. Some of the personal effects consisted of a mirror, one silver platter, two silver candlesticks, one silver soup tureen, a silver coffee pot, four crystal celery dishes, 101 German damask table napkins, two crystal flasks, 160 bottles of wine, and 23 empty wine bottles.[66]

As did their city cousins, planters in the isolated rural areas also entered into concubinage with Negro women. A typical case was that of Christopher Beard, who directed in his will that his slave, a little Mulatto girl named Venus, receive a good education and an equal dividend of his estate. Venus received her freedom and also six slaves from her White father and benefactor. This colored heiress also was to be properly educated in the Christian religion, taught to read and write, and when eighteen years old apprenticed to a mantua-maker to learn that business.[67]

Even members of the clergy were accused of living in concubinage with Negro women. Father Antonio Cirilo, a Spanish Capuchin, reported to his spiritual superior in Havana that eighteen Negro and Mulatto slaves lived within the confines of the rectory in New Orleans. The suspicious friar had stayed awake one morning until four o'clock to witness a White man furtively leave the room of the rectory slaves. What most shocked Father Cirilo, however, was the alleged concubine of the French Capuchin priests. According to his report only God knows who her husband was although she had three sons. The children were allowed "to eat at our table and off the plates of Father Dagobert, who, without shame or fear of the world at least, if not of God, permitted them to call him papa." The woman in question was described as a Mulattress who was employed as the rectory housekeeper and

---

66. Porteous (trans.), "Index to the Spanish Judicial Records of Louisiana," *loc. cit.*, XXIV (1941), 1260–1265.

67. *Beard v. Poydras*, 4 Mart. La. 348–353, (May 1816).

absolute mistress of the whole establishment. The friars had become so much attached to this woman that they "strive to send to the cherished paramour the best dish on the table, before anyone is allowed to taste it."[68]

It should not be assumed that Louisiana was a vast brothel; not all Negro free women lived in concubinage with Whites. Marriage records of the St. Louis Cathedral in New Orleans provide ample evidence that many persons of this class had their marriages performed with the blessing of the Catholic Church. These records also reveal that the Spanish priests classified free Negroes according to color, as Negro, Griffe (offspring of a Negro and Mulatto), Mulatto, and Quadroon. In 1777, the first entry of the recordings of Negro and Mulatto marriages was that of Juan Bautista and Mariana, both legitimate children who were "joined in holy wedlock," by Father Cyrilo de Barcelona. In another entry dated the same year, Francisco, a free Mulatto, was married to Carlata, a free Negress. The woman's father was listed as unknown, which indicated her illegitimate status. In 1793, Santiago LeDuffe, classified as a free Mulatto, was married to Josephina Reusève, a free Quadroon. A rather imposing marriage was performed in 1794, for Juan Pedro Claver, a free Negro, with Celeste Hugon, a free Griffe. Celeste Hugon was the daughter of Captain Bautista Hugon, the Mulatto commander of the colored militia who furnished his daughter with a guard of honor on the gala occasion.[69]

---

68. Father Antonio Cirilo to Don Santiago Hechevarria, Bishop of Cuba, August 6, 1772, quoted in Gayarré, *History of Louisiana,* III, 63–74.

69. MS. First Book of Marriages of Negroes and Mulattoes of the Parish of St. Louis in the City of New Orleans 1777–1830.

The French custom of allowing free Negroes to contract legal marriages with slaves was continued during the Spanish period of Louisiana. Free persons of color were also required to obtain permission from the slave's owner to legalize such a marriage. For example, in 1778, a free Negress named Angela was given permission from Fernando le Leiva to marry his slave, Louis. In 1786, the free Negro Pedro contracted marriage with Maria Theresa, after having first received the permission from the owners and parents of the slave, Juan and Nova Bautista.[70]

The amusements and social life of the free Negro were far from discouraged by the authorities, and in fact reached a high degree of development during the Spanish dominion. Dancing was one of the principal diversions of Louisianians during that period. In order to satisfy the demand, public balls were usually held twice a week in the city of New Orleans, on Sunday and Thursday nights.[71] There were several kinds of balls. One was for the children[72] while two others catered to the White and free Negro adults exclusively.[73] Quadroon balls, which were attended by White men only, were considered superior in fun and beauty to the White dances. Contemporary observers, however, differed as to the decorum of the colored affairs. The French sojourner, Berquin-Duvallon,

---

70. *Ibid.*
71. Berquin-Duvallon, *Vue de la Colonie Espagnole du Mississipi*, 31.
72. *Ibid.*, 38–39.
73. Charles C. Robin, *Voyages dans l'Intérieur de la Louisiane, de la Floride Occidentale, et dans les Isles de la Martinique et de Saint-Dominque, pendant les années 1802, 1803, 1804, 1805 et 1806*, II, 119. This work will hereinafter be cited as Robin, *Voyages dans l'Intérieur de la Louisiane*.

considered Quadroon balls as places where "saffron colored women danced with the scum of society,"[74] and went on to register keen disappointment over the quality of the musicians at one free Negro dance. To this sharp critic they consisted of five or six Bohemians or people of color, who he wrote seemed to "scrape their violins with all their might."[75] In sum it was hardly an exhilarating exhibition of talent.

Another type of ball was sponsored for the benefit of the free colored population exclusively. During the social season of 1801 a group of free Negroes asked the Governor for permission to hold a grand ball. The petitioners indicated a preference for the house of a White man named Coquet because it was not only more spacious, but so arranged that it would allow the dance committee to better regulate the conduct of the guests. Formerly, this group pointed out, "certain rascals had been wont to leave wads of tobacco on the seats thus spoiling the ladies' gowns; they also chewed vanilla sticks and scattered vanilla around, thereby creating an intolerable odor."[76]

Another diversion in which the free Negro enjoyed himself was the colonial theatre. In many respects this form of amusement afforded a more edifying entertainment than dancing, since comedy, drama and comic opera was "passably" presented in the theatres in New Orleans.[77] Without exception, the New Orleans theatres encouraged free Negro patrons by providing them with separate seating arrangements from the Whites. Usually the second or

---

74. Berquin-Duvallon, *Vue de la Colonie Espagnole du Misssissipi*, 32.
75. *Ibid.*
76. *Alphabetical and Chronological Digest of the Acts and Deliberations of the Cabildo, 1769–1803*, X, 181–184.
77. Berquin-Duvallon, *Vue de la Colonie Espagnole du Mississipi*, 29.

third gallery was set aside for the colored patrons.[78]

Free Negroes and White persons frequently mingled with one another in taverns. New Orleans was described by one visitor from abroad as having a tavern at every street corner where the persons of all classes and colors mingled indiscriminately. Very near these places were the bawdy houses with dirty smoking rooms, where "father and son of all classes and colors openly drank and gambled together."[79] On the night of August 5, 1781, a raid was staged against one gambling house. Here the police discovered the main attraction to be the game of twenty-one which was being played behind a heavily screened corner of the establishment. As the officers in charge entered the gambling nook, Mulattoes, Whites, artillery soldiers and others fled to the most convenient exits. Francisco Livaudais, who was listed as a free Negro, was unfortunate enough to get caught. He was booked at headquarters, jailed for a few days and released with a stern warning not to gamble in the future.[80]

Crime among free Negroes was not so common as might be supposed by the alarmists of that period. In fact, one visitor named Paul Alliot noted that "twenty whites could be counted in the prison at New Orleans against only one man of color."[81] In some instances, White persons connived with free Negroes to harass their White enemies. Such a case occurred in 1773 when a White planter named

78. "Dr. John Sibley of Natchitoches, 1757–1837," *Louisiana Historical Quarterly*, X (1937), 486.

79. Berquin-Duvallon, *Vue de la Colonie Espagnole du Mississipi*, 185.

80. Henry P. Dart (ed.), "Episodes of Life in Colonial Louisiana," *Louisiana Historical Quarterly*, VI (1923), 35–46.

81. Alliot, *Historical and Political Reflection on Louisiana* in Robertson, *Louisiana Under the Rule of Spain, France, and the United States, 1785–1807*, I, 71.

Alexander Dubreuil was charged with placing a free Negress on his plantation to annoy his neighbor, Antonio Bouligny. She sold spirituous liquors to the latter's slaves and encouraged them to run away. This woman's cabin was described by the plaintiff as a meeting place for thieves and murderers. Satisfied with the evidence presented by Bouligny, Governor Unzaga ordered Dubreuil to destroy the cabin along with a warning that if this was not done, the free Negress would be evicted and her cabin destroyed by the authorities.[82]

Among the most horrible crimes ever committed by a free Negro during the Spanish period of Louisiana was the homicide case of Mary Glass. In 1780 this free Quadroon from North Carolina had married a "renegade" White man who had deserted the English army and moved to the vicinity of Baton Rouge. In the indictment it was charged that Mary Glass had tortured to death her fifteen-year-old white indentured servant named Emilia Davis. John Glass, the husband of the accused, was named as an accessory. Details of the gory affair came to light in the various statements of witnesses and the continuous interrogations of the accused by a Captain Favrot, the Spanish officer in charge of the trial at Baton Rouge. Madame Françoise Gause, one of the many state witnesses, testified she had once heard that a White girl was tied up and cruelly whipped, and that Mary Glass was barbarous enough to heat a fork to put into Emilia Davis' mouth to pierce her tongue with it. On one occasion this witness had seen the child with an eye almost out of her head as a result of a severe beating administered by Mary Glass.

---

82. Porteous (trans.), "Index to the Spanish Judicial Records of Louisiana," *loc. cit.*, IX (1926), 546.

Sarah West, another witness, swore that on visiting the home of the accused, she had seen her abuse and beat the murdered girl, then tie the unfortunate victim to a ladder for Mr. Glass to witness. Sarah West also stated that she had complained of this torture, but was threatened and forced to leave out of fear of physical harm to herself.

Another free Negro named Samuel, testified that on one occasion he had heard groans coming from the house of Mary Glass and on investigating was told to mind his own business. Nancy, another free Negro witness, who was described as a "very sensible and intelligent woman" swore she had also heard pitiful groans one night and on inquiring was told by Mary Glass that the White servant had been a very bad girl and had to be punished. Thomas George, a free Mulatto boy, aged eleven or twelve years, was described as "a very sensible, solid and understanding for one of his years," testified that when Emelia Davis failed to wash her owner's clothes clean enough, she was punished by being stretched out, tied upon a ladder and then whipped. This minor witness told the court he had once seen the murdered girl whipped so violently that her "buttocks were as raw as a piece of beef and all bloody." Mary Glass, he said, stopped beating for a while and "washed her with salt and water." George also told the court that the whippings sometimes continued from noon until night, and that a few days after one of these whippings the white child became so full of sores he feared "maggots were getting into them." He knew all this because he had frequently played with the unfortunate White child.

Mary Glass testified in her own defense and while not denying having punished her servant, she denied having anything to do with her death. Under questioning, John Glass finally broke down and confessed that his wife had murdered the child. The free Quadroon was therefore found guilty, condemned to death by hanging, and afterwards to have her head severed and posted on a pole at Browns Cliffs in the Pointe Coupee district. John Glass was likewise found guilty as an accessory, but he was recommended to the mercy of the Governor. On July 26, 1781, Mary Glass was executed at about eleven o'clock in the morning; her right hand was cut off before she mounted the steps of the gallows, and afterwards her severed head was placed upon the pole indicated in the sentence.[83]

Free Negroes too suffered both indignities and physical harm from Whites and many brought civil action against their tormentors. For example, on March 27, 1809, a free Mulatto named Jean Villars, a resident of Baton Rouge, filed a complaint against a White planter named Pierre Charlot for stealing his cattle. In addition, the colored man accused Charlot of attacking him without provocation when he attempted to recover his property. According to the deposition of Villars, Charlot had branded his two cows and calves with his own mark and was milking and using them as if they were his own property. When the Mulatto offered to prove that the cattle in question rightfully belonged to him, the White planter became enraged and "took a stick and started beating me . . . forcing me to resist, although I did not use my strength, only to stop the blows."[84]

83. Henry P. Dart (ed.), "Trial of Mary Glass for Murder, 1780," *Louisiana Historical Quarterly*, VI (1923), 591–654.

84. *Archives of the Spanish Government of West Florida*, 1783–1812, XVI, 173–174.

At this point Charlot called the aid of two slaves to subdue the hapless free Negro who thought it wise to undergo the punishment meted out by the White man, until the issue could be settled by the Governor of the Baton Rouge post. Governor de Lassus, to whom the freeman had appealed for justice, rendered a verdict in favor of the plaintiff and condemned the accused to serve 24 hours in the fort, and also to pay a fine based on one-half the value of cattle.[85]

In addition to the regular or standing army, Spanish authorities continued their French predecessors' practice of making use of militia companies consisting entirely of free colored soldiers. In 1779, the first and most significant use of this branch of the provincial militia was made by Governor Bernardo de Galvez in his campaigns against the British in West Florida. The free Negro soldiers saw active service against the English as combatants at Manchac, Baton Rouge, Mobile and Pensacola. Since Spain had allied with France to fight the British in 1779, free colored militiamen took a part in an overall effort to help the American colonies win independence.

Galvez began his expedition against the British posts on the Mississippi in the late summer of 1779. The Spanish force was made up of 1427 men, among whom were 80 free Blacks and Mulattoes. After a minor engagement at Fort Manchac the English surrendered the fort to the Spanish commander. On September 20, 1779, the Spanish reached Baton Rouge, but the fort there proved to be much more formidable than the one at Manchac. It was surrounded by a deep moat and had high thick walls which made it impossible to take by a frontal assault.

85. *Ibid.*, 175.

Near the fort, however, was a grove of trees which appeared to be the most obvious position from which to attack. Under the cover of darkness, Galvez sent a detachment of militiamen, containing colored troops and Indians, to this place. The purpose of the group was to make as much noise as possible to simulate an attack, and thereby attract the attention of the English. The British defenders were completely duped, and wasted much ammunition firing into the grove of trees. It was this diversionary action that allowed the Spanish to install their artillery on the opposite side of the fort.

On the morning of September 21, the Spanish artillery opened up and the fort soon fell to the besiegers. Among the prisoners of war taken at Baton Rouge were a number of free Negro soldiers who had been employed by the English. The Spanish, however, released them, because there were no accommodations to handle the great number of prisoners. After the climax of the Mississippi campaign, Governor Galvez reported to his government that the companies of free Blacks and Mulattoes "who had been employed in false attacks and as scouts displayed as much valor as the Whites."[86]

After the fall of the British Mississippi posts, Galvez began preparations for an attack upon the English strongholds on the Gulf of Mexico. In the beginning of the year 1780, he left New Orleans with 754 men composed of regulars, the militia of the province and 107 Black and Mulatto troops, destined for Mobile. After being delayed by a storm, Galvez succeeded in landing his army on the

---

86. *Gazeta de Madrid,* January 14, 1780, quoted in Gayarré, *History of Louisiana,* III, 125–132; Bernardo de Galvez to Jose de Galvez, October 16, 1774, AGI, Cuba, 2351, quoted in John Walton Caughey, *Bernardo de Galvez in Louisiana 1776–1783,* 153, 156–157, 163.

eastern shore of the Mobile River and began operations against the fort. This English stronghold fell to the warrior governor on March 14, 1780.[87]

Galvez next launched an attack against Pensacola, then the chief British stronghold on the Gulf of Mexico. After a siege of two months (March 9, 1781–May 9, 1781) this citadel capitulated to the Spanish forces.[88] Free Negro troops were used to good advantage in the siege of this city, for at one time the Louisiana free colored militia, together with White troops, "beat off an attack by 400 Indians by the use of artillery fire."[89] It is, however, impossible to determine accurately the number of free Negro troops from Louisiana present at the siege of Pensacola. All totaled, about 500 Spanish colored troops took part in the battle and of this number approximately one-half were from the Louisiana province.[90]

When the colony was threatened by invasion, free Negro troops also were expected to garrison the forts that protected the city of New Orleans. In the event of an attack, Governor Carondolet issued an order in 1797 indicating the stations free Negro soldiers were to occupy in the several forts. At the Redoubt St. John there were to be 50

87. Gayarré, *History of Louisiana*, III, 135–136.

88. *Ibid.*, III, 135–146 *passim;* Caughey, *Bernardo de Galvez in Louisiana 1776–1783*, 200–214.

89. Gaspar Cusacks (ed.), "Bernardo de Galvez's Diary of the Operations Against Pensacola, May 13, 1781," *Louisiana Historical Quarterly*, I (1917), 59.

90. Martin Navarro, "Report of Troops Used in the Pensacola Expedition," New Orleans, February 28, 1781, translated in Kinniard (ed.), *Spain in the Mississippi Valley, 1765–1794*, I, 421–424. This report listed 130 Mulatto grenadiers and scouts; 134 black grenadiers and scouts along with 90 free Mulatto and Black militiamen. In addition to these the report included 150 free Negroes from Havana. It is therefore concluded that about 250 free Negroes listed above were from Louisiana.

Mulattoes under the command of Captain Francisco Darville. In addition to White soldiers, 30 Negroes commanded by Lieutenant Pedro Thomas were stationed at the Rampart St. John, while Fort St. Ferdinand contained 50 men from the company of the free Negroes, under the command of Captain Nöel Cariérè. Captain Carlos Simon commanded 40 men of the company of free Mulattoes stationed at Fort Burgundy. A first lieutenant was placed in command of 25 men from the free Mulatto troops which were to be garrisoned at Fort St. Louis.[91]

In times of peace the free Negroes, both in the capacity of militiamen and as vigilantes, were expected to help maintain order in the colony. They were most frequently called upon to apprehend fugitive slaves for which service they were paid from public funds. The first evidence concerning Spanish use of free Negroes to capture runaway slaves was in 1771. In that year Juan Felix, a free Mulatto, Jacobo Raphael, a free Negro, Juan Bautista Raphael, a free Mulatto, and Juan Legros, a free Negro, were summoned by the firing of a gun. This was a prearranged signal to assemble at a Mr. DeRocheblave's plantation to go in search of fugitives.[92] In recompense for such services the Cabildo appropriated two pesos each to eighteen free Negroes for going in pursuit of "savage negroes." This amount was paid them independent of what they had received from their former masters.[93] Free Negro militia units were often employed in apprehending fugitive

---

91. James W. Cruzat (trans.), "The Defenses of New Orleans in 1797," *Publications of the Louisiana Historical Society*, I (1896), 36–38.

92. Laura L. Porteous (trans.), "Trial of Pablo Rocheblave Before Governor Unzaga, 1771," *Louisiana Historical Quarterly*, VIII (1925), 380–381.

93. *Alphabetical and Chronological Digest of the Acts and Deliberations of the Cabildo, 1769–1803*, I, 192.

slaves. The Cabildo, for example, in its meeting of February 15, 1782, paid, at the request of acting Governor Piernas, a small stipend for the arrest of two slaves made by a detachment of free Negro soldiers.[94]

However, free Negro militia companies were not always successful in apprehending fugitive slaves. At the regular sessions of the Cabildo on May 5, 1784, Attorney General Lorenzo Mazange called attention to atrocities committed by a colony of fugitive slaves. For this reason, certain nearby plantations had been left uncultivated. The official went on to explain that these slaves had settled in a village named Gaillaré. Their stronghold was too close to the plantations for safety, and could only be reached by unknown and inaccessible paths. Furthermore, the slaves had elected as their chief one called "*Senor Malo*," who was noted for his cunning and murderous activity. *Malo* had as his lieutenant one called *El Cabellera de la Hacha* [knight of the hatchet] who had been given that title because he had killed a White planter by splitting his head open with an axe. Mazange urged immediate action against the village in question, because it constituted a serious danger to every White person in the province. In compliance with this demand, Lieutenant Colonel Bouligny was directed to take the necessary measures to destroy the slave stronghold of Gaillaré.[95]

Bouligny sent such a small expedition against the slaves that it was easily defeated. Encouraged by success, the fugitive Negroes increased their assaults against the Whites in the vicinity. In a meeting of the Cabildo on July 4, 1784, the Attorney General, greatly disturbed by

94. *Ibid.*, VI, 194.
95. *Ibid.*, 194–195.

the setback, told that body that it was unwise to continue sending out inadequate detachments of men against such a powerful enemy. He also mentioned the uselessness of sending expeditions of free Negroes and Mulattoes because of their reluctance in proceeding against these criminals, "who are themselves mostly Creoles of this province, which reluctance is due to fear of reprisals against their families." He concluded by recommending that Bouligny send all available troops to accompany the free Negro and Mulatto militia.[96] This suggestion was carried out and the fugitive slave stronghold was soon destroyed and the leaders captured and executed.[97]

Free Negroes were also expected to report for service in other capacities when the public welfare demanded it. Such an occasion was a break in the levee on the Tchoupitoulas Coast in 1790. The danger was so great that it was necessary to repair the break by using other forces than the customary slave labor; therefore a call was issued for "all free Negroes and Mulattoes in the city [New Orleans] and such slaves as their masters wished to hire out," to meet this emergency. The pay was fixed at 3 pesos per day for each person, and the work continued for one month. Soon after the levee was repaired, a free Negro named Pedro Bahi, presented a claim for one of his slaves, Felipe, who had died while working on the levee. The Cabildo rejected the claim because persons hiring slaves were never held responsible in the event of a natural death, "as this one had been under certification from the royal physician," and furthermore, "it was Bahi himself

---

96. *Ibid.*, 195–196.
97. *Ibid.*, 201–204.

who had been called to work on the levee, as was true of other free Negroes, therefore if his substitute had been accepted it had been only to accommodate him."[98]

Policing slaves or patrol duty also was a public service required of every able-bodied White man as well as free Negro men. Failure to show up for such duty subjected the delinquent to the full penalties of the law. A case among many derelictions of this obligation was that of Julian Jalio, a free Negro living at the Baton Rouge post; he was arrested by a White officer and two free colored patrolmen for refusing to do patrol duty. Jalio was released when he presented a doctor's certificate stating that he was too ill with rheumatism for such strenuous duty.[99]

Probably no other event during the Spanish domination frightened colonial administrators as much as the French Revolution and its bloody impact on Santo Domingo and Louisiana. Both of these upheavals produced a great amount of talk among Louisiana's French subjects, who made no effort in concealing their support of the ideas of "Liberty, Equality and Fraternity." French Creoles kept themselves informed of the minutest developments in France through correspondence from that country and its colonies in America.[100]

Even before the outbreak of revolution in Santo Domingo, Governor Estevan Miro, anticipating such an event, issued secret orders in 1790 to prevent slaves and

---

98. *Ibid.*, VIII, 110.

99. *Archives of the Spanish Government of West Florida, 1783–1810*, XVI, 321.

100. Manuel Gayoso de Lemos, "Political Conditions in the Province of Louisiana," Natchez, July 5, 1792, translated in Robertson (ed.), *Louisiana Under the Rule of Spain, France and the United States, 1785–1807*, I, 283.

"half-cast persons" coming from that French possession to the Louisiana colony. For his part he pledged to expel all of that category in the most "efficacious and opportune manner" so that the public would never know the true reason for their expulsion.[101] Miro's successor, Louis Hector, Baron de Carondolet, on learning that the French government had decreed freedom for the slaves of Santo Domingo, publicly prohibited the importation of slaves and free Negroes from that island. He also issued a proclamation forbidding the dissemination of revolutionary propaganda and the reading of radical French literature. In addition all gatherings in private homes for the purpose of discussing political questions pertaining to the French Revolution.[102]

Despite these precautions, enthusiasm for the French Revolution grew and Governor Carondolet turned his attention to investigating secret meetings that usually involved the free Negro element of the population. In these small gatherings, since it was alleged that plans were laid for revolutionizing the province and projects were formulated to enlist the support of the free Negro population.

In the Spring of 1793, Carondolet got wind of one such conspiracy in the German Coast district [later St. Charles Parish]. Concerning these events the Governor reported to Havana that he had obtained information that some

---

101. Estevan Miro to Don Luis de Las Casas (Captain-General of Cuba), August 21, 1790, in Works Progress Administration, Survey of the Federal Archives in Louisiana (trans. and ed.), *Despatches of the Spanish Governors of Louisiana,* XXI, 50. This work will hereinafter be cited as *Despatches of the Spanish Governors of Louisiana.*

102. Gayarré, *History of Louisiana,* III, 325; "Proclamation by Carondolet," February 15, 1793, in Kinniard (ed.), *Spain in the Mississippi Valley, 1765–1794,* IV, 139–140.

individuals who were in sympathy with the French Revolution were trying to poison the minds of Louisiana's free Negroes. At the same time the Governor reported that these persons were using all sorts of threats to terrify the colored people and instill in them a hatred for the Spanish people and its government. Yet he was sure that such effort would fail. They had threatened the Mulattoes and Negroes by telling them that when "the French come down the river" they would kill all free colored persons or reenslave them.[103]

The Governor's informants were four free Negroes who volunteered the information that a conspiracy against the government was in the making among the French planters of the German Coast. Charles Joseph L'Ange, a free Mulatto, informed the Governor that one rainy day while he and his father-in-law were located at their plantation they had a visitor named Monsieur Penn who spoke approvingly of the concepts of the French Revolution. Penn maintained that the French had the right to kill the "silly king" because he was "a rascal and a man like any other" person. Furthermore, the Queen did nothing but spend the taxpayers' money.

François de Lande replied to Penn that "the French killed their King, well, the Spanish will force them into subjection." The irate White man replied, "one Frenchman is worth four Spaniards. The word of the French is the word of God." Penn continued to speak of these matters and of what was taking place in the city regarding the declaration of war against France. He also informed

---

103. Carondolet to Las Casas, March 23, 1793, *Despatches of the Spanish Governors of Louisiana*, VI, 219.

the free Negroes that many Creoles had taken an oath of loyalty to the Spanish government,[104] but it was nothing because when the time came they would take up arms and turn against the Spaniards whose "heads they would cut off in the night." Penn also advised the two colored men not to support the Spaniards because the French would soon arrive in Louisiana "as the sea was then covered with French ships." François de Lande replied he would never side with any but the Spaniards because the French had "ill treated them too much in their slavery."

Following hours of questioning, François de Lande substantiated his son-in-law's testimony and added that on one occasion the revolutionist returned and talked to Madame de Lande. Penn had told her the free Negroes would do well to "hide in the woods and not stain their hands with the blood of Frenchmen," for it would only bring them misfortune when Louisiana once again became French territory. De Lande also informed the Governor that on another occasion while he and his wife were cleaning rice on their back porch someone had fired a shot at them, but he was unable to determine from which direction the bullet had come or who had fired it.[105]

Rene de Lande, another free Mulatto informer, implicated several White persons in his testimony before the Governor. He had been told by his friend, Pierre, a free Negro, that Alexander LeBranche Piseros, Pierre Trepannier and François Trepannier always leveled verbal blasts

---

104. Ernest R. Liljegren, "Jacobinism in Spanish Louisiana, 1792–1797," *Louisiana Historical Quarterly*, XXII (1939), 51. All persons who had come to the colony since 1790 as well as those who did not own property or have other permanent interests, were required to take an oath of allegiance to Spain.

105. Investigation by Carondolet, *Despatches of the Spanish Governors of Louisiana*, VI, 220–223.

against the free Negro population. He had heard these
individuals say that when the French took over the province, the free Negroes would be sold to them as slaves.[106]

Joseph Cabaret, another free Mulatto, stated that for
thirteen years he had lived in the house of his former
master, a M. Cabaret, who was loyal to the Spanish government. In his opinion, the free Negroes would remain
faithful to the Spanish government even to the extent of
"dying with guns in their hands for the Spaniards." Cabaret also testified that he had been informed by free Mulatto friends, Jacques Bellaire and Barnabe, that M. François Trepannier would like to have him for a slave. The
white planter also expressed a desire to own Bellaire, because he could make shoes for his family, and Barnabe,
because he could play the violin and amuse his friends.
According to this informant, the White revolutionaries
were accustomed to having drinking parties in which they
toasted the *Cocarde Nationale*.[107] Whether or not Carondolet took formal action against the suspects is a matter
of conjecture, but it is not unlikely that they escaped the
close observation of Spanish authorities. Then too, the
harassed Governor probably felt secure with the declaration of loyalty by the free Negroes of the German Coast
district.

The problem of the free Negro was not alarming except
when the disgruntled element combined with the unruly
slaves, and thus posed a serious threat in the minds of
Whites. Such a possibility occurred in 1795 when a conspiracy was discovered among the slaves at Pointe Coupee.
Here a number of slaves planned to rise up and massacre

---

106. *Ibid.*, 223–225.
107. *Ibid.*, 225–226.

their owners and declare themselves free persons of the
French Republic. Much of the extant evidence points to
the fact that this insurrection had been instigated by the
pro-French Revolutionary faction as part of their campaign for overthrowing Spanish rule in Louisiana. The
conspirators, however, were betrayed by one of their own
men and the Negro leaders captured and brutally executed.[108]

There can be no doubt that free Negroes were involved
in this attempted revolt. Governmental authorities found
enough evidence to expel Antonio Coffi, a free Negro
known in the province for his revolutionary ideas. In
ordering his exile Governor Carondolet offered the public
incontestable evidence of Coffi's help to the Pointe Coupee
plotters. Police officials had found a carbine, six muskets,
two swords, and a saber in his house. The Governor also
considered the free Negro as derelict in duty because he
know about the resolutions adopted by the slaves at Pointe
Coupee, but had failed to inform the authorities. "All of
this goes to prove," reported the Governor, "he is not
worthy to be trusted and when least expected he would
be ready to aid those of his color." At the same time,
Carondolet expelled Louis Benoit, a free Negro from
Santo Domingo, who also was suspected of being connected with the slave plot in Pointe Coupee. "Having such
a character around," the Governor wrote superiors in
Havana, "under the present circumstances in which I am
placed might produce bad results."[109]

If one takes into consideration the ratio between Whites
and Negroes, the Governor's anxiety had some basis in

108. Gayarré, *History Of Louisiana*, III, 377.
109. Carondolet to Las Casas, June 16, 1795, *Despatches of the Spanish Governors of Louisiana*, VI, 254–255.

fact. During the entire period of Spanish control the total Negro population exceeded the White. In 1785, for example, the White population was listed as 9766, slaves at 15,010 and the free Negroes numbered 1175. The areas of greatest free Negro concentration were as follows: New Orleans had 563 Negroes, while the rural districts counted 612 persons of that class. The greatest concentration of rural free Negroes were found in the Tchapitoulas Coast, where there were 203; Balize, at the mouth of the Mississippi, had 67; the German Coast had 60; Attakapas (Southwest Louisiana) had 22; and Avoyelles had 138 free Negroes. The remaining 52 free Negroes were located in St. Bernard, Second German Coast, Catahanose (First Acadian Coast), Baton Rouge, Pointe Coupee and the Natchitoches districts.[110]

Three years later, according to the census of 1788, the same conditions prevailed. In the two provinces (Louisiana and West Florida) there were 1701 free Negroes in a total population of 43,111. Among the free Negro population, 693 were males and 1008 were females. New Orleans had the greatest single concentration with 233 of the 693 males and 587 of the 1008 females. This census also indicated a greater free Negro rural population—881 lived outside New Orleans.[111]

During the greater part of his administration, Carondolet was constantly threatened with revolution, invasion and conspiracies in favor of the French Republic. In 1795, considerable anxiety was expressed by the authorities after

---

110. *Appendix to An Account of Louisiana*, lxxxiv.
111. Resumen General del Padron hecho . . . en 1788, quoted in Caroline Maude Burson, *The Stewardship of Don Esteban Miro 1782–1792*, 105. Burson suggests that the fire of 1788 in New Orleans may have caused the trend to rural life.

learning from a free Negro informer that a conspiracy existed in the Louisiana militia. Charles Joseph L'Ange, the free Negro who had reported the conspiracy in the German Coast, again supplied the information. According to L'Ange, it had been planned for some time; it had started when he had been sent with an expedition of free Negroes and Mulattoes to work on Fort Plaquemine. At that time, the informer said, he had met a French soldier named Joseph Roland, and had become friendly with him.

Roland had promised to give the free Negro some fencing lessons, but when his company was withdrawn the informer had no occasion to see his friend until he accidently met him in New Orleans during Easter week of 1795. On that occasion L'Ange was greeted by Roland with a "How are you brother?", a handshake and an invitation to have a drink. They went to a tavern, selected the darkest corner of the room and ordered large bottles of wine. For several hours the two men drank and always addressed each other as "brother." As the evening wore on, Roland began talking about the "rights of man" and the equality of persons regardless of color; he made it clear that equality for all would be guaranteed if the French could gain control of Louisiana. The White soldier confided in L'Ange that 40,000 Negroes were ready to "help return the province to France." After a few more rounds of drinks the two parted company, promising to meet for breakfast.[112]

Instead of breakfast, Roland was arrested and brought before the Governor to answer charges of treason. On being questioned, he swore under oath he had been in

---

112. Testimony of Charles L'Ange, *Despatches of the Spanish Governors of Louisiana*, VI, 256–258.

the province for only five years and, moreover, did not know a single Negro, slave or free. He, however, admitted having seen some Negroes in a tavern where he had gone for some bread and cheese, but testified he had not spoken or drunk with them.[113]

Sergeant Marcos Ribera supported L'Ange's testimony. He stated that he had seen the free Negro and the accused soldier drinking together in a tavern. He had noticed that while drinking they had been talking together in low tones.[114] In addition, five other witnesses swore they had seen L'Ange and Roland together in the tavern.[115]

Attorney General Vidal, who had been placed in charge of the investigation, was of the opinion that Roland was guilty of "inciting L'Ange with friendly words . . . so that he would convoke those of his race to an uprising." This official, however, did not recommend a public court martial because of the "delicate nature of the matter." Instead, he suggested that the Governor expel Roland from the colony "with as much secrecy as possible."[116]

During the Spanish regime custom as well as law created clear lines of distinction between different classes. The chapetones were European by birth and the first in rank and power; the Creoles were second; the free Mulattoes and free Negroes formed the third class; and the slaves and Indians the fourth.[117] Since Spain was never certain of the loyalty of the masses of the White people, it became the policy of the authorities to back free Negroes

---

113. Testimony of Joseph Roland, *ibid.*, 259–261.
114. Testimony of Sergeant Marcos Ribera, *ibid.*, 264–265.
115. *Ibid.*, 265–269.
116. Nicholas Maria Vidal to Baron de Carondolet, June 30, 1795, *ibid.*, 273–274.
117. Henry Rightor, *Standard History of New Orleans*, 187.

up to a certain point, thereby creating a class of people
who would maintain a balance of power between the
White and the slave populations. In order to keep the
affection of free Negroes, they were legally granted the
same advantages as the other members of the nation with
which they were incorporated. The law granted them
the same security as Caucasians. They could not be
molested in the possession of their property, injured or ill
treated. However, this group of people were watched
with the same suspicion as were Whites and slaves.
Spanish administrators were especially watchful of their
conduct, and diligently required that deference and attention "which was due from them to the members of that
society whom they formerly served, and which had admitted them to its bosom."[118]

The color line was clearly drawn in the area of public
social services. In making a donation to the Cabildo for
a hospital to care for bind people, Don Andres Almonaster
y Roxas stipulated that separate rooms be provided for
White and free colored persons.[119] The traveler Robin
mentioned that Black blood was by nature so impure that
the slightest amount degraded White blood. It was his
opinion that free Negroes should be kept in a subordinate
position as a necessary precaution for the preservation of
the institution of slavery. He recommended that the
Creoles conduct themselves more like Spartans who had
been successful in conserving their "authority over slaves
for more than 600 years."[120] Mulattoes, on the other hand,
were considered even more dangerous, and from time to

---

118. Proclamation of Governor Carondolet, June 1, 1795, *Appendix
to an Account of Louisiana*, lxxxii.

119. *DePontalbo v. New Orleans*, 3 La. An. 661, (November 1848).

120. Robin, *Voyages dans l'Interiéur de la Louisiana*, 210.

time campaigns were initiated with the idea of forming them into a colony on some uninhabited part of the continent. Proponents of the scheme argued that such a plan would not only free the colony of undesirables, but would at the same time bring to an end the intemperate conduct of the Whites toward this class of persons.[121]

Free Negro women formed a redoubtable class. Mulattresses and the nearly white Quadroons, with their yellow or bronze-tinted complexions, vied with White women for the attention of men. For this reason these so-called "priestesses of illegitimate love" incurred the everlasting enmity of the White women of the province.[122] As an example of this animosity Robin recounts an experience he witnessed while visiting a ball in New Orleans. Here he describes how White women of questionable reputation had sensed that "a woman of mixed blood" was present at the dance and when two Quadroon women were discovered, they were required to leave because the sensitive lady would be "offended by their presence." The Quadroon ladies in question had two brothers who were officers in the merchant marine. Aboard their vessel they could have White sailors whipped, "but ashore they dare not look them in the face."[123]

Some of the ordinances of the Spanish period demonstrate the attempts made to define, if not maintain, the color line. Among these ordinances are those which forbade women with the least trace of Negro blood to show any excessive attention to dress: the wearing of feathers

121. Perrin Du Lac, *Travels through the Two Louisianas and among the Savage Nations of the Missouri; in the United States, along the Ohio and the adjacent provinces, in 1801, 1802, and 1803*, 95.

122. Baudry des Lozières, *Second Voyage a La Louisiana, faisant suit au premier de l'auteur de 1794 à 1798*, 281.

123. Robin, *Voyages dans l'Interiéur de la Louisiane*, II, 120–121.

or jewelry, or in any way copying the dress of White women, was forbidden. The wearing of caps, coiffures and Spanish mantillas was against the law. Since their heads were required to be bound, the handkerchief turban became a badge of distinction for the free Negro women, although in this matter as in others there was a great laxity in enforcing the law.[124]

Thus midway between the White and slave population of Spanish Louisiana stood a caste known as the free Negro or free people of color. Planters, merchants and government officials regarded them as necessary in managing their complex households, to warn them of plots among the slaves and Whites, and to serve as soldiers whenever the public welfare was endangered by invasion. Yet, like the French, the Spanish preserved the color line. In so doing they reduced the free Negro's social and economic status. Yet despite these drawbacks imposed upon them, free Negroes made history, and just as evidence of their color persisted in Louisiana, so did their influence continue in the years to come when the area reached the status of an American territory and finally that of a state.

---

124. Gayarré, *History of Louisiana,* III, 179.

3

An American Dilemma: Growth of the Free Negro, 1803-1860

WHEN the American territorial governor, William C. C. Claiborne, took possession of Louisiana in 1803, he found a messy and uncertain situation. The structure of government successfully created by Spain and France had crumbled almost beyond repair, and the few remaining caretaker officials were corrupt and suspicious of the American republic. Most of the inhabitants were woefully uninformed about their new status and were quite naturally confused as to whether their loyalty should be to Spain, France, or the United States. As if to compound an already serious affair, the shy Virginia-born Governor was brought face to face with the sudden crisis of what to do about the great influx of free Negroes from Haiti.

This movement, which represented the largest single migration into Louisiana, began about the time of Haitian independence in 1804 when many free persons of color fled their homeland to escape hostile action by the island's ex-slaves. This exodus continued during a five-year period and accounted for a more than doubling of the territory's free Negro population. Quite predictably, this increase aroused great fear among White citizens lest the Negroes spread revolutionary notions of freedom among Louisiana slaves. The fear of a repetition of the scenes which "wrapped in flames and drenched in blood the beautiful island of Santo Domingo" conditioned the attitudes of Louisianians toward any Negro regardless of color from that island for the next half century.[1]

During the high point of this movement excitement reached epidemic proportions when a free Negro named Marseille, who had served in Haiti's army, was found living among the recent immigrants in New Orleans. He was immediately apprehended and deported to prevent any contact with the territory's slaves.[2] Following other cases of a similar nature, steps were taken by the municipal authorities to halt the entry of such persons from Santo Domingo. The City Council received permission from Governor Claiborne to inspect all incoming ships suspected of having free Negro passengers.[3] This body also passed regulations requiring all such persons coming into the port city to register with the municipal officials under penalty of fines or expulsion.[4]

These measures proved insufficient, and the Mayor,

1. Mary Treudly, *The United States and Santo Domingo, 1787–1866*, 125.

2. MS. Proceedings of the City Council of New Orleans, November 30, 1803 to March 29, 1805, Session of July 27, 1804, 124.

3. *Ibid.*, 82.

4. MS. Ordinances and Resolutions of the City Council of New Orleans, March 11, 1805 to November 20, 1815, Session July 24, 1805, 63.

John Watkins, called upon the territorial authorities for aid. Watkins admitted his failure to prevent "many worthless free people of color" from coming into the city or "to drive them away after they have come."[5] The territorial government also was urged to take action when in 1806 a free Negro named Stephen informed the Governor of the existence of a plot to help the Spaniards win back the Louisiana territory. According to the informer, a great number of free Negroes were armed and stood ready to march against Americans whenever the Spaniards gave the necessary instruction.[6]

Faced with such an emergency the Territorial Legislature hastily enacted a measure to prevent Negro immigration from the French West Indies. This law denied admission to all except free Negro women and children under fifteen years of age. Those already in the Territory had to give evidence of their freedom or suffer the chance of being classified as fugitive slaves.[7] With this legislation begins a long list of discriminatory measures against the immigration of free Negroes into Louisiana.

While the excitement continued to rage, a year later the Legislature passed a general law prohibiting free Negroes from any part of the world from coming into Louisiana. If caught and convicted of violating this statute such migrants were subject to a fine of $20 for each week that they remained in the Territory. If the Negroes failed to leave or pay the fine at the end of a two-week grace

---

5. John Watkins to John Graham (Secretary of the Territory), September 6, 1805, Clarence E. Carter (comp. and ed.), *The Territorial Papers of the United States; The Territory of Orleans, 1803–1812*, IX, 503.

6. Statement of Stephen to Governor Claiborne, January 23, 1806, *ibid.*, 575–576.

7. *Laws of the Territory of Orleans* (1806), 1st Leg., 1st Sess., 128.

period, judges and justices of the peace had the power to jail them as felons. To help defray expenses of the trial and incarceration, judges could hire out free Negro prisoners for a sum sufficient to pay all costs.[8]

During the year 1809, the number of French immigrants reached over 10,000—including Whites, slaves and free Negroes. This influx from Cuba came after Napoleon invaded Spain and war was declared against France. Patriotic Cubans had made these persons so uncomfortable that many sought refuge in the United States. Louisiana was a particularly desirable place because both the language and religion were more suited to their needs than were other areas of North America. In 1809 the movement reached an especially high rate. During a thirty-day period, over thirty ships from Cuba landed 10,342 refugees in New Orleans, among whom were 3428 free Negroes.[9]

These unfortunate persons received permission to land because Governor Claiborne could not humanely enforce the laws excluding free colored persons. He justified his stand on the ground that they had suffered so many hardships and discrimination in Cuba.[10] Meanwhile all males of color over fifteen years old were required to give bond for good behavior and guarantee their departure as soon as possible. Yet, in the one source in which this incident is mentioned, only 64 are reported as having given bonds to that effect. In reporting this number the Mayor of New Orleans went on to lament that he knew

8. *Ibid.*, (1807), 1st Leg., 2nd Sess., 180–182.

9. William B. Robertson (Secretary of the Territory) to Robert Smith (United States Secretary of State), July 8, 1809; James Mather (Mayor of New Orleans) to W. C. C. Claiborne, August 7, 1809, Dunbar Rowland (ed.), *Official Letter Books of W. C. C. Claiborne,* IV, 381, 409, 482.

10. Claiborne to Robert Smith, May 20, 1809, *ibid.,* 363–364.

of "but few men of color who have left this place."[11] Governor Claiborne was so greatly disturbed by the arrival and continued residence of such large numbers of this class that he wrote consular officials in the West Indies to inform prospective free Negro emigrants of the Louisiana law restricting their migration into the territory. The chief executive also reminded the consuls that "we have at this time a much greater proportion of that kind of population than comports with our interest."[12]

Despite these measures free Negroes continued coming, and since few left the Territory, this class of the population grew at an even larger rate than before the ban. That the majority settled and remained in Louisana is attested to by a comparison of census figures. For example, in 1803—when the United States took charge of the Louisiana Territory—the free colored population amounted to 1566;[13] by 1806, their number had risen to 3350[14] and in 1810 there were 7585 inhabitants classified as free persons of color.[15]

It is therefore apparent that efforts to keep free Negroes out of Louisiana were a failure either because of laxity in the administration of the law or a humane attitude on the part of government officials.

To Louisiana also came the free Negro emigrants from other areas of the South and from the free states of the North. Then came the sailors and the employees of river

---

11. James Mather to Claiborne, August 8, 1809, *ibid.*, 406.

12. Claiborne to William Savage (Commercial Agent of the United States for Jamaica), November 10, 1809, *id.* to Vincent Grey (Acting Consul at Havana), *ibid.*, V, 3–6.

13. *Appendix to an Account of Louisiana*, lxxxv.

14. Census of the Territory of Orleans, December 31, 1806, Carter, *op. cit.*, 923.

15. *Third Census of the United States*, 1810, 82.

vessels. A great variety of routes were taken in entering the state. Some came usually under the cover of night by way of Lakes Pontchartrain and Borne, and the swamps that surrounded the city of New Orleans. In fact such method of entry became so common that one New Orleans mayor pleaded with the Governor to issue orders to officers in command of the military posts along the ways leading to the city "to arrest and ship back under proper escort on the first boat, all strangers of color, whether equipped or not with passports who might attempt to effect an entrance through this medium."[16]

As the railroad mileage expanded, the free Negroes began to use this means of entering the state, though it was more expensive and chances of detection were greater. That some came by railroad is indicated by an ordinance passed by the East Feliciana Parish Police Jury in 1846. This regulation provided that all free Negroes coming into the state by way of the Clinton and Fort Hudson Railroad without a written permit would be considered as runaway slaves.[17]

The largest number, however, used the water routes afforded by the river systems of Louisiana. Although there is little doubt that the majority entered by way of the Mississippi River from its southern approaches, the northern Mississippi also was utilized mainly because there was little likelihood of detection in those isolated parts of the state. It was an era of exciting movement

16. MS. Mayors' Messages to the City Council of New Orleans, 1812–1813, Message of Mayor Nicholas Girod to the Council, November 14, 1812. n.p.

17. D. B. Samford (ed.), *Police Jury Code of the Parish of East Feliciana, Louisiana, Containing a Digest of the State Laws, Relating to Police Juries, and also a Digest of the Ordinances, of the Parish of East Feliciana, Having the Force of Laws, Up to May 1, 1859, Inclusive,* 101.

westward and the vigilance of law officers was hampered by the great variety of persons passing through Louisiana. One observer from Shreveport in 1850, for example, reported seeing on board a Red River steamer bound for Texas, "men, women, and children," of every "hue, variety, color and country under the sun," and their occupations and ideas varied as much as the different "tinges of color."[18]

Another favorite route was to cross the river at Natchez. This route was especially safe because of the sparsity of population on the Louisiana side. It was also the most inconvenient. Beyond a doubt many came into Louisiana from Texas after 1840, when that republic passed a law requiring all free Negroes to depart.[19]

The efforts to prevent the entry of free colored persons into the state continued to find expression in various legislative enactments. Such measures not only reflected the increase in the number of free Negroes in the population but also revealed the fear White citizens had for the growing abolitionist movement in the North. As this Northern directed crusade pressed harder after 1830, it became the prevailing attitude of most slave owners that free Negroes were among the most dangerous representatives of the Northern anti-slavery forces.

Yet before the first third of the 19th Century had passed, discriminatory measures found their way into law. In 1817, for example, laws came into being making it unlawful for free Negroes who had a criminal record to come into Louisiana. All masters of vessels, boats, flatboats, pirogue, rafts, or "other water craft," knowingly

---

18. New Orleans *Daily Delta*, April 23, 1850.
19. Harold Schoen, "The Free Negro in the Republic of Texas," *The Southwestern Historical Quarterly*, XL (1936), 101.

carrying former Negro convicts were subject to having their water craft confiscated and were liable for a fine not to exceed $500.[20]

In 1830 Louisiana's free Negro population came to 16,710 inhabitants.[21] Since the slaves numbered 109,588 and there were 89,441 White inhabitants, the possibility of an alliance of the Negro race loomed as an ever-present threat to the white "master class." On March 8, 1830, excitement reached fever pitch when a free colored merchant of New Orleans named Robert Smith was arrested and charged with not only possessing but circulating "a dangerous and revolutionary pamphlet" dealing with slavery. It was discovered to be the David Walker's "Appeal to the Colored Citizens of the World," which reputedly advocated world revolution for the Negro population. Another free Negro and several slaves also were apprehended with copies of the same pamphlet in their possession.[22]

Faced with the prospect of mass insurrection, Louisiana authorities sprang into action. In short order the General Assembly passed an act extending the list of conditions prohibiting free Negro migration into the state. Accordingly, any free persons of color who had arrived after January 1, 1825, in violation of the act of 1807, were subject to deportation within sixty days. The penalties called for one year's imprisonment for the first offense, and life imprisonment for the second. Regardless of motive, if a

---

20. *Laws of Louisiana* (1816–1817), 3rd Leg., 1st Sess., 44–48.
21. *Fifth Census of the United States* (1830), 105–106.
22. Baton Rouge *Gazette,* March 20, 1830. The Pamphlet alluded to full title is David Walker, *Walker's Appeal in Four Articles Together with a Preamble to the Colored Citizens of the World but in Particular and Very Expressly to Those of the United States of America.*

native-born free Negro left the state, on returning to Louisiana he was subject to the law. Those free Negroes who came under the scope of this law, were given one year to dispose of any taxable property and leave the state. As an added safeguard, the act made it compulsory for all free persons of color who had arrived between 1812 and 1825 to enroll their names with the parish judges. A particularly stringent clause referred to free Negro seamen. Such persons remaining longer than thirty days in the ports of the state were subject to the full penalties of the law.[23]

The discovery of Walker's pamphlet on one's person was also punishable by this law, which prescribed a fine ranging from $300 to $1000 and imprisonment from six months to three years for White citizens "who by writing, printing, or speaking disturb the peace of the state." Fines up to $1000, and imprisonment at hard labor from three to five years, were provided for free Negroes guilty of the same offense. The state printer was ordered to publish this law every six months, and district attorneys were required to prosecute violations of the statute.[24]

Although the act of 1830 was passed during a period of unusual fear of the native and immigrant free Negroes, its harsh provisions were seldom enforced to the letter of the law. Southern legislators often made extreme laws for emergencies, which were later moderated by the good nature or the inefficient practice of the Southern people. Some draconic measures were also tempered by the liberality of court decisions.[25]

A case in point was the interpretation by at least one

---

23. *Laws of Louisiana* (1830), 9th Leg., 2nd Sess., 90–92.
24. *Ibid.*, 92–94.
25. Clement Eaton, *A History of the Old South*, 269.

editor of the 1830 measure regarding native free persons of color. When a group of free Negroes of Baton Rouge expressed concern over the operation of the law, they were assured by the editor of a local newspaper that it referred only to "suspicious and arrogant" non-native persons of color and that they had nothing "to apprehend from its operation."[26]

The Supreme Court also took a broad view of those features which called for heavy penalties on persons, who by speaking or writing might cause a slave revolt. In 1850, for example, a certain White citizen named Read was charged with inciting the free Negroes and slaves to insurrection and insubordination by using seditious language. He reportedly said that "the negroes are as free as white men. This is a free country, and the negroes have no right to call any man master."[27] The local court found Read guilty and sentenced him to the penitentiary for a term of five years. When the case reached the state's Supreme Court that body reversed the sentence on the technicality that the word "feloniously" had been omitted from the indictment; in addition, it had not been charged or proved that his words were spoken directly to either slaves or free Negroes.[28]

The matter of the coming of Negro emigrants came before the 1831 session of the Legislature by the chief executive of the state for serious and "permanent" solution. In his message to the Assembly, Governor Jacques Dupre called the lawmakers' attention to the fact that he did not know whether it was apathy on the part of the officials or a fault in the law of 1830 that made it

---

26. Baton Rouge *Gazette*, April 17, 1830.
27. *State v. Read*, 6 La. An. 227 (March 1851).
28. *Ibid.*, 228.

ineffective in preventing free Negroes from entering Louisiana. He therefore recommended an amendment to the act, which was designed to remedy these shortcomings.[29] Instead of imposing any additional restrictions on immigration the legislature approved an amendment which had the effect of modifying the 1830 act. This amendment exempted all free persons of color who had become permanent residents and owners of property or those who were gainfully employed from that section of the act which prevented them from returning to Louisiana after having once left the state. In the future such persons could travel anywhere in pursuit of business affairs, except "to go to or return from, the West India Islands."[30]

In the summer following this action, a mass meeting of 330 citizens of New Orleans protested that neither city officials nor parish authorities were enforcing the existing laws. They registered the grievance that only persons who had been found guilty of crimes had been expelled from the state. This group went on to predict that if the local officials would only use the power vested in them and expel those free Negroes who were already in the state, "it will be easy to stop others from entering the country. . . ."[31] Soon after their petition, the Nat Turner insurrection broke out in Virginia, and even though the press and orators of Louisiana gave considerable attention to the affair, the Legislature did not deem it necessary to pass additional measures forbidding immigration of

29. *Journal of the House of Representatives* (1831), 10th Leg., 1st Sess., 11.
30. *Laws of Louisiana* (1831), 10th Leg., 1st Sess., 98.
31. Petition of the Inhabitants of the City to Council Protesting Against the Introduction of Strange Negroes into the city, June 1831, in MSS. Documents of the City Council of New Orleans, 1823–1835, Record Book # 4084.

free Negroes. Apparently content with the laws on the books, the matter remained quiet for over a decade, when again the course of events compelled the General Assembly to address itself with restrictive legislation.

The census of 1840 showed that Louisiana contained 25,502 free colored inhabitants. The total number of slaves was listed at 168,502, while the White population numbered 158,457.[32] On the basis of these figures the combined Negro population of the state outnumbered the white inhabitants by 35,547 persons. However, J. D. B. DeBow, the director of the 1850 census, maintained that an error had been made in recording the number of free Negroes in the sixth census. It was his contention that an error had occurred in the third municipality of New Orleans, where free persons of color were probably counted as White.[33]

While the census figures of that year failed to give a true picture of the growth of the free colored population, many Whites thought that the increase in the number of that class in 1840 was due mostly to immigration. This fact, coupled with the exaggerated fear of Northern abolitionists, stirred a group of slaveholders in Concordia Parish into action. At a mass meeting held in the Parish seat of Vidalia on August 7, 1841, this group strongly urged the Legislature to take immediate steps to prevent

32. *Sixth Census of the United States 1840*, 258, 262.

33. J. D. B. DeBow (comp.), *Statistical View of the United States, Embracing its Territory, Population—White, Free Colored, and Slave— Moral and Social Condition, Industry, Property, and Revenue; the Detailed Statistics of Cities, Towns and Counties; Being a Compendium of the Seventh Census; to which are added the results of every previous census, beginning with 1790, in comparative tables, with explanatory and illustrated notes, based upon the schedules and other official sources of information*, 62. Hereinafter this work will be cited as *Compendium of the Seventh Census*.

any further migration of free Negroes into the state of Louisiana. This demand was based on the conviction that a large majority of the abolition agents in the South were free persons of color. As a salutary measure, the Concordia group recommended legislation which would authorize public officials to sell into "perpetual bondage" any free Negro immigrant who refused to leave the state after being given one day's notice to do so.[34] The New Orleans *Picayune*, which also reported this incident, approved the action of the Concordia citizens and laid the blame on those free persons of color employed on steamboats who "prowled about . . . forming a dangerous body of incendiaries."[35] Since free colored seamen were singled out as especially dangerous persons in the abolitionist movement, it was suggested that they not be employed on steamboats, on the grounds that it "virtually licenses the free blacks to carry out all the instructions and artifices of the abolitionists."[36]

When the General Assembly met in 1842, the attitude of many White citizens, the press, and ministers of the gospel was expressed in an act designed to stop free Negro immigration. Despite the bill's passage, however, the enactment failed to meet the extreme demands of those who urged stringent measures. According to this act, free persons of color were prohibited from coming into Louisiana on board any water-craft as employees or passengers and persons found guilty of such offense were to be confined in the parish jail until the vessel was ready to leave a Louisiana port. Masters or commanders were required,

34. Baton Rouge *Gazette*, August 28, 1841.
35. August 22, 1841.
36. Natchez *Free Trader* quoted in Baton Rouge *Gazette*, August 28, 1841.

upon receipt of a written permit or order of the judge or justice of the peace in that jurisdiction, to carry out of the state the Negroes in question and be held responsible for all expenses entailed in their apprehension or detention.[37]

The act also included specific regulations as to the amount of security to be given by ships' officers bringing such persons into the state. They were required to deposit with the parish judge or justice of the peace a bond not to exceed $500 for each free Negro. If such officials failed to supply the necessary bond within three days after arrival in a Louisiana port, they were liable to a penalty of $1000 for each free Negro. If they did not have the means to supply bond, the Negroes in question were to be transported out of the state at public expense.[38]

Should a free person who had been expelled from the state, according to the 1842 measure, return, he would be subject upon conviction to five years' imprisonment at hard labor in the state penitentiary. After the expiration of this sentence such a colored immigrant would be given thirty days to depart or incur the danger of imprisonment at hard labor for life.[39]

Free Negroes who were permanent residents did not come under the scope of the law, nor were those who had lived in the state since January 1, 1825. Persons of this category were allowed to leave and return to Louisiana provided such persons did not establish legal domicile in a free state of the United States.[40]

The 1842 statute also made provisions concerning the

---

37. *Laws of Louisiana* (1842), 15th Leg., 2nd Sess., 308.
38. *Ibid.*, 310.
39. *Ibid.*, 312.
40. *Ibid.*

entrance of those slaves entitled to freedom at a future period (a *statue liber*). Accordingly, it was made unlawful to bring into Louisiana any such slave, and anyone bringing in one would be subject to a fine of $1000 and imprisonment not to exceed six months. In addition the guilty party would have to pay the expense of transporting the slave back to his place of origin.[41] It was also made unlawful for any person to purchase a *statu liber,* under penalty of forfeiting such a slave and assuming the burden of transporting him out of Louisiana. All *statu liberi* currently living in Louisiana were required to leave as soon as their freedom went into effect. Such removal was to be done at the expense of their last owner.[42]

In the following years, however, amendments were enacted which had the effect of softening the harsh 1842 law. For example, in 1843, an act passed the Legislature that allowed all free Negroes who had immigrated prior to 1838 to remain in the state. However, such dispensation required the permission of the Municipal Councils of New Orleans and the Parish Police Juries. After the registration of his name and other relevant information, permission to remain was granted if the immigrant could supply evidence that he was of good character, and promised faithfully to observe all state laws governing free persons of color.[43] Again in 1852, the Legislature found it necessary to amend the act of 1842 by allowing free Negro employees aboard steamboats, upon due execution of bond, to remain on board while the ship was in port. If the duties of such persons necessitated their going

41. *Ibid.,* 316.
42. *Ibid.,* 318.
43. *Ibid.* (1843), 16th Leg., 1st Sess., 45–46.

ashore, a passport was to be supplied by the authorities for that purpose. Failure to have this passport on their persons at all times while in the state would incur the penalty of imprisonment until the ship left port and a fine of $1000.[44]

The formulation of new restrictive measures did not interfere with the granting of special privileges to certain free persons of color. By a series of special legislative acts, non-native freemen residing in contravention of the law were allowed to remain as residents of Louisiana. In 1846, for instance, Julie Vigoureau and her daughter were given legislative permission to remain in the state after giving bond of $2000, sufficient to insure their good behavior.[45] At the same session, Harriet Mitchell received the right to remain in Louisiana upon "giving good and sufficient bond for five hundred dollars."[46] In another case, the Legislature approved a special act in 1848 to allow Nancy Flournoy and her son to remain in the state. Such permission was dependent upon the posting of a $500 bond by each of the two parties in question.[47] An act of 1850 permitted Frances Townsend and her seven children to remain in Louisiana. In this case no posting of bond was required.[48] A similar privilege was granted to Cornelia Carter together with her five minor children.[49]

Besides special legislation allowing certain exemption from immigration laws, it often happened that White citizens petitioned the authorities for similar privileges in

---

44. *Ibid.* (1852), 4th Leg., 1st Sess., 193–194.
45. *Ibid.* (1846), 1st Leg., 1st Sess., 19.
46. *Ibid.*
47. *Ibid.* (1848), 2nd Leg., 1st Sess., 90.
48. *Ibid.* (1850), 3rd Leg., 1st Sess., 13.
49. *Ibid.*, 102.

behalf of Negro friends and acquaintances. In vouching for their good character and conduct these White persons not only served in the capacity of friend and protector, but by so doing became factors contributing to the growth of the free Negro population. An example of such a testimonial can be found in the following letter (dated 1843) from a White citizen named James A. Caldwell to Mayor William Freret of New Orleans:

> Henry Bradford is the son of the Woman whose free papers he carries and he came out with me in 1822 from Norfolk Virginia—I know her son Henry to be a free man and that he has been here since the year 1829—that is since the winter of 28–29–. . . . P.S. Henry Bradford has called up my recollection that his Mother who was waiting maid to Miss Placide did go to Virginia in 1823. . . . I came back out with her in the winter of 1823–24 during his residence in the City. I do remember him coming occasionally to see his Mother, and he was waiting on Doctor Kearny of the Navy— My seeing him so seldom at that time made me forget all about his final residence here in 1828–29—He is very orderly, respectable colored man . . . he being a barber in Exchange Place and very well liked by all he serves.[50]

In 1853, a White citizen named William H. Hanks wrote a letter to the Mayor of New Orleans requesting residential privileges be given the free Negro, John Jones, whom he had personally known for seven years and because he could "answer for him as a person of good habits and respectability."[51]

Four White citizens wrote in a letter in 1855 their

---

50. MS. Register of Free Colored Persons Entitled to Remain in the State, Mayor's Office, 1840–1857.
51. *Ibid.*

opinion of the good conduct and orderly disposition of Priscilla Williams, a free Negro from Philadelphia whom they described as "always conducting herself well and had complied to all the requirements of the laws relative to free persons of color."[52]

Other White citizens went further in behalf of their free Negro friends and resorted to extra-legal means in obtaining resident rights for particular free Negroes. In 1850 one such case occurred: a White woman named Phoebe Black had managed to persuade the free Negress, Sarah Johnson of Indiana, to come to Louisiana disguised as a slave in order to dodge the immigration laws. The Negress was hired as a slave servant of a White woman in New Orleans. Yet, when Phoebe attempted to put a mortgage on the "slave" with a Mr. Kathman, the former proclaimed herself free and revealed the entire ruse to the authorities. At the trial witnesses swore that the Negress in question was free and that they had known her in that status back in Indiana. Although the woman gained freedom, the affair was used to the advantage of militant pro-slavery forces. "The idea of a free person of color smuggling herself into a slave state as a slave," reported a New Orleans journalist, "is a commentary upon the condition of the free colored persons in Northern States."[53]

Free Negroes used all sorts of devices to remain in Louisiana; they would even resort to disguising themselves as White. One such case was that of J. M. Brown, who had succeeded in convincing the authorities he was a White man by swearing his mother was a White woman.

---

52. *Ibid.*
53. New Orleans *Daily Delta*, September 19, 1850.

When the conditions of the oath were discovered to be false, Brown's immunity from the laws was changed, and he was arrested as a free Negro illegally residing in the state of Louisiana. In default of a $500 bond the erstwhile White man was sent to prison.[54]

From time to time the state authorities made attempts to prevent the entry of free Negroes into Louisiana, by expelling or imprisoning those found in the state in violation of existing laws. Very often these officials were forced to invoke the law by the disorderly and contumacious conduct of especially loud persons. In 1841, for example, it was reported in the Baton Rouge press that the New Orleans police were enforcing the laws "with commendable vigor."[55] Frequent attacks by free Negroes on White citizens were the reasons given for this action. As a result of this vigilance several free Negroes were condemned to the state penitentiary. In 1849, a free man of color named Lewis Eddington, who was described as a "great scoundrel and a thief," was arrested for not leaving the state after he had been warned to do so. He was thereupon turned over to the district court for trial.[56] On another occasion a certain James Bruce was sentenced to one year at hard labor for being in the state in contravention of the law.[57]

The spasmodic enforcement of immigration regulations was ever conditioned on the growing fear that free Negroes were nothing but disguised abolitionist agents. A case of this nature was that of the Reverend John Brown when he was tried in New Orleans on the charge of being

54. New Orleans *Daily Crescent,* March 3, 1857.
55. Baton Rouge *Gazette,* July 21, 1841.
56. New Orleans *Daily Picayune,* February 9, 1849.
57. *Ibid.,* June 30, 1844.

dangerous to "the servile population and as an abolition emissary." Authorities were convinced that he had been sent south to do mischief among slaves and he was sentenced to leave the state within sixty days or be made to feel the full weight of the law.[58]

During the 1850s feeling against the presence of free Negroes grew more and more intense as Northern anti-slavery forces stepped up their campaign. Any addition to what was considered an already-too-large colored population was viewed as a patent contradiction and a serious threat to the peace of the state. The Seventh Census only served to substantiate such fears when it showed that 17,462 inhabitants were free colored, 244,809 slaves, and 255,471 were Whites.[59] The press of the state was cognizant of these figures and constantly called the public's attention to this fact and repeatedly stressed the dangers of abolitionism; allegedly this movement would have mischievous effects on the slaves of the state.[60] In addition, legislation passed by other Southern states, which provided for the expulsion of free Negro immigrants, was held up as an example for Louisiana to emulate.[61] Aroused White citizens took pens in hand and wrote letters to newspapers, emphasizing the need for effective measures to prevent free Negroes from coming to Louisiana from other states. A typical letter was sent to a New Orleans editor from a citizen of East Feliciana. He wrote, under the signature of "A Southerner," calling for the adoption of regulations so severe as to make free Negro migrants

58. New Orleans *Daily Crescent*, March 18, 1857.
59. *Seventh Census of the United States 1850*, 473.
60. New Orleans *Weekly Delta*, July 19, 1853.
61. Franklin (La.), *Planters Banner*, January 5, 1854.

"unhappy and discontented with their present condition."[62]

Acting under pressure from the public, the General Assembly, in 1855, sought to alter the laws dealing with free Negro migrants by passing "An Act Relative to Slaves and Free Colored Persons."[63] This statute represented a codification of all previous measures concerning slaves and free colored persons, but strangely enough no changes were made in regard to the entry of Negro immigrants. In 1856, however, the Supreme Court of Louisiana declared this legislation unconstitutional on the grounds that "its title expressed two distinct objects; to wit, slaves and free colored persons, because many of the sections of the act embraced objects not expressed in the title." The wording of this bill, said the court, was a violation of Article 115 of the 1852 Constitution which stated: "Every law enacted by the Legislature shall embrace but one object, and that shall be expressed in the title."[64]

Immediately after this decision demands were made either to enforce the existing laws prohibiting free colored immigration or to pass legislation to rid the state of even the native-born persons of that class. The country parishes, and particularly the press of St. Landry, was adamant on the latter proposal, on the grounds that the welfare of the White race depended upon the expulsion "from among us all free Negroes or people of mixed blood."[65] When the legislature convened in 1857, Governor Robert C. Wickliff recommended that the lawmakers give their

62. New Orleans *Semi-Weekly Creole*, November 5, 1854.
63. *Laws of Louisiana* (1855), 3rd Leg., 2nd Sess., 377–391.
64. *The State v. Harrison, a slave,* 11 La. An. 722, (December 1856).
65. Opelousas *Courier*, December 20, 1856.

attention to this matter. The Governor said, "the immigration of free Negroes from other states of this Union into Louisiana, which has been steadily increasing for years, is a source of great evil and demands legislative action." He went on to stress the fact that "public policy dictates, the people require, that immediate steps should be taken at this time . . . to remove all free Negroes who are now in the state, when such removal can be effected without violation of the law." The Governor thought such action necessary because such a population was having the "most pernicious effect upon our slave population."[66]

Attorney General E. Warren Moise reported to this same body that the laws forbidding free Negroes from coming into the state were not effectively enforced. He went on to urge more stringent measures to decrease the number of those in the process of entering the state. "The immigrant free Negro," he said, "engendered crime and disaffection among the slaves and in no way contributed to the wealth and good order of society." Moise, however, made it clear that his observations were not applicable to the "respectful and useful" native free colored population. According to this official, there were many free Negroes in Louisiana who did not rightfully belong there and some had come with forged passes describing them as slaves and thus permitting them residence in the state. There were other migrants, such as seasonal workers from the North who came during the winter for work and then returned North for the summer. In light of these conditions the Attorney General demanded that an immediate effort should be made to plug up loop-holes in the law.[67]

---

66. *Louisiana Legislative Documents* (1857), 4th Leg. 2nd Sess., 15.
67. *Ibid.*, 11–12.

When these recommendations were not followed up by the lawmakers Moise persisted and repeated his demands for action in 1858 and again the following year.[68]

When the Legislature failed to take action, the movement to rid the state of all free Negroes regardless of status was renewed with greater intensity. In demonstrating the need for such action, irate private citizens launched individual campaigns of vilification and hatred against free Negroes. They urged legislators to concern themselves with restricting the growing number of this race, because such persons, as one writer wrote, were an "idle, lazy, vagrant" class whose presence engendered "a spirit of dissatisfaction and insubordination in the breasts of slaves." Slaveholders were described as being "a unanimous unit" in wanting the "speedy removal of this cancer upon society."[69]

Just before the Legislature convened for its 1859 session, the advocates of strong measures pointed out the weaknesses of Louisiana's laws in comparison with that of other Southern states. One editor requested the Assembly attend to this matter at once and called into play the following action taken by a neighboring state:

> Texas has adopted some very stringent regulations to free herself of this population. Virginia is perfecting a plan to cure this evil, so is Mississippi, South Carolina, Georgia, and Alabama. Shall Louisiana remain an idle spectator to this great work of safety and reformation, and make no move in self defense, though experiencing the effect of this curse upon her population.[70]

---

68. *Ibid.*, (1858), 7, (1859), 3.
69. Opelousas *Patriot*, December 4, 1858.
70. *Ibid.*, January 15, 1859.

This sentiment was not by any means unanimous among the citizens of the state. The few who looked upon the situation more dispassionately thought native-born free Negroes as just as orderly and well-behaved a class as the White population. Moreover, their interests in the sympathies toward Southern viewpoints were the same as those of White citizens. Although this group was in favor of restrictive immigration laws they suggested that the Legislature elevate the status of the native free Negroes and declare slaves who were sufficiently removed from African extraction "free men at a proper age." It was further contended that such enactments would give the "best evidence of our right and our Christian mercy to the world."[71]

Other friends of the Louisiana free Negro were not so bold as to suggest emancipation, but they opposed the forcible removal of such persons on the grounds that they had become property owners and many were a "quiet and industrious people." They argued that "if native free Negroes were removed, why not include the degraded white men as well."[72] All groups, however, were in accord that effective if not rigid measures should be adopted to prevent the flow of free Negro immigation from other states.

Popular sentiment against the free Negro immigrants reached fever pitch during February of 1859—in St. Landry Parish where two public meetings of slaveholders were held to devise "some means to secure the observance of the laws relating to the free colored population of the State." Forming themselves into an organized body made up of a president, vice presidents, and secretaries they

71. Baton Rouge *Daily Gazette and Comet,* January 28, 1859.
72. *Messager de St. Jacques* quoted in *Le Courier des Opelousas,* Fevrier 12, 1859.

proceeded to draft a set of resolutions calling for the expulsion of these people. In regard to the immigrant free Negro this group recommended the following for the approval of the Legislature:

> That if any free persons of color shall enter within the limits of the State he shall be sold as a slave at public auction, one-half of the proceeds of which sale shall inure to the benefit of the informer, the remaining half deposited in the State Treasury after paying all costs. That all free persons of color who are now in the state in contravention of its laws shall also be sold as slaves for life at public auction and the proceeds to be applied as set forth in the forgoing. . . .[73]

This anti-free-Negro sentiment, so largely molded by the press and pressure groups, found expression in the Immigration statute of March 15, 1859. This final act before the Civil War abolished the pass system for Negro seamen and required that they be lodged in parish jails until their ships or vessels were ready to leave port. Captains or ship masters who brought either free Negro seamen or passengers had to underwrite the expenses of incarceration up to the amount of forty cents a day. Failure to accept this stipulation could result in Negro seamen or passengers being considered as deserters. Such deserters were given five days to leave the state or suffer the penalty of twelve months' imprisonment for the first and five years' for the second offense. In an effort to bear down upon violators, provision was made to encourage persons to inform against a free Negro residing in Louisiana illegally. A reward of ten dollars was offered for any White

73. Opelousas *Patriot*, February 19, 1859.

reporting the culprit. The Governor was instructed to send copies of this act to chief executives of the United States as well as to the diplomatic officials of the major ports of foreign nations. The act was to become effective on September 1, 1859.[74]

However the advocates of the extreme policy of complete removal of the free colored population expressed keen disappointment with this act. The vitriolic Opelousas *Patriot* stated that "the people of Louisiana know that they are unfortunately cursed with an internal free Negro population, which if not removed will blight the fairest prospects of the state. The Legislature has failed us. They should apply their powers to the removal of all free negroes within the limits of the State and they will have acted as wise and intelligent members of society."[75] More will be said later concerning the campaign for removal of the free Negro population from Louisiana.

After the passage of the 1859 immigration law, the authorities began to enforce it vigorously. Doubtlessly, police officers were made more diligent because of the reward offered for apprehending Negroes illegally in the state. On September 8, 1859, for example, five free Negroes were arrested and ordered to leave Louisiana.[76] Three months afterward twenty more Negroes of the crew of the steamer *Southern Light*, and claiming to be slaves, were arrested by the Chief of Police of New Orleans under suspicion of attempting to violate the 1859 act. Upon close investigation, all of them were found to be free colored persons and ordered deported.[77] The successful raid in-

---

74. *Laws of Louisiana* (1859), 4th Leg., 2nd Sess., 70–72.
75. March 19, 1859.
76. New Orleans *Daily Delta*, September 8, 1859.
77. New Orleans *Daily Picayune*, November 11, 1859.

spired law enforcement officers to keep a "bright lookout for the arrival of vessels from foreign and northern ports, likely to have free Negroes on board," disguised as slaves. In 1860, Officer E. Salvatory arrested sixteen men of that class on board the ship *Senator*. They were confined to prison until the ship was ready to leave port.[78]

In the final analysis, the act of 1859, proved as unenforceable as previous laws on the matter of free Negro migration. This is attested to by Governor Robert C. Wickliff's message to the Legislature, in which he said: "the Law of 1859, though thus far zealously enforced, has not accomplished its object." He went on to say that those colored persons who were "designing and cunning" found it easy to evade the provisions of the law.[79]

Thus, despite laws prohibiting immigration, free Negroes continued to come into Louisiana, and except for a few isolated cases they remained there. Attempts to solve this problem by legislation had been in vain. From time to time the laws were vigorously enforced, especially when free colored persons were suspected of abolitionist activity, but for the most part restrictive legislation lay fallow or unenforceable.

Manumission of slaves, which had been the main source of the free Negro class during the colonial period, continued uninterrupted during the early years of American independence. The existing laws regarding the freeing of slaves remained relatively the same after the transfer to the United States, except for those parts which contradicted the laws of the United States.[80] Although there

---

78. *Ibid.*, August 3, 1860.
79. *Official Journal of the House of Representatives* (1860), 5th Leg., 1st Sess., 8.
80. Albert Phelps, *Louisiana: A Record of Expansion*, 195.

were some differences in procedure from the French and Spanish laws, as the years went by there emerged a peculiarly Louisianian system of emancipation, which included much of the French, Spanish and English customs and regulations.

In 1807 the first act of American Louisiana dealing with the emancipation of slaves was enacted by the Territorial Legislature. According to this measure certain provisions had a tendency to mildly restrict manumissions. To be qualified for liberty, a slave had to be at least thirty years old and present proof of good behavior for four years preceding emancipation. However, exceptions were granted for any slave who had saved the life of his master or his master's family. When an owner desired to free a slave, he was required to render a declaration with the parish judge together with proof of age and a certificate of good behavior. When these conditions were met, a notice would be posted in French and English on the parish bulletin board attesting to the fact that the pending manumission was the wish of the owner. Anyone having objections to the proceedings was required to make his position known within forty days. If no objection was made, the judge would usually declare the slave free provided all other legal requirements had been filled. Manumission was considered valid unless it was later proved that the master had liberated his slave to defraud creditors, minors or persons either absent or residing out of the parish when the notice of emancipation was given. Then too, if at the time of manumission the slaveholder did not possess sufficient property to meet his financial obligations, an attempt to defraud creditors was also presumed. Any emancipation contrary to these provisions was deemed null and void. This act also carried the specific obligation on the part of the master to maintain and support the freed slave during his lifetime if he should need it. If the former master failed to perform this duty, any judge was empowered to order former owners to pay the freedman sufficient money to assure a subsistent livelihood.[81]

One of the first recorded incidents of a long series of requests to manumit underage slaves which required legislative permission was that of a free colored woman. In 1823, Marie Martha of West Baton Rouge Parish, was granted legislative permission to free her two slave sons.[82] An act was approved by the General Assembly during its 1825 session to enable Marie Louise Lecompte to set her 22-year-old son free from slavery.[83] Similar permission was secured by a free colored resident of St. Mary Parish to emancipate her two underage slave children.[84]

Eventually, requests of this nature became so numerous that the legislature began to incorporate a number of such cases into a single bill. On March 22, 1826, for example, the Legislature approved such a bill providing for the manumission of 24 underage slaves. Four of the petitioners were free people of color who owned sixteen of the slaves concerned in the act.[85]

In an astonishing number of cases manumission came as a reward for meritorious public service. With such liberation there was always compensation to the slaveowner along with provision for the freedom of such slaves who had discovered slave conspiracies.[86] In 1813, the Legisla-

81. *Laws of the Territory of Orleans* (1807), 1st Leg., 1st Sess., 82–88.
82. *Laws of Louisiana* (1823), 6th Leg., 1st Sess., 36.
83. *Ibid.* (1824–1825), 7th Leg., 1st Sess., 46.
84. *Ibid.*, 137.
85. *Ibid.* (1826), 7th Leg., 2nd Sess., 106.
86. *Laws of the Territory of Orleans* (1806), 1st Leg., 1st Sess., 304.

ture of Louisiana conferred freedom upon three slaves named Charles, Louis and Samson, for "their fidelity and for the discovery they made of certain plots among the slaves in St. John the Baptist Parish."[87] The state paid $1000, $800 and $1200 to the respective owners of these slaves. Again in 1838, the General Assembly appropriated funds to buy the freedom of a slave named Louis for reporting a slave conspiracy in Rapides Parish. The lawmakers also voted the sum of $500 to enable this Negro to leave the state, and provide him with enough money to ensure security.[88] Legislative permission to free young slaves and those who rendered meritorious service to the state accounted for an appreciable number of persons entering the ranks of the free Negro class.

In 1827 the General Assembly passed an act changing the method of manumitting slaves under thirty years of age. According to this enactment, opportunity was given to the slave's owner, in his petition to the parish judge, to outline his motives for freeing the slave. After this condition was met, the matter would then be considered by the police jury of the parish. If a three-fourths vote of that body favored the emancipation, the petitioner then proceeded with the usual formalities. Furthermore, only those slaves who were natives of the state could obtain freedom.[89]

In 1830, the discovery of David Walker's pamphlet in the possession of slaves and free Negroes caused the Legislature to set in motion legal means for restricting the number of slaves manumitted in Louisiana. Accordingly, any slaveowner who wished to free his slaves was required

---

87. *Laws of Louisiana* (1812–1813), 1st Leg., 2nd Sess., 100.
88. *Ibid.* (1836), 13th Leg., 1st Sess., 119.
89. *Ibid.* (1827), 8th Leg., 1st Sess., 12–14.

to post a $1000 bond for each slave freed in order to insure the freedman's departure from the state within thirty days after the passage of the act of emancipation. If the emancipated Negro refused to leave, the posted bond was forfeited and the slave became subject to the payment of the forfeit. Exceptions were made for any slave who had rendered meritorious service in behalf of the state, his master, or his master's family.[90]

In the following year, the 1830 statute was amended to allow slaveowners to dispense with posting bond provided they could obtain the consent of the parish police jury. Another important change was the one in which permission might be granted to deserving persons to remain in the state after emancipation. Such permission also could be accomplished by a three-fourths vote of the police jury at two successive meetings.[91] The obvious intention of the Legislature in framing such laws was to eliminate any responsibility that might be placed on that body by numerous private petitions for manumission of underage slaves. At the same time it was designed to restrict the number of domestic emancipations which contributed to the increase of the free Negro class which slaveowners had begun to consider as both harmful and dangerous to their interests. By placing the burden of responsibility upon parish authorities, it was assumed that such officials, who were in a better position to know the merits of a particular case for emancipation, would exercise a more rigid control, and consequently grant or reject such petitions in terms of the welfare of a slaveholding society.

In general the parish police juries followed the simple

---

90. *Ibid.* (1830), 9th Leg., 2nd Sess., 92–94.
91. *Ibid.* (1831), 10th Leg., 1st Sess., 98–99.

procedure of considering emancipation petitions for two successive readings. If the application was approved, a certificate of freedom could be secured from the clerk of the jury for a five dollar fee.[92] If the petition be denied, the slaveowner was allowed to submit another petition before the police jury for a reconsideration of the case.

The police jury minutes of West Feliciana Parish contained the petitions of slaveowners wishing to free slaves, and thereby they served as a catalogue of the various reasons given by masters for manumitting their slaves. For example, a certain James Fair appealed, on April 20, 1841, for the freedom of his 22-year-old Mulattress slave and her infant son. He stated that for the past four years her conduct had been above reproach, and since they were natives of the state, he desired their freedom. The jury accepted the petition with the recommendation that the Negroes be allowed to remain in the state without posting bond. When this petition failed to carry the necessary three-fourths vote at the next meeting, freedom was lost. Fair did not appeal the decision.[93] In the same year, a Robert Stanley requested permission to emancipate four of his slaves who were under thirty years of age. Their conduct was described as good, but more important was the fact that they had nursed Stanley during a long illness, and for this service, the slaves were freed and allowed to remain as residents of the state.[94]

Charles LeBlanc, a White person of Lafayette Parish, was authorized to proceed with the emancipation of his

92. See, for example, MS. St. Martin Parish Police Jury Minutes, Volume 1, 1843–1858, 95.

93. MS. West Feliciana Parish Police Jury Minutes, Volume I, 1840–1855, 6, 11.

94. *Ibid.*, 18.

slave, Lecende, and permission was granted by the police jury to allow the Negress to remain in the state. The causes which inspired that body to make the grant were, "first, the conduct of the slave and next, that it had been satisfactorily proven that Lecende was the first to reveal a conspiracy of slaves in the year 1840."[95] Apart from this extraordinary case, the parish granted relatively few requests for manumissions. During the ten year period from 1823 to 1833 for example, only three emancipation petitions were approved by the police jury.[96]

After a delay of over a year, Leandre Guillot, a White citizen of Avoyelles Parish, was granted the right to manumit his four colored children. The conditions set were that he post bond of $1000 to insure that the Negroes in question would never become a financial burden on the community.[97] Cupid Hankins, a free colored woman living in the same parish, was given permission, without comment from the jury, to free her husband and their four infant children.[98] In 1847, a slaveowner named Jacques Raudin presented an emancipation petition stating that his nine-year-old Mulatto slave, Claire, had rendered "long and faithful services" to his wife. The jurors thought this such an "extraordinary case" that they tendered their permission to free the slave in question. At the same time, that body granted Claire permission to live in Louisiana.[99]

St. John the Baptist Parish stands out for the large number of slaves emancipated and permitted to remain in the

---

95. MS. Lafayette Parish Police Jury Minutes, Volume I, 1823–1853, 164.

96. *Ibid.*, 42, 73, 85.

97. MS. Avoyelles Parish Police Jury Minutes, Volume I, 1821–1843, 364–365.

98. *Ibid.*, 282.

99. *Ibid.*, Volume II, 1843–1852, 75.

state. At a meeting on June 5, 1837, for example, the police jury approved the emancipation of five slaves. These were found to be "good and faithful subjects and not dangerous" to the community.[100] Among this number was the petition of Jean Gasparu, a White citizen, to emancipate his slave named Ursule and their Mulatto daughter. Three days later, six other slaves were liberated by police jury action and given permission to remain in Louisiana.[101]

The police jury of Pointe Coupee Parish demonstrated little opposition to granting petitioners the right to liberate underage slaves. In most cases the emancipated Negroes were given permission to live in the community. In fact, the jurors of this parish were exceptionally lenient in granting the demands of slaveholders even if such petitioners were free persons of color. In 1830, an owner named M. A. Martin represented his slave, Margaret, as a well-behaved girl who was entitled to her freedom as well as the right to remain in the parish. The reasons advanced by Martin indicated that he wished "to increase in her favor some act of benevolence." The members of the police jury, "knowing the benevolent intentions" of the slaveowner, approved his petition after two successive readings.[102] Seldom did the clerk of the Pointe Coupee jury record the reasons for freeing slaves of free persons of color. For example, the petition of a free colored woman named Augustina to emancipate her daughter was granted in 1840 on the grounds that "such a demand was just."[103] In this parish, between 1848 and 1850, sixteen

100. MS. St. John the Baptist Parish Police Jury Minutes, Volume 1834–1847, 11–12.

101. *Ibid.*

102. Pointe Coupee Parish Police Jury Minutes, Volume I, 1829–1840, 228.

103. *Ibid.*, Volume II, 1840–1848, 101.

slaves were emancipated without the posting of bond by their master, and with permission to live in the parish.[104]

In Ascension Parish every slaveholder who had received permission to emancipate a slave was required to post a $250 bond with the police jury clerk. Almost without exception such a bond was required of all persons emancipating their slaves. Louis Colomb, for example, was granted the right to emancipate his slave named Hebee and her six children in consideration of their "good conduct and faithful services." Colomb was, however, required to post the necessary bond to insure the future good conduct of these Negroes. After this requirement had been fulfilled, Hebée and her offspring were allowed to live in the parish.[105]

In 1850, to avoid posting the required bond, a free Negro named Jacques Thomas offered to send his slave son out of the state within thirty days after the act of emancipation. This offer was unanimously accepted by the jurors.[106] Although the police jury of Ascension Parish consistently adhered to the regulation requiring the posting of bond as surety for good behavior of emancipated Negroes, the jurors were especially liberal in granting the requests of masters desiring to free their slaves. For example, eleven petitions for the manumission of slaves were approved on June 2, 1851, and all the individuals freed were permitted, after the posting of bond, to remain as residents of the parish.[107]

The police juries of Lafourche and St. James Parishes

---

104. *Ibid.*, 75: Volume III, 1848–1857, 99, 113.
105. MS. Ascension Parish Police Jury Minutes, Volume I, 1837–1856, 123, 135.
106. *Ibid.*, 173.
107. *Ibid.*, 281.

created special committees to investigate the conduct and feasibility of manumitting slaves for whom emancipation petitions had been submitted. In 1841, a committee of the Lafourche jury recommended the liberation of a slave belonging to a certain White woman named Nancy Tabor. It had found the slave's conduct exemplary because "she has always shown obedience and respect to white persons and has ever acted according to her state of subordination."[108] In some cases, however, the committee system operated to discourage emancipations. Only the very determined slaveowner appealed his case beyond the instance of first rejection by the special committees. For example, after a three-year delay, a certain Alfred Millard, acting in behalf of a free Negro, was able to obtain a favorable committee report for the freedom of the latter's daughter. Millard, who was the owner of the young slave in question, had submitted three petitions before the committees, each time stating that he desired the slave's freedom on the grounds that "proper care and attention be best bestowed on her by her parent."[109]

On the other hand, the committees of the St. James police jury were far more lenient. In 1851, for example, one such special committee reported favorably on the petition of two slaveowners who wished to free their slaves, because of "meritorious service and good respect to white persons" of the parish. At the same time the slaves were granted the right to remain in the parish "if they so desired."[110]

---

108. MS. Lafourche Parish Police Jury Minutes, Volume I, 1841–1852, 13.

109. *Ibid.*, 35.

110. MS. St. James Parish Police Jury Minutes, Volume 1849–1855, 150.

In Iberville Parish, the governing board demonstrated reluctance in approving emancipation petitions and resident privileges for slaves unless such persons were known personally by members of the jury. For example, a White planter named Don Louis R. Orillion, presented a manumission petition in which he represented his slave as "a sober, quiet and industrious man" who had rendered him "long and faithful service." After the petition was taken into consideration, it was found that the slave was well known to the jurors and they unanimously resolved that he be set free and be permitted to remain in the state of Louisiana.[111] The slave of a certain Honor Roth was doubtlessly unknown to the jurors since his emancipation petition was rejected three times by the police jury. No reasons were given for this action.[112] On the other hand, a P. A. Degelas was unanimously granted the right to emancipate his "sober, quiet and industrious" slave named Baptiste, because he was "well known to all members of the jury to be a harmless person."[113]

Free Negroes frequently held their wives, children and other relatives in slavery with the intention of setting them free. Such efforts were well illustrated by the petitions to the police juries. In East Baton Rouge Parish a free Negro barber named Victor Vincent presented a petition to the jury in 1841 asking that "honorable body" to emancipate his two children, "which looked as much like him as two small drops look like a large one." Among other allegations, he stated the "startling fact that he had given them birth." A member present, thought that this

---

111. MS. Iberville Parish Police Jury Minutes, Volume I, 1850–1862, 3.
112. *Ibid.*, 8, 47, 52.
113. *Ibid.*, 50–51.

such an "extraordinary phenomen, the jurors should, under the circumstances of the case, grant the prayer of the petitioner." It was agreed to on June 8, 1847.[114] This same jury, however, refused Vincent permission to free his wife Nancy, even though he had obtained a petition signed by several White citizens of Baton Rouge attesting to her good conduct.[115]

According to the records, the jury of East Baton Rouge did not freely grant requests for manumission. Requests of freedom in behalf of her daughter from January 6, 1851, to September 7, 1853, were received by the jury from Patsy Hébert, but in each case the colored woman's requests were rejected without comment from the police jury.[116] Rejections were also the net results of the efforts of Louisa Lange, George Robinson and J. B. Kleinpeter to emancipate their slaves.[117] This strictness may be attributed to the fact that Baton Rouge as a river port town was receiving free colored immigrants from other states and seamen of that class as well.

In 1841, the system of freeing underage slaves by police jury action was attacked in the press of Baton Rouge. In an article signed "A Subscriber" the "evils of the partial abolition law of 1831" were held up as a source of an "already growing free Negro population." The author singled out the police juries of the state for condoning this practice and went on to say that "however peaceful our free colored population may be, they are always a

---

114. MS. East Baton Rouge Parish Police Jury Minutes, Volume I, 1847–1867, 11.
115. *Ibid.*, 60–61, 84, 125, 142.
116. *Ibid.*, 119, 146, 165, 174.
117. *Ibid.*, 96–97, 149.

subject of comparison for the slave, present before the eye at all times." The writer made the analogy that "we find the same comparison going on amongst the free [Whites], giving rise to the feelings of jealousy and hatred between the rich and the poor, and, where the laws impose restraints on the latter, frequently occasioning bloodshed and revolution." It was suggested that only the "law of God" allow for the emancipation of slaves.[118]

In at least one case a Louisiana police jury emancipated the slave of a Texas slaveowner. This extraordinary case was acted upon in 1851 by the jury of Calcasieu Parish. In that year they unanimously resolved that:

A certain negro boy named Jack belonging to John Hampshire of Liberty County, State of Texas, be emancipated after complying with the formalities required by Louisiana law.[119]

The slaveowner was required to post bond "with good security domiciliated in this parish for future good conduct and maintenance and support" of the freedman.[120]

Although they used a variety of practices to discourage manumission, the police juries, which were comprised of slaveowners, seldoms refused applications that would free Negro slaves and allow them to remain in Louisiana. Even if strict practices were the policy of such parishes as East Baton Rouge and Lafayette, the leniency of the jurors in St. John the Baptist and Ascension parishes acted as a counterbalance and thus contributed to the growth of the

---

118. Baton Rouge *Gazette*, October 16, 1841.
119. MS. Calcasieu Parish Police Jury Minutes, Volume 1847–1856, 66.
120. *Ibid.*

free colored population. Once freed by police jury action, the emancipated persons were entitled to the "right of doing whatever is not forbidden by law."[121]

The increase in the number of free Negroes in Louisiana came not only from manumissions by state and local legislative bodies and individuals, but also from the emancipation of slaves in slaveowners' wills. When emancipation was provided for by testamentary action, the usual legal formalities prescribed by law were required of the testamentary executors, administrators, heirs or representatives of the testator.[122]

Few masters in Louisiana ever revealed the conviction that slavery was morally wrong. In liberating their slaves, neither religious scruples nor the liberal philosophy of the natural rights of man so characteristic of other areas of the South at an earlier period appear to have had much influence. More often than not emancipation came as a reward for good and faithful services to owners, or because of blood relationship between the master and slave. There were to be sure a few slaveowners who in their wills expressed disapproval of holding human beings as slaves. One such case was that of Stephen Henderson. In his 1837 will he indicated his opposition to slavery, but at the same time he recognized slaves as property guaranteed by the United States Constitution. "To take that away," wrote Henderson, "would at once destroy the greatest government in the World." He went on to blame the preaching of the "fanatic abolitionists" against slavery as responsible for "turning the heads of the unfortunate Negroes" to

---

121. Thomas G. Morgan (ed.), *Civil Code of the State of Louisiana; with the Statutory Amendments, From 1825 to 1853, Inclusive,* 6.
122. *Laws of the Territory of Louisiana* (1807), 1st Leg., 1st Sess., 86.

commit crimes of every kind. In Henderson's opinion it was this factor which had dissuaded many slaveowners from emancipating their slaves although such persons were opposed to the institution itself.[123] In another instance, in 1854, believing that "mankind was not entitled to human chattel," Margaret Bird of Baton Rouge made provision in her will to emancipate her slave servant.[124]

By far, the largest number of liberations came about as a reward for services rendered to masters, and not infrequently manumission was accompanied by bequests in lands, goods and moneys. In 1827, for example, William Inrufty, a resident of Avoyelles Parish, made the following provision in his will:

> I desire my faithful servant, Unity, who is a slave for life to me, who I raised and who had served me faithfully and honestly should be set free and to that end, I will and give . . . freedom . . . to her and her child, George Washington. . . . I will . . . to Unity all my household furniture, the stock marked in her brand, consisting of seven head of cattle, and my riding horse, saddle, and bridle.[125]

By testamentary action, a planter of Natchitoches Parish named William Sutherland freed his three slaves in 1817 for faithful services and further provided that the "bulk of my estate go to them."[126] In 1829, a sugar planter of Iberville Parish named John Erwin manumitted his

---

123. *Heirs of Henderson v. Rost and Montgomery, Executors,* 5 La. An. 441–448 (May 1850).

124. MS. Succession of Margaret Bird, in East Baton Rouge Parish Probate Records, Record No. 382, 1854.

125. MS. Will of William Inrufty, in Avoyelles Parish Alienations Book F 1827, No. 2401, 329–331.

126. MS. Succession of William Sutherland, Natchitoches Parish Succession Records, Record No. 2, 1817.

house servants, Jobe Walker and his family, for "good service rendered to me over a period of years."[127] In addition to freedom, the White planter bequeathed $1000 and six acres of land to insure the future security of his former servants. Before making a "long and dangerous voyage by sea," Mary C. Moore of West Feliciana Parish made a will providing for the freedom of her maidservant, Louisa. The White woman also stipulated that the Negress be free "without labor or servitude during her life and that the sum of fifty dollars be given her during her natural life, annually for her own use."[128]

Several large planters made provision in their wills for the liberation of slaves after the lapse of a certain number of years. Three prominent Louisiana planters who made such conditions were Julien Poydras, Stephen Henderson, and Martin Wood. Julien Poydras, who died in 1824, ordered his administrators to sell his six plantations together with the slave staff,[129] under contracts so as to secure the freedom of each slave after a 25-year period of service to the purchaser. In addition an annual pension of $25 was provided for each slave over sixty. He also asked that all persons in the "name of humanity," and particularly the state authorities to "cause this request to be executed."[130]

---

127. MS. Succession of Joseph Erwin, Iberville Succession Records, Record No. 85, 1829.

128. MS. Will of Mary C. Moore, Weeks Papers.

129. Carter G. Woodson (comp.), *Free Negro Owners of Slaves in the United States in 1830 together with Absentee Ownership of Slaves in the United States in 1830*, 52. In 1830 the Poydras estate in Point Coupee Parish was listed as containing 106 slaves.

130. *Moosa v. Allain,* 4 Mart. NS. 99–100 (December 1825); *Poydras v. Mourrain,* 9 La. An. 492 (December 1835). The will is quoted in both these cases.

Another celebrated case was that of Stephen Henderson, a sugar planter and owner of "six or seven hundred slaves" whose will, probated in 1837, called for the following: ten and twenty slaves respectively were to be chosen by lot at periods five and ten years after his death to be freed and sent to Liberia, and at the end of 25 years the remainder were to fare likewise; but any who refused to be deported were to be kept as apprentices on the various plantations. These benefits, however, were not to extend to slaves guilty of "murder, theft, or confirmed runaways."[131]

It frequently happened that when a master cohabited with a slave woman he would manumit the woman and the children from such unions. In 1855 a White citizen named Turnbull made a will to the effect that his five natural children should be freed at his death. Turnbull's executors was directed to:

> . . . take the necessary steps to obtain their emancipation according to the laws of this State, or to send them to some country or state, . . . where slavery is not recognized, if their emancipation with leave to remain here cannot be obtained. Expenses to be borne by the mass of my estate.[132]

Other slaves were manumitted by testamentary document for personal and sentimental reasons. General Philemon Thomas of Baton Rouge willed freedom to his slave, Sukey, "for hir Honest and Upright Conduct from hir youth up and also on account of hir being much afflicted

---

131. *Executors of Henderson v. Heirs*, 12 Rob. La., 549–550 (February 1846); *Heirs of Henderson v. Rost and Montgomery, Executors*, 5 La. An. 458–462 (May 1850). The will is quote in both these cases upholding the bequests of the testator.

132. *Turner, Curator v. Smith et al.*, 12 La. An. 417 (June 1857).

and wishing hir to be able to take care of hir old mother and to help each other."[133]

As has been shown, a considerable number of free Negroes effected the freedom of their slave relatives by approved deeds, after receiving permission from parish police juries. Some few persons of this class also made wills providing for this purpose, and in rare cases for faithful services from slaves not related to them. In 1810, for example, a free Mulatto named Louis Rodin willed freedom to his natural daughter and also made provision for the payment of 300 piastres to a certain Sr. Etienne for the liberation of the slave Bahe, who had rendered him "good services."[134] Pierre Profit, a free Negro resident of New Orleans, willed freedom to his natural son in 1825.[135] In 1837, Ulyses York, by testamentary action gave freedom to his common-law wife and their two children.[136]

Aside from the practice of holding slave relatives with the objective of ultimately giving them freedom, an appreciable number of colored masters in the rural areas of Louisiana owned slaves as a source of revenue. A case in point was the free Negro ownership of slaves at Iberville Parish in 1830. The smallest number of slaves owned by a colored family was 18, while the largest holding was listed as 46.[137] In St. John the Baptist Parish, of the five

---

133. Frances Robertson, "The Will of General Philemon Thomas." *Proceedings of the Historical Society of East and West Baton Rouge,* I (1916), 26. Philemon Thomas was the military commander in the West Florida Revolution of 1810.

134. MS. Will of Louis Rodin, 1810, Orleans Parish Will Book No. 1 (1805–1810), 346.

135. MS. Will of Pierre Profit, 1825, Orleans Parish Will Book No. 4 (1824–1833), 365.

136. MS. Will of Ulyses York, 1837, Orleans Parish Will Book No. 5 (1833–1837), 421.

137. Woodson, *Free Negro Ownership of Slaves in the United States in 1830,* 6.

colored slaveowners listed, only two held slaves that could conceivably be considered as relatives of the owners. The other three proprietors had holdings amounting to 49, 52 and 38 slaves respectively.[138]

Another type of emancipation that tended to increase the free Negro population occurred in the practice of permitting slaves to purchase their own freedom. This right proceeded from French and Spanish laws, and was made valid in Louisiana provided the contract between master and slave was in the form of a written instrument.[139] In 1824, Louis Doubrérè, an alleged slave, brought suit against the heirs of his former master to uphold an agreement made in 1819 for his emancipation. The Negro asserted that he had purchased his freedom with the assistance of friends and by his own industry. To prove this contention, Doubrérè produced two written documents attesting to this fact. One of them indicated the payment of a note for $1700 towards the emancipation. The other was a license, signed by the collector of the port of New Orleans, authorizing Doubrérè to carry on trade in a coasting vessel and also bearing the surety of his late master that he was a free man. The Supreme Court of Louisiana held the documents to be sufficient proof that a written agreement had been executed and declared Doubrérè a free man.[140]

Yet, such an interpretation was not always placed upon the principle of written contracts, and some Negroes gained their freedom by verbal agreement with their

138. *Ibid.,* 7.

139. *Victoire v. Dussuau,* 4 Mart. La., 212 (March 1816). In this case the high court proclaimed that slaves were incapable of making any contract except for their freedom.

140. *Doubrérè v. Grillier's Syndic,* 2 Mart La. 171–172 (February 1824).

owners. Evidence by parole for self-purchase was declared admissible as proof of an agreement for emancipation, since Article 1783 of the Civil Code of Louisiana, which allowed slaves to contract for their freedom, stipulated no particular formality to be followed. With this reasoning, the Supreme Court granted freedom to a slave named Gaudet based on a verbal agreement she had made with her owner.[141]

There were other cases in which the high court upheld the right of slaves to enter agreements for emancipation. For example, Angelina brought suit against her master for failure to fulfill the terms of a contract he had made, promising emancipation for her and her children when she reached thirty. The Negress had already paid her owner $150 toward redemption. When the lower court decided in favor of the slaveowner, Angelina appealed her case to the Supreme Court of the state. This tribunal held that the contract was binding because a sum of money had been accepted towards manumission, and furthermore it was within the rights of slaves to contract for their liberty under the laws of Louisiana. Accordingly, the court ruled that Angelina and her children were *statu liberi* until the final payments were made. Once that was accomplished the defendants were ordered to proceed immediately to free the Negroes in question.[142]

It was not uncommon for Negro slaves in Louisiana to claim prescriptive rights in order to effect their freedom. By the laws of Louisiana, if "a master suffered a slave to enjoy his liberty for ten years during his residence in

---

141. *Gaudet v. Gourdain et al.*, 3 La. An. 136 (February 1848). In this case the court upheld the principle that a child born of a free woman was free.

142. *Angelina v. Whitehead, et al.*, 3 La. An. 556 (August 1848).

this state or for twenty years while out of it, he shall lose all right of action to recover possession of the slave unless the slave be a runaway or fugitive."[143] In 1818, Adelaide was at first denied freedom, because the court refused to recognize her residence in Haiti as applying to the requisite number of years necessary to claim freedom by prescription.[144] The Supreme Court, in an appeal suit, reversed its previous decision on this matter, and allowed the woman to reckon the time she enjoyed freedom in Haiti in establishing her right to liberation by prescription. Justice P. Derbigny, in rendering the decision for the court, reasoned that Adelaide Metoyer [spelled Metayer in some records] did not live in a state of slavery in Haiti, because the maintenance of general emancipation in that republic had been "sanctioned by the successive supreme authority of that country." It was determined that the Negress had complied with all requirements pertaining to prescription and was declared free of slavery.[145]

The case of Eulalie presented an especially significant point because it demonstrated that the Louisiana high court upheld the right of slaves to sue for freedom through the device of prescription as late as 1854. According to Eulalie's testimony she and her seventeen children and grandchildren had been held unlawfully in slavery by two Whites named Zacharia Mabry and Daniel Long. She further testified that she and her family had lived as free persons for 45 years in Pointe Coupee Parish. Then one night in 1852 they were abducted by unknown White

143. Moreau L. Lislet and Henry Carleton (trans.) *The Laws of Las Siete Partidas Which are Still in Force in the State of Louisiana*, I, 591.
144. *Metayer v. Noret*, 5 Mart. La. 556 (June 1818).
145. *Metayer v. Metayer*, 6 Mart. La. 16–19. (January 1819).

persons and sold as slaves to the defendants. The question before the court was whether Negroes who had been free for years could be reduced into slavery without some redress of grievances before legal authorities. Judge Ogden expressed the opinion that "the affirmation of this proposition was repugnant to the natural dictates of reason and humanity," and denied the defendants' brief that prescription was "idle [and], without meaning or applicability," in Louisiana. The justice went on to state the court's position regarding prescription by saying: "we see nothing in the relation subsisting between master and slave, or the laws which undertake to regulate the status of the slave in reference to his right and privileges as a freeman, incompatible with the prescriptive title to freedom which he may acquire under that law. The law recognizes this as one of the modes in which a slave may acquire his right to freedom. . . ."[146]

In Louisiana slaves frequently obtained freedom as a result of suits, based on various grounds. There were an amazing number of cases contending freedom by virtue of being transported to a state or foreign country where slavery was illegal. In France, for example, the law of 1791 provided that "every individual is free as soon as he is in France."[147] Accordingly, Josephine, who had been taken to that country by her owners and there "placed under the direction of a hair-dresser, to learn his art," upon her return to Louisiana was imprisoned by her masters. It was held by the Supreme Court of the state, in December 1835, that Josephine was entitled to her free-

---

146. *Eulalie and Her Children v. Long and Mabry*, 9 La. An. 9–15 (January 1854).

147. Helen Tunncliff Catterall (ed.), *Judicial Cases Concerning American Slavery and the Negro*, III, 389.

dom. "Being free for one moment in France, it was not in the power of her former master to reduce her again to slavery."[148] Likewise, Priscilla was declared free, in 1839, after a sojourn in France with her owners, even though she returned to Louisiana "on her [Mistresses'] entreaty." Her wish in the matter was immaterial.[149]

Yet at no time did the court hold that a mere sojourn in a free state or territory bestowed freedom on a slave. Residence in a state or territory whose constitutions prohibited slavery has that effect only if the slaveowner gave express permission for such residence.[150] In her suit for freedom in 1840, Elizabeth Thomas contended that she had been sent to Illinois at her own request, and with the express consent of her master, for the purpose of receiving medical "care of an eminent physician." While in Illinois she had lived in a house belonging to her master for a period of five years. After returning to Kentucky, she was sold as a slave in Louisiana, and basing her case on the grounds that since Illinois prohibited slavery she brought suit for her freedom in a Louisiana court. The Supreme Court of the state declared the Negress *ipso facto* free because of her residence in a free state with the permission of her owner "and being once free could not be made a slave."[151] Once again the old maxim, stretching back to ancient times, "once free for an hour, free for ever" received full support in Louisiana.

---

148. *Marie Louise (f.w.c.) v Marot et al.*, 8 La. An 475 (March 1835).

149. *Priscilla Smith v. Smith*, 13 La. 441 (April 1839).

150. See *Lunsford v. Coquillon*, 2 Mart. 401 (May 1824); *Louis (f.m.c.) v. Cabarrus et al.*, 7 La. 170 (August 1834); *Frank (f.m.c.) v. Powell.* 11 La. 499 (January 1838).

151. *Elizabeth Thomas (f.w.c.) v. Generis et al.*, 16 La. 483–484 (December 1840).

However, in 1846, this principle was changed by an act of the Legislature. This legislation spared Louisiana the possibility of any Dred Scott cataclysm. The law implicitly provided that thereafter "no slave shall be entitled to freedom under the pretence that he or she has been, with or without the consent of his or her owner, in a country where slavery does not exist, or in any of the states where slavery is prohibited."[152] The high court, however, in making an interpretation of the 1847 statute declared the act was not retroactive, so that Eugénie, who was in France from 1830 to 1838, and Arsene, who lived there from 1836 to 1838, were adjudged free, even though their suits were brought after the passage of the act in question.

In these two suits, however, the residence of the master or mistress in France was stressed, for a mere sojourn there, as in the cases of Josephine and Priscilla, evidently was no longer sufficient by that time. The facts for the first case revealed that Eugenie's mistress had married a French officer, who remained in France after his wife had returned to Louisiana, and thus established her residence in the French nation where slavery was prohibited by law.[153] Arsene's owner claimed that her two years' stay in France was a mere sojourn, but the court did not agree with him and set the Negress free. Chief Justice Eustice declared further:

> We cannot expect that foreign nations will consent to the suspension of the operation of their fundamental laws, as to persons voluntarily sojourning . . . for such a length of time. As to those thrown on foreign coasts by Shipwreck,

152. *Laws of Louisiana* (1846), 1st Leg., 1st Sess., 163.
153. *Eugénie v. Préval et al.*, 2 La. An. 180–181 (February 1847).

taking refuge from pirates, driven by some overwhelming necessity, or perhaps passing through . . . their personal condition may remain unchanged; but this is the extent to which an immunity from the effect of a foreign law could be maintained under the law of nations.[154]

By 1850 Chief Justice Eustice was citing the law of 1846 in declaring the inability of any slave to claim freedom by being carried by his owner to a free territory.[155] Henceforth, slaves were categorically prohibited from claiming freedom merely by the fact of having resided in free territories or states.

In the decade preceding the Civil War Louisiana slaveholders became convinced that the practice of manumitting slaves constituted a serious menace to the institution of slavery. Placing restrictions upon emancipations, it was argued, would operate to reduce the number of free Negroes whose presence, it was felt, had a tendency to make slaves restless and insubordinate. In this connection, considerable effort was exerted either to stop manumission altogether or at least render it so tedious as to make it almost impossible of achievement. The Legislature was urged to take this matter into consideration for the welfare of the "citizens at large." Slaves who had been set free by well-meaning masters were held up as "a pest of every community" and "none acknowledge this more freely than the most raving abolitionists." Slaveowners were, however, conceded the right to emancipate their slaves, provided they sent the Negroes out of the state. As an added safeguard, the General Assembly was urged to pass measures

---

154. *Arsène v. Pigéguy*, 2 La. An. 620–621 (June 1847).
155. *Bernard Conant, Tutor of Mary (a negro woman) v. William Guesnard and Wife*, 5 La. An. 696 (November 1850).

that would not only restrict manumissions but would also include provisions for reenslavement of any free Negro who returned to the state after emancipation.[156]

This sentiment found a sympathetic echo in the legislative halls of the state. In 1852, a heated debate broke out in the Louisiana House of Representatives, as it began consideration of a bill which provided that no more slaves be manumitted, except those who were to be sent to Liberia when emancipated. Representative F. D. Richardson of St. Mary Parish, who wrote the bill, reminded his fellow lawmakers that the "constant increase of free negroes" was a cause of "corrupting the slaves and an absolute nuisance" to the state. Richardson contended that there was "no humanity in liberating a good slave, and thus condemning him to drag out an irksome and precarious existence."

U. B. Phillips of West Feliciana Parish opposed the bill on the grounds that it would discard all previous regulations on the subject and prohibit, by the expense involved in transporting freed slaves to Liberia, all pending emancipations. Although he was aware of the "evil accompanying a free negro population," Phillips suggested that "hereafter no further emancipation shall be allowed." E. W. Moise of Plaquemines Parish favored the passage for the reason that the free Negro population was increasing in the state. "This population," he said, "corrupts the morals of the slave . . . and forms a constantly augmenting nucleus of mischief and evil." T. Vaughn of Claiborne spoke in opposition to the measure because he was satisfied with the present legislation as it operated in the country parishes. In his opinion the bill was unjust because

---

156. Baton Rouge *Gazette*, February 7, 1852.

it would "cut off the right of those slaves who have already contracted for their liberty."[157]

Finally, on March 16, 1852, an act was approved by the Governor making it mandatory for all slaves emancipated in the future to leave the state of Louisiana within one year after the manumission date. The act was to take effect six months after it received the approval of the Governor. Police juries and the municipal governing bodies of New Orleans were instructed to demand a $120 bond for each slave emancipated by either White or colored slaveowners. This money was to be applied toward paying the expense of transporting the freed Negro to Africa. If the emancipated Negro was not sent to Africa within the stipulated time, or returned to the state after emancipation, he was subject to reverting to the state of slavery under his former owner.[158]

By passing this measure, it was obvious that the Legislature sought to discourage manumissions. In anticipation of the effective date of the 1852 act, many masters rushed emancipation petitions. In St. Martin Parish, for example, on September 3, 1852, 46 cases for emancipation were approved for slaveowners, with the accompanying provisions that the free persons be permitted residence in the state without posting of bond. In this group of petitions a certain J. F. Miller was able to obtain permission to liberate twelve slaves.[159] In the same month, the jurors of Lafourche granted permission for the emancipation of thirteen slaves without the posting of bond, together with

---

157. *Journal of the House of Representatives* (1852), 4th Leg., 1st Sess., 7–8.

158. *Laws of Louisiana* (1852), 4th Leg., 1st Sess., 214–215.

159. MS. St. Martin Parish Police Jury Minutes, Volume I, 1843–1855, 158.

permission for such persons to remain as residents in that parish.[160] It is significant, however, to note that none of the parish police juries approved emancipation petitions after the 1852 act went into effect. Yet, this did not prevent slaveowners from requesting, and often receiving, such permission from the state legislature.

Soon after the passage of the 1852 emancipation act, a special bill to manumit a slave of a Concordia Parish White citizen brought a storm of protest from the lawmakers. Representative Hunt of Concordia Parish, who had introduced the act to set aside the emancipation laws in favor of his constituent, proceeded to justify legislative approval on this matter. He represented his constituent as "an old frontier man, whose home was in the wilderness far from the ameliarating and chastening influences of society, [who] made a friend of a colored woman, by whom he had an offspring." Since the White man in question had failed to take advantage of the law providing for the liberation of his child, the representative asked in the "name of humanity" for the legislature to pass the special bill freeing the slave in question. Representative Sandusky opposed the measure for he had "no sympathy for men who take negresses to their brest." He urged his colleagues to "frown upon all such unmitigated levity," and reminded them that the 1852 law required the expulsion of emancipated Negroes. G. B. Miller called the attention of the legislators to the "already clogged parishes of free negroes," and he could not see the necessity of any "further increase of this population" by favoring the bill. In Miller's opinion, if the bill was approved, it "would

---

160. MS. Lafourche Parish Police Jury Minutes, Volume II, 1852–1862, 1–3.

lead others to follow suit and the law will, in effect, be a nullity." H. A. Wailes supported the "old frontier man" as having acted in a way that any member of the legislature would have acted under similar circumstances. Representative Wilder, apparently enraged by this remark, retorted that the bill was unconstitutional and besides "he [old frontier man] was able to find his way into the woods, he was able, certainly, to find his way out." "This is an age of progress," continued Wilder, and "I for one did not wish to see Louisiana making a retrogradable movement" by approving such a bill. In the face of so much opposition, the bill was withdrawn and permanently placed on the table.[161]

All petitions for emancipation with permission to remain in the state before the General Assembly did not, however, receive this kind of reception. In 1853 that body approved the emancipation with state residential privileges for Patsy, a child of a free woman of color living in East Baton Rouge Parish.[162] At the same session of the Legislature, a certain Baptiste Dupeyné was allowed, by a special act, to emancipate his slave, Zoe, with the same privileges.[163] Besides these two exemptions from the 1852 law, the Legislature granted four other requests for the emancipation of slaves.[164] It would appear that the forces, benevolent or otherwise, which motivated emancipation for certain slaves were much stronger than the barriers which had been erected by the law.

The Legislature on this matter, however, was inconsis-

---

161. *Official Reports of the Proceedings of the House of Representatives* (1853), 1st Leg., 1st Sess., 24–25.
162. *Laws of Louisiana* (1853), 1st Leg., 1st Sess., 162.
163. *Ibid.*, 163–164.
164. *Ibid.*, 51–52, 272, 273–274.

tent, since it approved some cases for manumission and rejected others. In 1854, considerable opposition was voiced against a bill providing for the manumission of certain slaves belonging to a St. Tammany Parish slaveowner. During the course of the debates, reference was made to the necessity of restricting manumissions because the large numbers of free Negroes already in the state constituted "a blighting and burning curse," and because "liberty given to a slave is his worst enemy."[165] The bill in question was lost because of the overwhelming hostility of the legislators.

The next year, Governor Paul O. Hébert, in vetoing several emancipation acts, reprimanded the House of Representatives for spending too much valuable legislative time on such matters. The irritated Governor stated that "judging from the number of special acts annually passed, one would be led to the conclusion that the [general] laws are defective. If this be the case, in the opinion of the undersigned . . . let the fundamental law be amended so as to meet public opinion and the exigencies of the time."[166]

The lawmakers heeded the suggestion of the chief executive and passed the comprehensive 1855 act relative to slaves and free persons of color in Louisiana. A new manumission procedure was adopted: An owner who wished to emancipate his slave had to enter suit in the parish court. All suits for manumission were to have a jury trial, and the jury had the power to decide whether

---

165. *Official Reports of the Proceedings of the House of Representatives* (1854), 2nd Leg., 1st Sess., 15.

166. *Journal of the House of Representatives* 1855, 2nd Leg., 2nd Sess., 9–11.

the slave was to remain in the state after his emancipation. If freedom was approved by a twelve-man jury, the parish judge would then execute the manumission. On the other hand, if the jury failed to give the slave permission to remain in the state, the judgment of freedom was to be without effect so long as the slave remained in Louisiana. If the emancipated slave returned to the state, the plaintiff in a suit for emancipation was required to pay the district attorney $20, along with all costs of the suit regardless of the decision.[167] It will be recalled that this act was declared unconstitutional and consequently was never effective insofar as manumission by jury trial was concerned.[168]

After the 1855 act was declared unconstitutional, demands to prohibit emancipation altogether were raised by the press of the state. In vehement language the point was made that manumission of slaves gave rise to the "existence of a third class which produces discontent among the enslaved, corrupts, makes them refractory, and debauches their morals."[169] Urging legislative action on this matter in 1857, the editor of the Baton Rouge *Advocate* wrote:

Our contemporaries all over the State concur in the belief that the next session of the Legislature will be asked to pass an act prohibiting further emancipation of slaves in this State or at least one prohibiting their remaining among us after emancipation. Public opinion is almost unanimous for a policy of this kind, and we recommend the subject

167. *Laws of Louisiana* (1855), 2nd Leg., 2nd Sess., 378–388.
168. *Cf. supra*, 111.
169. Opelousas *Courier*, December 20, 1856.

strongly to the attention of the members of the Legislature.[170]

When the General Assembly met in 1857, Attorney General E. Warren Moise, in his annual report to that body, called attention to additional reasons for more stringent regulations limiting the liberation of slaves. That ever cautious official argued that too many freed slaves had been able to remain in the state and had created a "deplorable situation" insofar as a rise in the crime rate was concerned. He therefore recommended regulations designed to restrict the emancipation of slaves in Louisiana.[171] On March 6, 1857, an act was passed to prohibit any future emancipation of slaves.[172] For the first time, there were no ways or means legal or otherwise by which a slave might hope to win freedom. Long and faithful service to master, blood relationship with the master class, self-purchase, or even an act of meritorious service no longer sufficed in freeing Louisiana slaves. Neither special legislative act, police juries, district court, nor the State Supreme Court had any power to free a slave under this absolute prohibitive law.[173]

In congratulating the General Assembly for enacting the measure the editor of the Opelousas *Courier* said, "It will show the abolitionists that, instead of yielding a hairs breath to their clamorous demands, we are only made

170. Baton Rouge *Advocate,* quoted in Opelousas *Courier,* January 3, 1857.

171. *Louisiana Legislative Documents* (1857), 3rd Leg., 2nd Sess., 11.

172. *Laws of Louisiana* (1857), 3rd Leg., 2nd Sess., 55.

173. This law was upheld by the Supreme Court in the following cases: *Oreline v. Heirs of Haggerty,* 12 La. An. 880 (August 1858); *Delphine (f.w.c.) v. Mrs. Guillet et al.,* 13 La. An. 248 (April 1858); *Jones v. State,* 13 La. An. 406 (July 1858).

more earnest, more diligent, more careful, and more determined in resisting them, and that every movement on their part towards emancipation will be promptly answered on ours by a more decisive movement in the opposition direction."[174] Intoxicated with success in preventing emancipation, the anti-free-Negro forces urged consideration of legislation which would enable free persons of color to voluntarily select masters and become slaves for life.[175] Such an act was passed in 1859.[176] Under this reenslavement action a free Negro named John Clifton chose a Mr. Green L. Bumpass as a master and then legally proclaimed himself a slave of that White man.[177]

It has been shown that the emancipation of slaves by private owners accounted for a sizeable number of Negro slaves entering the free ranks. Although it is not possible to determine just how many entered through this method and allowed to remain in Louisiana, the continued residence of significant numbers of emancipated slaves could be seen even to the casual observer. The emancipation policy was, of course, seemingly always conditioned by the deepening hatred between the Northern and Southern people over the issue of slavery. Northern abolitionists and their fellow travelers constantly irritated Louisiana citizens whether they were slaveowners or not. Many Whites were undeviatingly convinced that the very presence of Negroes not in slavery was an especially bad example for those held in chattel ownership. Even worse

---

174. March 14, 1857.

175. *Messager St. Jacques* quoted in *Les Courier des Opelousas,* Fevrier 12, 1859.

176. *Laws of Louisiana* (1859), 4th Leg., 2nd Sess., 214–215.

177. New Orleans *Daily Delta,* May 18, 1860. This is the only case the author could find in which a free Negro returned to slavery, under the act of 1859.

to many was that the free Negro population might serve as agents or allies of the dreaded Anti-slavery forces of the North.

However, in the years before 1830, only mild conditions had been imposed on owners desiring to free slaves. But, soon after that date as the sectional controversy reached ever-spiraling crises, almost every session of the Legislature entertained countless numbers of measures aimed at curtailing emancipations. In 1857 the day of the pro-Slavery forces had come into its own. After that date no emancipations were permitted to any slaveowner in the state of Louisiana. Yet, it must be recognized that even though both police juries and Supreme Court had the effect of moderating harsh features of state laws, these instruments of government were silenced in 1857. From that time on emancipation could no longer account for the increase of the free Negro population in Louisiana.

Some slaves attempted to pass as free persons and when successful contributed to the growth of the free Negro population. Even though they never did so in great numbers such instances did occasionally take place during the early decades of the 19th Century. Advertisements of the time indicated that slaveowners suspected that their runaway slaves would attempt to pass as free persons. In 1821, for example, a fifty-dollar reward was offered for the return of:

Nanette and her infant daughter Euphrosine who are now lurking about this city [New Orleans] or its environs. She is about 40 years, middle size, rather lightish complexion, looks young for a woman of her age—being creole wench she speaks French and English—she is an excellent laundress, and I am persuanded she is now pursuing that occupation in some part of this city or its suburbs. She has the address to pass herself for a free woman and calls herself Nannette Revoie.[178]

Another slaveowner offered a ten-dollar reward for the return of his Mulatto slave, Paul, "who speaks English, French and Spanish with facility." This slave was also described as "endeavoring to pass himself as a free man."[179]

Nearly every runaway slave who attempted to pass as a White man was Mulatto or of even lighter complexion. Many country slaves considered the city of New Orleans as the least likely place for detection and apprehension and fled there in sizeable numbers. In 1827, a P. Browing, who owned a plantation in West Baton Rouge Parish advertised a ten-dollar reward for the return of his Mulatto slave. He described this slave as "a well built, good-looking fellow with a fine head of hair" who told other slaves on the plantation that "if he was in New Orleans, he would there pass for a free man."[180] A $100 reward was offered in 1859 for a runaway from the Crescent Plantation near Donaldsonville, who was described as having "straight black hair and mulatto skin and who will probably pass himself for a white man in New Orleans."[181]

There are cases in which such runaway slaves were captured and returned to bondage. In 1855, for example, a $500 reward was offered for the return of George Allen Blackson, "a light griff or yellow boy" whose features

---

178. New Orleans *Friend of the Laws and Commercial Journal,* May 22, 1820.
179. New Orleans *Gazette and Commercial Advertiser,* February 6, 1817.
180. Baton Rouge *Gazette,* June 9, 1827.
181. New Orleans *Daily Delta,* August 11, 1859.

were described as "very sharp and with a kind of crooked or Roman nose." On a previous occasion, he had attempted to pass as a free person of color and was again suspected of "making out he is free."[182] In 1844, the sum of $100 was offered for Helene, "a fair complected mulattress who had attempted to pass as a free woman on three different occasions. The first time was in St. Landry Parish and the other two attempts were in Pointe Coupee Parish."[183]

There was a fairly large number of Negroes confined in parish jails claiming to be free persons. Such persons were often imprisoned when they failed to produce sufficient evidence of free status. In 1830, for example, a free Mulatto named John Brown was imprisoned in the East Baton Rouge Parish jail when he failed to furnish sufficient proof to satisfy the authorities of his status.[184] Frequently, if the person claiming free status was black, even more doubt was expressed as to his being a free person. Two Negroes of that description were confined in the Baton Rouge jail in 1827 despite their claims to the contrary.[185] In the same year, three other Black men were committed to the parish prison of Iberville for failing to produce free papers, and they were suspected of being runaway slaves from Mississippi.[186]

On occasion, the jailer of the Louisiana slave depot at Baton Rouge was convinced that the claims of certain Negroes were spurious. Such an instance occurred in 1844 when the jailer inserted the following announcement in the local newspaper:

---

182. *Ibid.*, January 14, 1855.
183. Opelousas *Courier*, April 9, 1859.
184. Baton Rouge *Gazette*, January 9, 1830.
185. *Ibid.*, March 17, 1827.
186. West Baton Rouge, *The Capitolian Vis-A-Vis*, September 29, 1852.

Committed to Baton Rouge Slave Depot, negro man calls himself Elisha, 5 ft. 9½ in. high, about 25–30 year old, was taken with a white man . . . John Eldridge, says he is free, but I have reason to believe that he was brought to the country by a trader named Davis and sold at a brick yard opposite New Orleans and was called Henry Austen when sold.[187]

It was not unknown for clever slaves to gain a period of freedom by the use of forged papers. In advertising for his "yellow boy Henry Wilson and his wife Harriett," the owner of Azucena Plantation in Tensas Parish indicated that "it is supposed that they have forged free papers."[188] Some Negroes even claimed to be of Indian origin to effect their escape from bondage. In 1847, Elizabeth Parsons of New Orleans made such a claim, but was unable to prove this to the satisfaction of the law and was remanded into slavery.[189]

Some idea of the growth of the free colored population can be seen in census reports. When the first federal census of Louisiana was taken in 1810, 1858 of the Negro population living in rural Louisiana were classified as free, and by 1860, the number had grown to 7708 inhabitants.[190] Although the rural population of this class more than doubled during the fifty year period from 1810 to 1860, there was no actual numerical decline in the last two decades of the ante-bellum period.

---

187. Baton Rouge *Gazette*, July 13, 1844.
188. New Orleans *Daily Picayune*, September 2, 1857.
189. *Ibid.*, January 16, 1847.
190. *Third Census of the United States, 1810*, 82; *Eighth Census of the United States, 1860*, 193.

TABLE I

Free Negro Population in Louisiana, 1810–1860.[191]

Year	Rural Population	Decade	Numerical Increase of Rural Population from Previous Census	Orleans Parish	Aggregate
1810	1858	1810–20	1457	5727	7585
1820	3315	1820–30	1444	7161	10476
1830	4759	1830–40	1517	11951	16710
1840	6276	1840–50	1225	19226	25502
1850	7501	1850–60	207	9961	17462
1860	7708			10939	18647

The increases in the rural free Negro population from 1810 to 1860 were due in part to a natural increase by excess of births over deaths; and in part to an increase from among the slaves through manumissions and self-purchase. The dramatic numerical decline after 1840 may be attributed to several factors. For example, the free Negroes were a bit older and therefore subject to a higher death rate. They also were less normally distributed by sex, and consequently more or less characterized by a marital condition less conducive to any great natural increase. The census lists from 1820 to 1860 indicates fewer males than females. In 1850, for example, the ratio of the sexes was 3524 males to 3977 females.[192] But in 1860, this

191. Figures compiled from *ibid. Fourth Census of the United States, 1820,* 31; *Fifth Census of the United States, 1830,* 107; *Sixth Census of the United States, 1840,* 256; *Seventh Census of the United States, 1850,* 473. It is evident that Orleans Parish contained the largest concentration of free Negroes in Louisiana. Henceforth all census figures will be concerned chiefly with the numbers and location of the rural free Negro population of the state.

192. *Seventh Census of the United States, 1850,* 473.

ratio came to 3696 males to 4012 females.[193] The significant reduction in numbers in the last decade may also be attributed in large part to the hostility of the White citizens in the rural areas, which caused many to migrate to the Republic of Haiti. Of this matter more will be said later.

Although the rural free colored population did not increase in numbers so great as in New Orleans, there was a steady growth in certain country parishes. As early as 1810, the census reports show clearly marked concentration in certain parishes. For example, the concentration was greatest in Natchitoches, Opelousas [later St. Landry], Attakapas [later St. Martin and St. Mary], Pointe Coupee, St. Charles, East Baton Rouge, Rapides and Plaquemines. Altogether, the free colored population in these localities in the first census amounted to 1423 free Negro inhabitants out of a total rural free colored population of 1858. The largest single concentration was found in Opelousas with 384 free persons of color.[194] Moreover, throughout the ante-bellum period these parishes continued to contain the largest number of free Negroes. It is significant that there seems to be no fixed pattern for the geographical location of the free Negro in the rural parishes. Natchitoches, Opelousas, Attakapas and Rapides are inland parishes, located in the southwestern and northcentral section of Louisiana. On the other hand, Plaquemines, St. Charles, East Baton Rouge and Pointe Coupee are Mississippi River parishes.

The number of free Negroes continued to grow in these

193. *Eighth Census of the United States, 1860,* 192.
194. *Third Census of the United States, 1810,* 82.

areas. In 1820, for instance, this group of parishes had a free colored population amounting to 2226 out of a total rural population of 3315.[195] The census of 1830 showed 3006 out of a rural population of 4759;[196] and 3730 out of a rural total of 6276 in the 1840 census reports.[197]

The census of 1850 is an especially pertinent point at which to study the growth of the free Negro in provincial Louisiana. The number had increased by 1225 in the ten-year period just preceding the sixth enumeration, and the total of free Negro inhabitants living in the country parishes of the state had reached 7501.[198] The concentration followed lines similar to those of preceding censuses. Four of the eight parishes of greatest concentration had more than 500 free Negro inhabitants: St. Landry, with 1242, had almost doubled its free colored population; Natchitoches, located in the northcentral part of the state, had 881, marking a gain of 224 free Negroes over the previous census; Pointe Coupee, in southeastern Louisiana, had 560, while in St. Martin Parish, the free colored population numbered 529 persons. Nine other parishes contained 100 or more free colored inhabitants, while 21 had less than this number. Five northern parishes—Bossier, Claiborne, Caldwell, Sabine and Union—listed no free Negro inhabitants.[199]

Free Negroes were also an important factor in the Negro population of parishes where the plantation system [with its many slaves] existed and flourished. In 1850, for example, Natchitoches, Pointe Coupee, St. Landry and

---

195. *Fourth Census of the United States, 1820,* 31.
196. *Fifth Census of the United States, 1830,* 107.
197. *Sixth Census of the United States, 1840,* 256.
198. *Seventh Census of the United States, 1850,* 473.
199. *Ibid.*

St. Martin parishes had 7881, 7811, 10,871, and 6489 slaves respectively. By way of contrast, of the five small land-holding northern parishes reporting no free Negro inhabitants, two of them—Claiborne and Caldwell—had only 2322 and 1231 slaves respectively. Similar small slaveholdings were reported in the other three parishes listing no free Negro inhabitants.[200]

In the census reports for 1860, the eight most populous parishes contained 4293 free Negroes out of a total rural free colored population of 7708. Appreciable increases were registered in all but St. Landry and St. Martin parishes, where losses of 277 and 218 respectively were reported. Despite the decrease of free Negroes in St. Landry, it was still ahead of the other parishes. The total free colored population was listed as 965; Natchitoches was second with 959, and Point Coupee was third with 721. In that year, East Baton Rouge ranked fourth with 532. Ten parishes in 1860 counted more than 100 free Negroes, while 23 had less than that number of free Negro inhabitants.[201] The continuance of parishes with less than 100 free Negroes may be attributed to the fact that such areas were continuously in the process of reorganization. Thereby, a parish with more than 100 free Negroes may have found itself dismembered for the purpose of creating one or more parishes. Thus, a part of its free colored population would be counted as that of the new parish in the next census. Twenty-two new parishes were created between 1810 and 1860.[202]

The census returns in 1860 for towns reveal that free

---

200. *Ibid.*

201. *Eighth Census of the United States, 1860,* 191.

202. See Works Progress Administration, Historical Records Survey, *County-Parish Boundaries in Louisiana,* 17–74.

Negroes, living outside Orleans Parish, remained essentially a rural people. In that year no town contained as many as 500 free colored persons. Table II illustrates the extent to which there was a lack of concentration of free Negroes in the towns of Louisiana.

TABLE II

Free Negroes in Louisiana Towns, 1860[203]

Town	Free Negroes	Slaves	Whites	Total
Alexandria	131	350	980	1,461
Algiers	250	1,099	4,467	5,816
Bastrop	1	163	317	481
Baton Rouge	468	1,247	3,693	5,428
Bayou Sara	28	152	360	540
Delhi	1	21	153	175
Donaldsonville	168	7,376	3,940	11,484
Floyd	0	113	185	298
Homer	2	590	859	1,451
Jefferson	131	720	4,256	5,107
Minden	0	675	471	1,146
Opelousas	163	—	623	786
Pineville	10	90	293	393
Plaquemines	130	508	1,025	1,663
Providence	8	144	430	582
Thibodeaux	39	302	1,039	1,380
Vermillionville	56	137	305	498
Washington	26	—	510	536
Shreveport	46	—	2,144	2,190
Total	1,658	13,687	26,050	41,415

Other areas of free Negro concentration in the country parishes were communities made up almost entirely of members of that class. Notable among such concentra-

---

203. *Eighth Census of the United States, 1860,* 195. It is evident that less than 2,000 of the 7,708 rural free Negroes lived in the towns of Louisiana.

tions of free Negro population were "Niggerville" in St. Landry Parish, Isle de Breville in Natchitoches, and a free Negro settlement located near the Louisiana–Texas border, known as the Ten Mile district.[204] There was also a free Negro settlement in Lafayette Parish called Prairie Marronne, where a free Negro patriarch named Coco and his numerous descendants lived.[205]

In summary, a study of the figures gleaned from the census reports shows that the greatest concentration of free Negroes was in Orleans Parish. Outside of that metropolitan area, free persons of color were found in greater numbers in the rural areas rather than in towns. Hence it may be said that throughout the ante-bellum period, those free Negroes who lived in provincial Louisiana remained essentially a rural rather than an urban people. The greatest concentration of these people was found in eight inland and Mississippi River parishes where the slave population was most numerous.

---

204. Frederick Law. Olmsted, *A Journey in the Seaboard Slave State, in the Years 1853–1854,* II, 294.

205. Alexandre Barde, *Histoire des Comités de Vigilance Aux Attakapas,* 217, 223.

4

Quasi-Citizenship

AMONG the most enduring colonial legacies carried over into American Louisiana was the peculiar legal status of free persons of color. At best it was a patent contradiction of the concept of equal justice under law. On the other hand, in some limited respects it guaranteed the same protection of life, liberty, and property as was afforded the ruling White population. Yet at no time were non-Whites ever deemed wholly equal; they were generally recognized by law as second class citizens.

The Territorial Assembly proved quite active in assigning an anomalous position to Louisiana's Free Negro race. Among a long list of measures was the 1808 law which required all such persons to place "free man of color" or "free woman of color" following their names in all business transactions, wills, and other forms of legal instruments.[1] In this way all free Negroes were earmarked and set apart from White persons and slaves for the remainder of the

---

1. *Laws of the Territory of Orleans* (1808), 2nd Leg., 1st Sess., 138.

Old Print of Flower Girls in New Orleans, circa 1850. Print in possession of author

Nicholas Augustin Metoyer f.m.c. Artist J. F. Fuille painted in 1836. Metoyer, planter and Church patron. Donated land for St. Augustine Church located in Natchitoches Parish, Louisiana. Original church constructed in 1803 is shown in background. Original painting located in St. Augustine Church. Courtesy John Guillet and François Mignon

Jules Hudson (f.mc.) "Self Portrait" New Orleans Artist. Courtesy Collection of the Louisiana State Museum.

ante-bellum period. Seldom did they escape the brand and both public and private records of the period carry the designation required by law.[2]

Free Negroes were always the objects of very close regulation and inspection in matters pertaining to owning and carrying arms. In 1806, any of that class wishing to bear arms was required to possess freedom papers or suffer the confiscation of the weapon.[3] Even though this regulation did not categorically forbid either the ownership or possession of weapons, it made certain that free Negroes had proof of their emancipation. Such was deemed necessary in order to prevent slaves from possessing weapons, which could be used in revolting against White persons.[4]

In some offenses against the law, White persons and free Negroes received equal puishment. For example any person, regardless of color, who concealed goods stolen by a slave would be "exposed to public shame," and forced to pay the person who suffered the loss a sum of money equal to the value of the stolen property.[5] All persons found guilty of selling intoxicating liquors to slaves were subject to a $25 fine.[6] The same severe penalties were provided for men and women of both races judged guilty of causing or joining slave insurrections. In an effort to discourage servile uprising, the Territorial Assembly in 1806, enacted the following measure:

If any persons shall, by words, action or writing, or any

---

2. See, for example, *Official Journal of the Senate* (1857), 3rd Leg., 2nd Sess., 6.
3. *Laws of the Territory of Orleans* (1806), 1st Leg., 1st Sess., 164.
4. *Ibid.*
5. *Ibid.*, 200.
6. *Ibid.*, 164

other manner whatsoever, persuade, encourage or advise any slave or slaves to insurrection against the white inhabitants of this State, or government thereof, such persons, on conviction thereof, shall suffer death.[7]

Frequent contact of free Negroes with slaves and White persons became the subject of legislation. One example is the passage of a law prohibiting gambling between Whites and Negroes of whatever status. The act also provided that any White man "who shall play any game of chance, or make any bet" with a free Negro or slave, "upon conviction . . . for the third time shall be fined $1000 and imprisoned for one year in the parish jail."[8]

Besides suffering discrimination in matters relating to offenses against the peace of the commonwealth, free Negroes were also prohibited from engaging in certain types of businesses. By an act passed in 1859, for instance, free persons of color could not legally operate billiard halls, coffee houses or retail outlets in which alcoholic beverages were sold.[9] At the same session of the General Assembly legislation was passed forbidding any free colored person from seeking employment as captains of "vessels navigating the Rivers, Bayous, and Lakes in the State of Louisiana."[10]

In addition to state legislation, free Negroes were also subject to further regulation by city and parish ordinances that greatly interfered with their freedom of person. A Lafayette Parish ordinance, for example, prohibited free

7. Levi Peirce, Miles Taylor, William W. King (comps.), *The Consolidation and Revision of the Statues of the State of a General Nature,* 208.

8. *Laws of Louisiana* (1852), 4th Leg., 1st Sess., 16.

9. *Ibid.* (1859), 4th Leg., 2nd Sess., 18.

10. *Ibid.,* 172.

persons of color from being in the company of slaves at any time under penalty of a $30 fine.[11] A similar measure was passed in Pointe Coupee Parish.[12] Dances conducted by free Negroes were made the subject of special regulation by local authorities. In St. John the Baptist and Lafayette Parishes, if a slave was found at a dance given by free Negroes the person in charge of the dance would be fined $10 for the first offence, and $20 and two months imprisonment for the second.[13] Horse racing on the public roads within the limits of Jefferson Parish was prohibited to all free Negroes under penalty of a $10 fine.[14]

One of the most severe restrictions on members of the free colored group were local ordinances forbidding them to move from place to place freely. A regulation to this effect was passed by the police jury of St. John the Baptist Parish and was quite specific in providing the following:

> Any negro or negress, mulatto or mulattress who should declare himself or herself free but who should not prove it, either by copy of his or her act of emancipation, or certificate from a competent authority or an attestation sworn to by two respectable persons, proprietors of the neighborhood or well known in the parish, shall be provisionally considered as a slave and as such conveyed to the parish prison . . . and shall get out from it but upon proving his or her emancipation and paying the cost of arrest, conveyance and detention.[15]

---

11. MS. Lafayette Parish Police Jury Minutes, Volume I, 1823–1857, 4.
12. Pointe Coupee *Democrat*, May 18, 1860.
13. MS. St. John the Baptist Parish Police Jury Minutes, Volume 1814–1817, 20; Lafayette Parish Police Jury Minutes, Volume I, 1823–1867, 5.
14. MS. Jefferson Parish Police Jury Minutes, Volume I, 1834–1843, 221.
15. MS. St. John the Baptist Parish Police Jury Minutes, Volume 1849–1882, 308.

The regulation further provided for the advertisement in the newspapers of the notice of arrest and detention of such persons. If, at the end of one month, such persons had not supplied required proof of emancipation, they would be sent to New Orleans for deportation from Louisiana.

The city of New Orleans enacted its own special regulations pertaining to the free Negro population under municipal jurisdiction. None could reside in the city limits without obtaining permission from the mayor or someone acting in his place. Permits were made when the mayor received sufficient evidence that the person in question was legally free of slavery.[16] Permission for staging balls was given to free Negroes only when they complied with the ordinance forbidding the presence of slaves at such affairs. In addition a fee of ten dollars was deposited with the mayor.[17] The personal conduct of free Negroes was further regulated by a city ordinance prohibiting gambling between them and the slaves of New Orleans. Even before the state enacted anti-gambling laws, the City Council prohibited this diversion between the races. In 1814, an ordinance provided that any slave found guilty of gambling with a free colored person could be whipped, and a free Negro could be fined at least $100 for the same offense.[18]

---

16. MS. Ordinances and Resolutions of the City Council of New Orleans, March 11, 1805 to November 20, 1815, Session of July 24, 1805, 63.

17. MS. Ordinances and Resolutions of the City Council of New Orleans, December 24, 1816, to February 9, 1821. Session of November 26, 1820, 18.

18. MS. Ordinances and Resolutions of the City Council of New Orleans, March 11, 1805, to November 20, 1815. Session of May 26, 1814, 318.

Free Negroes could not legally vote in ante-bellum Louisiana. Every ante-bellum constitution limited the suffrage to White males who were at least 21 and could meet other qualifications.[19] Constitutional limitation did not discourage Whites of the liberal frame of mind from favoring the voting of free Negroes. As was generally true throughout the South in the 1840s Louisiana felt the wave of liberalism engendered by Jacksonian democracy. This sentiment found expression in a new constitution, which lowered suffrage qualifications and enlarged the number of elective offices in the state.[20] A leading liberal in the Constitutional Convention of 1845 was Bernard de Marigny who unashamedly advocated that free colored persons should be given all the privileges of citizenship enjoyed by Whites. This suggestion failed badly, mainly because the majority of constitution-makers feared that such a proposal would lead to voting rights and thereby contest the White control of government. In the face of extremely strong opposition Marigny beat a hasty retreat, but not before declaring that his real intentions "were pure; and that the state would have benefited from it."[21]

Often times Louisiana state elections were so close that politicians called on free Negroes to help in winning a particular contest. Voting free Negroes took place on several occasions in Rapides Parish between 1830 and 1860. In the southeastern part of the parish was located a settlement of free Negroes known as the Ten Mile Creek.

---

19. See, *Constitution of Louisiana of 1812, '45 and '52; Also the Constitution of the United States with Amendments and Articles of Confederation and the Declaration of Independence*, 26, 38, 56.

20. J. K. Greer, "Louisiana Politics, 1845–1861," *Louisiana Historical Quarterly*, XIII (1930), *passim.*

21. *Official Report of Debates in the Louisiana Constitutional Convention 1844–1845*, 761, 831.

Most of these people were descendants of a group who had migrated there in 1804, and had taken up residence on public lands in the poor land of the hilly pine section. Many were so very closely related by blood that when about fifty of them cast votes less than a dozen bore different names from each other.[22]

The fact that the Ten Mile community of free Negroes voted came to light in an exposé by the Know Nothing party newspapers. It was a considered campaign to defeat the Democratic candidate for the state treasurer's post in 1857. The Democratic nominee, Colonel Robert A. Hunter of Alexandria, was not only accused of voting Negroes, but of arming them as well during the presidential election of 1856. He also was charged with repeating the same offense in the 1857 contest for state officers.[23] A committee of Know Nothing leaders reported these allegations, and also submitted the testimony of several White residents of the Ten Mile district. According to these depositions scores of free Negroes had been voted by Democrats in several elections. It also was alleged that they had not only been illegally registered but that the Ten Mile precinct had been purposely set-up to provide them with a polling place. A member of the American Party investigating commission submitted the most detailed account of Robert A. Hunter's activities. According to Edward Johnson he wrote of the following:

> I did see Robert A. Hunter, armed with a double barrelled shot gun and a revolver, rallying the free Negroes around him, all armed with double barrelled shot guns and rifles, for the purpose, as I believe, to force in their ballots,

22. New Orleans *Daily Crescent*, September 14, 1857.
23. *Red River American*, September 19, 1857.

regardless of all consequences. I heard Hunter say to the negroes 'let them come on, and we will make them smoke,' meaning the committee. . . . I further believe that Hunter has attended the said precinct at every election held at it for the past three years, and know that he gave a ball at one of their houses, near Ten Mile precinct, for the benefit or pleasure of said free negroes, and danced with them, and met them on an equality.[24]

Johnson's recital was backed by other members of the committee and a White Democrat.

In anticipation of denials or countercharges Know Nothing leaders secured written depositions of nine elderly citizens, who swore that the voters in question were undeniably of Negro origin. One old White resident, James Johnson, spoke at length of the inhabitants of Ten Mile, and testified to the following:

Old Joseph Willis, the Baptist preacher, was the first of that tribe of people that I knew. He was a mulatto, and was born a slave in North Carolina and it was reported that a few years previous to the first of my acquaintance with him he sold his mother. He was considered a free man of color, and, in fact, I called him a negro. He was not allowed to vote. All the Willises now living near Ten Mile precinct are descendants of the said Joseph Willis. The Perkins, Sweats, Johnsons, Rays, Royals, and Gibsons, are all more or less connected with the said Joseph Willis, and were all considered free men of color . . . none of them were allowed to vote or send their children to the public schools, nor to muster. I was very much surprised to hear that some few of them were allowed first to vote in the parish of Rapides, I think in the year 1841.[25]

24. *Red River American*, August 29, quoted in New Orleans *Daily Crescent*, September 14, 1857.
25. *Ibid.*

The Democrats of Rapides denied these charges. They cited as evidence of their denial the failure of a court trial to convict the free Negroes of voting in the 1856 election. According to the American Party newspapers this was little more than a travesty of justice and truth since the Democratic district attorney had failed to introduce bona-fide evidence, which would have proved that the persons in question were Negroes. It also was charged that the presiding judge had refused to allow the jury to conclude the voters Negroes despite their obvious Negroid features.[26]

Robert Hunter did not flatly deny seeking voters in the Ten Mile community. In a long speech before a gathering of Madison Parish citizens he proclaimed that in 1838 the predecessor of the Know Nothing party had voted Negroes in violation of the 1812 state constitution. In 1841 Hunter pointed out that "some of the Democratic boys got in among them and changed them over to their side." The Whigs then, he continued, "kicked up at it, and a trial ensued," to find out whether his party had been guilty of voting Negroes, but in every case the Democratic party and its leaders were exonerated. In attempting to justify this action, Hunter admitted taking 33 men to the Ten Mile precinct during the presidential election of 1856 solely for the purpose of preventing armed Know Nothing "vandals" from depriving citizens of their right to suffrage. He ended with a statement that he was "always willing to lay down my life in defense of the constitutional rights of my fellow citizens.[27]

---

26. *Ibid.*
27. Madison *American,* September 8, quoted in New Orleans *Daily Crescent,* August 14, 1857; West Baton Rouge *Sugar Planter,* August 29, 1857.

"Ten-Mile Bob," as he was dubbed by his opponents, nevertheless won the election for State Treasurer. He carried Rapides Parish by 68 votes, and along with the rest of the Democratic ticket polled the majority of the state vote.[28] There is little doubt that the free Negro vote in Rapides held the balance of power at the polls. Even as late as 1860 one traveling correspondent, J. W. Dorr who represented the New Orleans *Daily Crescent,* reported that approximately "eighty colored men are voted at Ten Mile by the unterrified Democracy whenever an emergency demands their loyal aid in carrying an election."[29]

Free Negroes did not, however, cease to be factors in Louisiana elections even though they were specifically disfranchised by the several constitutions of the state. In the 1852 constitution, for example, the Negro population was counted in the apportionment of representation to the General Assembly.[30] This had the practical effect of giving the southern parishes, where large numbers of slaves and free Negroes were concentrated, the decided advantage of greater representation to the legislature than the Northern or "Piney Woods," parishes.[31] In fact, great concern was expressed on this matter when the constitution in question was submitted for popular approval. At a meeting held in Baton Rouge in October of 1852, a group calling themselves Loyal Democrats went on record in opposition to the adoption of what they dubbed the "free nigger Constitution." It was their considered opinion that the apportionment of representation to the Legislature

---

28. New Orleans *Daily Crescent,* December 4, 1857.
29. Walter Prichard (ed.), "A Tourist's Description of Louisiana in 1860," *Louisiana Historical Quarterly,* XXI (1938), 1160.
30. *Constitution of 1852,* Article 8, n.p.
31. New Orleans *Daily Delta,* July 30, 1852.

based on the free colored population would ultimately result in racial equality and Negro suffrage.[32] The Constitution of 1852 was, however, approved by the electorate of the state despite the prediction of the Baton Rouge Democrats.

Louisiana free Negroes were never allowed direct participation in the affairs of government to the extent enjoyed by White citizens. They were, nevertheless, permitted a kind of left-handed representation through the right of petition. Petitions were used not only for redress of wrongs pertaining to residence and emancipation, but also in personal matters as well. In 1810, for example, a free woman of color named Marie Louise Lacoste petitioned the Territorial Assembly for the sum of $300. This was her estimated amount of the value of her slave, who had been killed by police authorities while resisting arrest as a runaway. The Assembly passed a special act granting the amount demanded by the woman of color.[33] In another case, a free Negro resident of West Feliciana Parish named George Clark petitioned the legislature to relinquish the state's right in an estate left him by his parents while he was in the state of slavery. The lawmakers unanimously passed a bill in favor of the colored petitioner during the 1830 session of the legislature.[34]

Although the free Negro was subjected to discriminatory legislation that made him inferior to White citizens before the law, certain privileges and immunities were never denied him. There were certain rights guaranteed to all citizens of Louisiana. By availing themselves of these

---

32. Baton Rouge *Daily Gazette and Comet,* October 29, 1852.
33. *Laws of the Territory of Louisiana* (1810), 2rd Leg., 1st Sess., 8, 10.
34. *Laws of Louisiana* (1830), 9th Leg., 2nd Sess., 42.

rights free persons of color or their White fellow citizens could secure considerable protection under the law. In making the distinction between a free Negro and a slave, the Supreme Court of the state called attention to the civil rights of the former by declaring the following:

> In the eyes of the Louisiana law, there is with the exception of certain political and social privileges, and the obligation of jury and militia service, all the difference between a free man of color and a slave that there is between a white man and a slave. The free man of color is capable of contracting. He can acquire by inheritance and transmit property by will. He is a competent witness in all civil suits. If he commits an offense against the laws, he is to be tried with the same formalities, and by the same tribunal, as the white man.[35]

Free Negroes of Louisiana, then, can be considered as possessing the status of quasi-citizenship and as such enjoyed a better legal position than any of their counterparts in other states of the South.[36]

The right of entering suit against White citizens was frequently exercised by free Negroes, especially in cases involving matters of property. For example, in 1832, a free colored man named Deslande won a damage suit against a White planter for killing his slave.[37] In another case of similar circumstances, the high court awarded a free woman of color the sum of $1000 for the death of her slave while employed by a riverboat captain.[38] Suits in-

---

35. *State v. Harrison (a slave)*, 11 La. An. 722 (December 1856).

36. "Emancipation at the South—Tolerance of Louisiana," *The African Repository and Colonial Journal*, XXXII (1856), 276.

37. *Deslonde (f.m.c.) v. LeBreret*, 5 La. 96 (December 1832).

38. *Burke (f.w.c.) v. Clark*, 11 La. 210 (March 1837).

stituted by free Negroes against White persons were not always successful. In 1812, the heirs of the free Negro, Jacob, entered suit against the Ursuline Nuns for a piece of property which they claimed was given to their father for his services during his tenure as a slave. Even though the court recognized the plaintiffs' right to sue, the plaintiffs lost the case on the grounds that the Ursulines could not alienate convent property without permission from the bishop of the diocese.[39]

It was not uncommon for free persons of color to exercise their prerogatives of entering suit for damages to property. A case in point was the suit of Zozine Audige, in 1853, against her neighbor, Manon Gaillard, to recover the cost of a slave killed while employed by the White woman. Damages were granted the plaintiff on the grounds of negligence on the defendant's part. The slave had been killed "by a loaded gun resembling a walking stick," which was the property of the defendant. The incident occurred while the Negro played on the White woman's premises.[40]

The right of free Negroes to own property did not go uncontested during the pre-Civil War period, but most of the gestures to deprive them of this basic right of all Americans met with failure. Yet, militant anti-free Negro forces tried plan after plan. In the Constitution Convention of 1852, for example, W. J. Lyle of the Iberville and West Baton Rouge parishes delegation, introduced a proposition to prohibit free Negroes from acquiring real

---

39. *Jacob et al. v. Ursuline Nuns*, 2 Mart. 269 (Fall 1812).
40. Zozine Audige *(f.w.c.)* v. Manon Gaillard *(f.w.c.)*, 8 La. An. 71 (January 1850).

estate by inheritance or purchase.[41] This proposal was denounced by most members as too radical and dangerous since such measures might operate to deprive all citizens of their property rights. It also was contended that free Negroes of comfortable circumstances regarded slaves with "more disdain and antagonism than the white man" and those in less fortunate circumstances were "in a worse condition than the slave, and, therefore, will never excite the slave's envy."[42] However, the 1852 constitution went into effect, but minus the controversial Lyle proposition.

Louisiana laws and court decisions on the right of free Negroes to bear witness in court differed substantially from every slave state in the United States. This was especially noticeable in nearly every state court where free Negroes, freely and unhindered by law, gave testimony in cases involving White citizens. This extraordinary practice came through the guarantee of law and a score of decisions of the state's high court. The law defining competent witnesses in civil suits as "freemen, whether free born or legally enfranchised who were at least fourteen years of age, of good character, and who had no interest in the case." Regardless of color, if a person could meet such qualifications his or her testimony was accepted as valid in the courts of Louisiana.[43]

From time to time there were efforts to deprive free

41. *Official Journal of the Convention to Form a New Constitution for the State of Louisiana,* (1852), 26.

42. New Orleans *Daily Delta,* July 17, 1852.

43. Edward R. Alcott and Henry W. Spofford (eds.), *The Louisiana Magistrate, and Parish Officer's Guide Containing Copious Forms and Instructions for Justices of the Peace, Administrators, Executors, Clerks, Sheriffs, Constables, Coroners, and Business Men in General. Together with the Constitution of the United States,* 39.

Negroes of such rights. During the 1846 session of the Legislature, for example, a campaign was launched to prohibit anyone but Whites from giving evidence in courts of law. As chairman of the Judiciary Committee, E. Warren Moise of Plaquemines reported out an act that would have deprived free colored persons of the right of bearing witness in courts as unwise and, in the committee's opinion, illegal. In strengthening his argument Moise noted that there is a vital distinction between the "better class and lower class" of free Negroes and closed his recommendation with the thought that "so long as persons of color are permitted to reside among us, the law should tend to elevate, not degrade," them. The bill also failed because it would not only "work a great practical inconvenience in the administration of the laws, but because of its general scope and policy is founded on principles at variance with the true interests of the State."[44]

At the same session, a group of West Feliciana citizens petitioned the General Assembly to enact legislation making it illegal for the courts of the state to accept the testimony of free Negroes. Accordingly, a bill was introduced which incorporated the demands of the West Feliciana citizens. The majority of the committee reported in favor of the measure on the grounds that the current law was harmful to the public welfare since it encouraged perjury and tended to obliterate the line which should distinctly mark the separation of races in a state where African slavery is recognized by law." In pointing out other reasons why colored persons should be disqualified as witnesses, the committee called attention to the low standard of living of such persons in the country parishes where

---

44. *Journal of the House of Representatives* (1846), 1st Leg., 1st Sess., 22.

"many of them marry slaves, and are identical with them in habits, principles, feelings and motives of action." According to the committee such individuals recognized no moral obligation in an oath and consequently served as tools of "vicious persons who desire to avail thmselves of the testimony of such witnesses." It was further pointed out that although the law was clear regarding free Negro testimony in civil cases it was not "equally clear" whether they were permitted to serve as witnesses in criminal cases.[45]

The minority of the committee reported in opposition to the bill in question by pointing out that such a measure would mean a departure from long established policy of the state. It was also contended that free Negroes were not lacking in proper understanding of the responsibilities incumbent upon them as witnesses, since there was inconclusive evidence to "single them out as the universal enemy of the whites" which would "denounce them as unsafe witnesses in all cases where the interest of white persons are concerned." In the opinion of the minority committee the free colored population of Louisiana was mainly composed of manumitted faithful slaves and their descendants whom the legislature was bound to protect. Many of this class, it was argued, was composed of Quadroons who were themselves slaveowners and as "peaceful, industrious, educated and truthful" persons sufficiently competent as witnesses in the courts of law.[46] With such formidable arguments the bill failed to pass the Legislature and free colored persons could continue to serve as witnesses.

---

45. *Ibid.*, 70.
46. *Ibid.*, 71.

Free Negroes were not only allowed to give evidence in civil cases, but they also were deemed by law to be qualified witnesses in criminal cases. In 1850 this right received the approval of the Supreme Court in an epochal decision. In rendering the judgment, Justice King said that among the large population of the free colored class of Louisiana could be found many of intelligence, education and wealth. Moreover, many of them were just as trustworthy as White citizens. He found them to be "worthy of credit, and their testimony may be safely received and weighed by the courts and juries," in both civil and criminal cases in which White persons are parties.[47] The Justice went on to cite colonial and Louisiana laws recognizing free Negroes as competent witnesses regardless of the nature of the case. This decision firmly established Louisiana as the only slave state that in 1850 permitted free colored citizens the privilege of bearing witness against White persons in both civil and criminal cases.

The ruling of the Supreme Court did not, however, go uncontested; concerted effort by anti-free Negro factions gave battle to disqualify this class as witnesses. The question again came before the General Assembly in 1852. No doubt chafing at the court's favorable decision, White solons took up a measure for prohibiting free Negroes from testifying in criminal cases involving White persons.[48] No action was taken on the proposition.

However, there were those who expressed keen disaffection in the matter. These persons urged the enactment of laws making it altogether illegal for free Negroes

---

47. *The State v. Henry Levy and Jacob Dreyfous*, 5 La. An. 64 (January 1850).

48. *Official Report of the Proceedings of the House of Representatives* (1852), 4th Leg., 1st Sess., 85.

to ever give witness in cases in which Whites were
an interested party. To this end, a group of St. Landry
Parish planters petitioned the Legislature in 1859 to prohibit "free persons of color to appear or testify as witnesses
against any white person whatsoever."[49] Again the Legislature failed to take action, and so during the entire ante-
bellum period testimony by free Negroes was accepted in
the courts of Louisiana.

During the territorial period slaves were allowed to
testify in all cases involving free persons of color.[50] But
the following years amendments against the practice came
under consideration. In 1870 a law came into existence
prohibiting slaves from giving testimony if they were the
property of free persons of color involved in the case.[51]
Free Negroes were finally granted the same immunity
from slave witnesses that was accorded to White citizens.
In 1816, the legislature passed the following act:

> No slave shall be admitted as witness against a free per-
> son of color, except in each case such free person of color
> be charged with having raised or attempted to raise insur-
> rection among the slaves of the State; or adhering to them
> by giving them aid or comfort in any matter whatsoever.[52]

The same regulation applied to White citizens as well.

The Supreme Court of Louisiana proved to be the
greatest protector of the free Negro class. This can be
seen in decisions handed down by that body in several
important cases. In 1824, for example, the court held that
a White person could not legally reduce a free Negro to

---

49. Opelouses *Courier*, March 5, 1859.
50. *Laws of the Territory of Orleans* (1806), 1st Leg., 1st Sess., 198.
51. *Ibid.* (1807), 1st Leg., 2nd Sess., 188.
52. *Laws of Louisiana* (1816), 2nd Leg., 2nd Sess., 146.

slavery following the legal formalities of emancipation. Justice Alexander Porter, in sustaining this principle, cited the Spanish law disallowing reduction of free persons to slavery. Porter specifically called into the case "the third Partida, title 29, law 24 providing that if a man be free, no matter how long he may be held . . . as a slave, his condition cannot be thereby changed; nor can he be reduced to slavery in any manner whatever, on account of the time he may have been held in servitude."[53] In another decision rendered in 1855, Justice John Slidell declared a free Negro named Sukey Wormley a free person on the basis of Spanish and Louisiana laws on the ground that the White plaintiff's acceptance of payment from the woman in question was sufficient evidence that she was entitled to liberty. In denying the White plaintiff's claim, Slidell declared that this particular case exhibited "a cruel experiment upon the liberty and hard earnings of an humble and deserving woman."[54]

Another right consistently upheld by the Supreme Court concerned the guarantee of free Negroes to make contracts with White persons. In 1834, this principle received emphatic approval as "a common privilege of all parties to a contract," and their "capacity to enter such an agreement cannot be questioned" on the basis of color.[55] A marriage contract entered into by free Negroes was also declared binding in the eyes of Louisiana law even though such contracts had been made while the persons in question were in the state of slavery. The high court in presenting its reasons stated among other things that with emancipation, "certain civil rights came as a matter

---

53. *Delphine v. Deveze*, 2 Mart. 650 (June 1824).
54. *Hardesty v. Sukey Wormley*, 10 La. An. 239 (April 1855).
55. *Grounx et el. (f.p.c.) v. Abat*, 7 La. 17 (June 1834).

of course," and among them was the privilege of having marriages legalized.[56]

The right of inheritance was subject to certain limitations imposed by state law and decisions of the Supreme Court of the state. For instance, a free colored concubine of a White man was deemed incapable of inheriting any immovable property from the latter's estate. Requests of any kind to women in this category had to be in the form of movable property, which could not exceed one-tenth of the total value of the estate—a strange formula, but one that lasted throughout the ante-bellum period.[57]

The making of a will when illegitimate children were involved became even more complicated and seemingly unreasonably harsh. Whenever a White citizen wished to leave a legacy to an illegitimate offspring the law required such a person to acknowledge paternity before a notary public in the presence of two witnesses.[58] Once the illegitimate offspring had been legally acknowledged, such person was known as a natural child, while those whose parent failed to recognize them were automatically given the appellation of bastards.[59] A natural child was qualified to receive one-fourth of an estate, provided there were no legitimate children of the testator. This amount was increased to one-third, provided the surviving relatives were even more remote in kinship. In such an event, when the White had distributed the maximum amount to his natural children the balance of the estate went to any surviving legitimate relations.[60] These same provisions also were re-

56. *Girod v. Lewis*, 6 Mart. 559 (May 1819).
57. *Civil Code of the State of Louisiana, 1825*, 343. This regulation was upheld in the case of *Cole v. Lucas*, 2 La. An. 947 (October 1847).
58. Thomas G. Morgan (comp.), *Civil Code of the State of Louisiana; with the Statutary Amendments, From 1825 to 1853, Inclusive*, 37.
59. *Compiled Edition of the Civil Codes of Louisiana*, 118.
60. *Civil Code of the State of Louisiana, 1825*, 342–343.

quired of free persons of color wishing to legitimize their offspring for the express purpose of bequeathing properties to them.[61]

On the other hand, "adulterous or incestuous bastards" could not inherit from either parent, even though such offspring had been acknowledged with the usual formalities. The Supreme Court held that persons in this category were allowed nothing more than subsistence. Moreover, free colored bastards were declared under a double incapacity, and could not, under any circumstances, lay claim to an estate from which the law expressly excluded them. "A part of the population of this state," said the court, "has been placed by law under certain disabilities and incapacities, from which it is not the province of the courts of justice to relieve them."[62]

However ingenious attempts were made by certain White men to circumvent the law. In 1840, for instance, a White man named J. H. Gladding, on the day of his death, sent for a notary to make a will disinheriting his sisters in favor of his colored mistress and their child. When informed that such a will would be declared invalid, Gladding attempted to have the notary draw up a bill of sale for his house made out in favor of the colored woman. The notary refused to be a party to such a transaction and he was dismissed by the dying White man. Shortly before his death, Gladding signed a note for $4000 payable to the free Negress. When the will was probated in 1841, the executors of the estate refused to deliver the note and the free Negress entered suit against them. The case was

---

61. *Thomassin (f.m.c.) v. Raphael's Executor (f.m.c.)*, 1 La. 128 (March 1837).

62. *Jung et al. v. Doriocourt et al.*, 4 La. 175 (December 1831); see also, *Robinett et al. v. Verdun's Vendee (f.p.c.)*, 14 La. 542 (January 1840).

carried to the Supreme Court of the state and that body upheld the actions of the executors.[63]

In addition to a certain amount of judicial protection, free Negroes of Louisiana were also guaranteed the protection of the law against kidnapping. According to legislation on this matter, any persons found guilty of kidnapping free persons of color were liable to a fine of $1000 and a maximum prison term of fourteen years.[64]

Quite predictably, free Negroes sometimes were kidnapped, and no doubt some of them passed into bondage and were forgotten. Yet, many were rescued from such a fate. In 1829, for example, a Natchitoches Parish White man was murdered and his colored family was seized by a band of White persons and carried across the Sabine River into Texas for the purpose of selling them as slaves. A majority of the White citizens looked upon this incident as a "shameful outrage." They were so incensed that a vigilante party was formed to receive the unfortunate family after they had been rescued by some Texas ranchers. The editor of the newspaper reporting the affair showed no sympathy for such persons "who took part in this shameful transaction," and he recommended that when apprehended they be subject to the full penalties of the law.[65]

A more detailed account of this abortive attempt to kidnap the Natchitoches family was recorded in the following memoirs of an old resident of Texas:

There lived in Yocum's neighborhood [Natchitoches Par-

---

63. *Barriére (f.w.c.) v. Gladding's Curator*, 17 La. 144 (February 1841).

64. Peirce, Taylor and King (eds.), *The Consolidation and Revisions of the Statutes of the State of a General Nature*, 207.

65. Baton Rouge *Gazette*, December 19, 1829.

ish, Louisiana] an old Frenchman who had a negro woman for a wife, by who he had a large family of mulatto children. . . . The Yocum's association with Earpe Wingate and Colonel Govenor who at one time had been a soldier at Fort Jessup [Louisiana],—planned the killing of the old man, and taking his wife and children to western Texas, and selling them into slavery. Accordingly, they approached the old man one night and murdered him, and burnt him in a log heap. Then they drove his family across the Sabine into Texas, and secreted them in the Palogacho bottom . . . and placed them under a strong guard. . . . But a few nights before they were ready to go [to west Texas], they got drunk and one of the young women effected her escape, and made her way to the neighboring house and made known their dreadful situation. . . . [These] villains [were driven out] and the women and children . . . returned to their homes in Louisiana.[66]

As residents of Louisiana, free Negroes were obliged to share in the support of the government. In return for the protection they received, the authorities considered it only just that they render certain services when called upon to do so. In the territorial period, they served in the militia, but they were put in separate units, under the command of White officers.[67] When some White persons, expressed distrust of these units, the officers were ordered not to enroll any new members in the colored battalions. They were instructed instead to "diminish the corps if it

66. A. Horton, *History of San Augustin, Reminiscences of an Old Time Resident,* quoted in Harold Schoen, "The Free Negro in the Republic of Texas," *The Southwestern Historical Quarterly,* XLI (1937), 103–104.

67. Governor W. C. C. Claiborne to Henry Dearborn (Secretary of War), March 22, 1804, Rowland (ed.), *Official Letter Books of W. C. C. Claiborne,* II, 58.

can be done without giving offense."[68]

On several occasions, Governor Claiborne asked the Territorial Assembly to recognize the free colored battalion as a part of the regular militia, but each time his request was refused.[69] The legislative body did not share the Governor's opinion that, as part of the state militia, free Negro units could render valuable service to the commonwealth.[70] The Governor's faith in the loyalty of Louisiana's colored troops was demonstrated by the zealous way they performed their duty during the 1811 slave insurrection in St. John the Baptist Parish. The colored company sent against the slaves fought with such valor that Claiborne was moved to thank each soldier for his "bravery and patriotism" and for his contribution to public safety.[71]

During the War of 1812, the danger of a British attack on Louisiana became so imminent that the General Assembly passed a bill authorizing the Governor to form a new militia unit made up of select free Negroes of the state. The bill included the following stipulations:

> that . . . certain free men of color be chosen from among the Creoles, and from among such as shall have paid a State tax. . . . The Commanders . . . [had] to be white men and said corps shall not consist of more than four companies, each of which, officers included, shall not consist of more than sixty-four men . . . and [they] must have been, for two years previous, owners, or sons of owners of a landed property of at least the value of three hundred dollars.[72]

---

68. Claiborne to Major Michel Fortier, June 22, 1804, *ibid.*, 215.
69. Claiborne's Speech to Assembly, January 13, 1807, *ibid.*, IV, 92–93.
70. Claiborne to William Eustice, August 31, 1811, *ibid.*, V, 40.
71. Claiborne to Major Dubourg, January 14, 1811, *ibid.*, V. 100.
72. *Laws of Louisiana* (1812), 1st Leg., 1st Sess., 72.

In this way, the Legislature was making certain that only those colored persons who had a financial stake in the community would be trusted with its defense.

During the Battle of New Orleans, it was deemed necessary to enroll additional free Negroes for the defense of the city. Accordingly, a company was formed of refugees from Santo Domingo, and placed under the command of a free Negro named Joseph Savary. Andrew Jackson singled this unit out for special commendation for their bravery under fire of the enemy. Regarding colored troops in general, in his order of the day after the American victory over the British on January 8, 1815, Jackson had this to say: "The two corps of colored volunteers have not disappointed the hopes that were formed of their courage and perseverance in the performance of duty."[73]

The Battle of New Orleans was hailed throughout the nation as a great victory, and a grateful state tendered its appreciation for the part played by free Negroes by authorizing the Governor to form an auxiliary organization of colored troops in Natchitoches Parish. But again there were limitations. The unit was not to exceed 84 men, who were required to supply their "own arms and horses." The act further stipulated that only such free Negroes who owned property valued at $100 were eligible for service in this special unit.[74]

After the passage of this act, no further mention is made in the Legislature of Louisiana regarding free Negro sol-

---

73. Charles E. Gayarré, "The Blacks of Louisiana," Gayarré Papers.
74. *Laws of Louisiana* (1815), 2nd Leg., 1st Sess., 62–64. The writer has been unable to discover whether this unit was formed. No further mention is made of it in either the official records or newspapers of the period.

diers. Undoubtedly free colored military units which had been authorized during the emergency of 1812 were allowed to break-up for want of sufficient state appropriations. However, the lawmakers did pass a number of pension acts for the benefit of free colored veterans. In 1819, for example, Joseph Savary was granted a monthly pension of thirty dollars for four years in recognition of "his service in defense of the state."[75] The legislature granted the same amount to Savary at its 1823 session.[76] Similar payments were made from public funds for the benefit of Vincent Populus[77] and Isidore McCarty Honore.[78]

Free colored veterans of the Battle of New Orleans were held in special esteem throughout the ante-bellum period. Every January 8th, the press of New Orleans printed glowing accounts of the "valiant free colored soldiers who served the state in the Battle of New Orleans."[79] Even as late as 1860, when Negrophobe sentiment reached fever pitch, the city press carried accounts of the surviving colored veterans who took part in celebrations commemorating the American victory. In that year one newspaper focused attention on one "Jordan the Drummer who beat reveille on the morning of the Battle of New Orleans." It was reported that he received great applause when he was introduced at a banquet attended by White citizens. This colored veteran's speech on that occasion was hailed as the best of the evening and he terminated it with a sentiment in French: *"Je vous souhaite beau-*

75. *Ibid.* (1819), 4th Leg., 1st Sess., 9–10.
76. *Ibid.* (1823), 6th Leg., 1st Sess., 70.
77. *Ibid.* (1832), 10th Leg., 3rd Sess., 8.
78. *Ibid.* (1847), 1st Leg., 2nd Sess., 84.
79. See, for example, New Orleans *Daily Delta,* January 10, 1851; New Orleans *Daily Picayune,* January 8, 1857.

coup de retour de ce jour."[80] ("I wish you many happy returns of the day.")

In addition to military services during periods of emergency, various other duties were required of free colored persons of Louisiana. In some parishes, they were subject to patrol duty. A Jefferson Parish ordinance made it compulsory for all White and free Negro males above the age of fifteen to serve in patrol companies under penalty of a five dollar fine. In case of illness or other incapacity, such persons were either to furnish a substitute or suffer the penalty of the law.[81] In Calcasieu Parish, free Negro males from 18 to 45 could be enrolled in patrol companies to serve in districts where they lived. If a White planter gave his written permission, such persons were allowed to exercise patrol duties on his plantation. Regardless of the situation, patrol companies were always under the command of White citizens. Furthermore, when on duty, free persons of color were required "at all times and under all circumstances, to be obedient and subordinate to all leaders, captains or patrols of white persons.[82] A similar regulation was made in Pointe Coupee, but free Negro patrolers were permitted officers of their own color.[83]

In New Orleans, free men of color could be drafted for police duties. In this capacity, they had the responsibility of "preserving the peace, visiting cabarets and public houses," and "whenever necessary arrest all malefactors."[84]

80. New Orleans *Daily Picayune*, January 8, 1860.

81. MS. Jefferson Parish Police Jury Minutes, Volume I, 1834–1843, 29.

82. MS. Calcasieu Parish Police Jury Minutes, Volume A, 1840–1846, 22.

83. MS. Pointe Coupee Parish Police Jury Minutes, Volume 1857–1863, 177.

84. MS. Ordinances and Resolutions of the City Council of New Orleans, 1816–1821. Session December 18, 1817, 91.

The same practice was followed as in the country parishes, where White men were placed in command of free Negroes enrolled as city guardsmen. New Orleans became one of the first southern cities to make use of free Negro policemen. In 1820, the City Council authorized the formation of a free Negro volunteer firefighting company. Soon thereafter an organization composed of sixty colored firemen came into existence. This unit was smartly outfitted with distinctive uniforms along with badges.[85] Their devotion to duty received the recognition of the authorities in 1830 in the following resolution of the city council:

> Whereas . . . [they] have deserved the approbation and praise of the authorities of the city and its inhabitants for the zeal and loyalty they have always manifested in all the fires, be it resolved, that the Council grant to said company $200.00 as a token of appreciation for their behavior. . . .[86]

As residents of Louisiana, free Negroes were subject to the same state laws pertaining to criminal offenses as White persons. The press reports of the period show that many committed a great variety of crimes and also that they were frequently victims of crimes. Theft was among the most frequent infractions. In 1857, for example, William Chevis was arrested and ordered to appear before the district court of Opelousas for stealing cattle from one of his White neighbors. Although cattle rustling was considered a serious crime in St. Landry Parish, Chevis was placed under bail of $300 until his trial.[87] Another free

---

85. *Ibid.*, January 5, 1820 to December 30, 1821. Session May 1, 1820, 43–64, 73.
86. *Ibid.*, January 2, 1830 to December 31, 1930. Session of January 19, 1830, 11–12.
87. Opelousas *Courier*, July 18, 1857.

Negro, Jerry Hartwell, was not so fortunate. When the accused was charged with stealing thirteen milk cows belonging to two White citizens, Hartwell was committed to prison without bail until the disposition of the case before the Orleans Parish district court.[88]

Instances of petty larceny were very frequent in New Orleans, where both the temptation and opportunity were greater than in the country parishes. A free woman of color named Française Esclavon was found guilty in 1842 by the municipal court for stealing a wig from a barber shop located on Royal Street.[89] In 1849, Julia Armstrong and a White woman named Catherine Mulholland were both convicted for "burglarizing a lot of kitchen furniture from the premises of Elizabeth Crawford."[90]

There were to be sure more than a few instances in which free Negroes were convicted of grand larceny. At least one, Louis Ferrand, appears to have been especially talented in embezzling great amounts of money from persons of whatever color. This obviously charming man used the old ruse of passing bad checks and notes to a wide assortment of White and colored friends.[91] It came out in his trial that he had taken friends for about $50,000.

Other embezzlers went into alliance with White men. In 1848 such was the circumstances of Robert Lilly of New Orleans, when he sold a "slave" named William to a Leonard Kuhn of Alexandria for the sum of $3000. Following this transaction, Lilly booked passage on a steamboat bound for New Orleans. Meanwhile, the so-called slave escaped, and was in the process of rejoining Lilly

88. New Orleans *Daily Picayune*, April 17, 1852.
89. *Ibid.*, March 5, 1842.
90. *Ibid.*, May 17, 1849.
91. New Orleans *Bee*, March 15, 1852.

when captured. Under questioning by the district attorney of Rapides Parish, Lilly revealed that and the free Negro had utilized this fraud several times before in the country parishes.[92]

Although it became a serious offense to receive stolen goods from slaves, a considerable number of free Negroes engaged in that illicit practice. During the summer of 1851 one White citizen, using the pen name of "Indicator," wrote a New Orleans newspaper complaining that a group of free Negroes and slaves of Plaquemines Parish were openly dealing in stolen property. "Indicator" pointed out that:

> In the upper part of this parish from fifteen to twenty un-licensed individuals most of whom are free colored people of both sexes, engage in exchanging intoxicating liquors with the slaves for stolen objects. These own small crafts or carts which are well supplied with the necessary articles for carrying on such a trade. During the nights, these worth-less fellows are occupied either in purchasing or bartering for whiskey, sugar, molases, chickens, etc. What a find field for Judge Lynch.[93]

Free Negroes also were accused of raping White women, but only on rare occasions. In 1845, for example, James Berry was tried for this offense. According to the testimony Berry had attempted rape at the time the White female's husband was absent from home. The unfortunate Negro was defended by a Colonel T. G. Hunt, who secured an acquittal on the grounds of insufficient evidence.[94] The New Orleans *Bee* reported a case of rape

92. Alexandria *Red River Republican*, June 24, quoted in New Orleans *Daily Delta*, July 1, 1848.

93. New Orleans *Daily Picayune*, August 28, 1851.

94. New Orleans *Daily Delta*, November 8, 1845.

committed by a free Negro on the body of a small White
child who was employed as an aid to a blind beggar
woman. The victim was found near a roadside "ruined and
almost dead, the monster villain having succeeded in ac-
complishing his hellish design." He was lynched.[95]

On the other hand, there were frequent occasions when
White citizens were tried and convicted of crimes against
free Negroes. In 1845, Thomas Gibbon was tried on a
robbery charge preferred by a free woman of color named
Aimee Poitine; he was found guilty of this charge and sentenced to the state penitentiary at hard labor for two
years.[96] In 1859, Pierre Casanave, a wealthy funeral director, had two White men arrested for stealing over four
hundred pounds of lead from his premises. The inept
thieves were caught in the act, when their wheelbarrow,
which contained the lead, broke down.[97]

Besides theft, free persons of color charged their White
neighbors with insulting and attempting to do them
bodily harm. In 1847, a certain Mrs. Francis was ordered
to give a peace bond for her future good behavior, after
threatening to kill the free Negress Louisa Flora with a
kitchen knife.[98] In still another case, Claire Dupart preferred charges against a White man named John Fletcher
for threatening to beat her with a cowhide. Fletcher was
also accused of covering the colored person's home with
filth.[99]

As might be expected, free Negroes sometimes committed murder, and in turn were victims of this crime at

---

95. October 9, 1858.
96. New Orleans *Daily Delta,* December 21, 1845.
97. New Orleans *Daily Picayune,* December 6, 1859.
98. *Ibid.,* August 1, 1847.
99. *Ibid.,* October 26, 1851.

the hands of White persons and slaves. When a free woman of color named Arthemise Simion was found stabbed to death in bed on August 9, 1847, her colored husband was held for suspicion of murder.[100] A White overseer while employed by a Mr. Baine of West Feliciana Parish killed a free Negro named Hardesty. The motive was not revealed and the press merely reported that the unfortunate Negro had been shot with a pistol and "expired instantly."[101]

According to extant evidence, whenever free Negroes were employed as overseers on plantations, there existed the ever-present danger that they might be murdered by slaves. In 1856, for instance, a colored overseer on Daniel Smith's Catahoula Parish plantation was "chopped in pieces with an ax by a desperate slave." When thirty other slaves attempted to restrain the attacker, they were threatened with the same fate. At the time of the murder, the free Negro was the only authority present on Smith's plantation.[102] In at least one instance, friction between a slave and a free Negro became so bitter that the former hired a slave assassin for ten dollars to kill his enemy's nine-year-old son. The crime was frustrated by the cries of the child and the two slaves were arrested. Under questioning the hired killer confessed that he had taken the child in question into a field "to butcher him with a knife," but decided to strangle him instead and that while attempting to do this the intended victim's cries for help were answered by some White citizens.[103] Both slaves

---

100. *Ibid.*, August 18, 1847.
101. St. Francisville *Chronicle*, quoted in New Orleans *Daily Delta*, July 30, 1849.
102. Opelousas *Patriot*, March 29, 1856.
103. New Orleans *Daily Delta*, July 21, 1859.

were confined to jail to await trial before a jury of slave-holders in Jefferson Parish.

Press reports of the 1840–1860 period indicate that free Negroes had much difficulty getting along with each other. No doubt it was the intention of the reports to place the colored class in disrepute by making it appear that the class consisted of an unruly, criminal type of person. The indulgence by free Negroes in insulting language, street fighting, and disturbing the peace received considerable attention in the newspapers. In 1847, a free colored woman, Mary Jane Taylor, was arrested for using "highly improper language" towards "the favored object of her husband's affection." She was reported as "being affected with the green-eyed monster, jealousy." Mary Jane was put under a peace bond by an inferior court and bound "to keep quiet or go to jail."[104] On another occasion, in 1860, two "very pretty quadroons" were committed to a term in the city workhouse for calling each other names while arguing on a New Orleans street corner. The paper described them as especially "skilled in the use of foul words."[105]

Another example of a clash is that of an altercation between two free colored women in 1846 on the streets of New Orleans. Julia Hays, who was well known for her "belligerent disposition," was arrested at the request of Eliza Harris for having assaulted the complainant with "mud and brick-bats." The court ordered the aggressive Negress to post a $500 bond or be committed to the workhouse.[106]

It would appear that January 13, 1851, was an espe-

---

104. New Orleans *Daily Picayune*, March 14, 1847.
105. New Orleans *Daily Delta*, May 31, 1860.
106. *Ibid.*, March 12, 1846.

cially bad day for Louis Beaulieu. According to a newspaper account this free colored man had been "playing the beau to many ladies of color." On the aforementioned afternoon, he was approached by "three irate colored woman" who proceeded to knock him down "with the intent, as he thinks, to kill him." One of the jealous females, Mary Simon, pounded him on the head with a hammer while the other two repeatedly beat him with brickbats."[107]

Although free Negroes were often suspected of—and were at times even condemned—for instigating slave insurrections, there was, with few exceptions, little proof that very many of them actually had any connection with such conspiracies in Louisiana. It would seem that there were more free Negro informers than conspirators. It will be recalled that during the territorial period several free colored men were employed to win the confidence of a White man who was suspected of planning to incite the slaves to revolt. As a result of this service, the White conspirator was apprehended and the territory was spared the fate that had "encrimsoned the plains of St. Domingo."[108] Even as late as 1853, the editor of a country newspaper voiced the opinion that the great majority of such persons who tamper with slaves and incite them to insurrection were "depraved whites who deliberately speculate, for dishonest gain, upon the ignorance and excitability of the negro."[109]

There were, however, some instances in which free Negroes were implicated in slave conspiracies. In the

---

107. *Ibid.*, January 14, 1851.
108. John Watkins to John Graham, September 6, 1805, Carter (ed.), *The Territorial Papers of the Territory of Orleans,* IX, 501–502.
109. Franklin (La.) *Planters Banner,* June 23, 1853.

abortive uprising of 1856 in St. Martin Parish, it was proved to the satisfaction of the district court that a free boy of color was implicated, and following a trial was executed for the crime. At the same time a White man was executed as one of the leaders in the insurrection.[110] When the slaves of a Vermillionville planter conspired to rebel against their master in 1840, they were exposed by one of their own, who at the same time reported that a natural son of a certain Mr. Clouet and a free Mulatto named Prefere were among the leaders of the conspiracy. Both men were sentenced to be hanged.[111]

When convicted of crimes free Negroes of Louisiana were usually sent to the state penitentiary at Baton Rouge. Others were confined in either the slave depot in the same city, or in the parish jails throughout the state. In New Orleans, free colored malefactors were housed in the municipal work houses. In these places, they were segregated from White prisoners and classified according to the nature of their crimes. On Sundays, religious services were conducted for prisoners and during the week they were placed "at constant labor" on public projects.[112] A. B. Roman suggested to the state's Assembly, on December 1, 1841, that free men of color confined in the state penitentiary be transferred to public works.[113] Here they would be employed in chain gangs for work on such state projects as the construction of roads and levees.[114] Accordingly, an act was passed in 1842 which authorized

---

110. Franklin (La.) *Journal,* quoted in New Orleans *Daily Picayune,* December 2, 1856.

111. Baton Rouge *Gazette,* September 5, 1840.

112. B. C. Norman, *New Orleans and Environs, 1845,* 130–132.

113. *Journal of the House of Representatives (1841–1842),* 15th Leg., 2nd Sess., 5.

114. *Ibid.,* 42.

the transfer of colored convicts in the state penal institution for work on state projects under the supervision of the Board of Public Works. This agency, however, was prohibited from employing colored prisoners in parishes which objected to the use of such labor within their limits.[115] In February 1843, forty Negro convicts, "both slave and free," were transferred to the state engineer to be employed on public works.[116] By December 31, 1843, no free Negro prisoner remained in the state penitentiary.[117] However, the employment of these prisoners proved an unsuccessful experiment because of the high cost of maintenance,[118] and an act was approved in 1845 to return the colored convicts to the state institution at Baton Rouge.[119] The act further provided for the segregation of prisoners according to race and further required that Negro convicts be employed in the manufacture of bagging and rope as a step toward defraying the expenses of their upkeep.

Just as White citizens, free persons of color—if convicted of crime—could entertain the hope of escaping full punishment. They could appeal to the chief executive for clemency, since the Governor of Louisiana had the power to grant reprieves and pardons. The number of pardons granted by various governors of the state suggest that appeals were frequently made and won by free colored prisoners. On June 16, 1806, for example, Governor W. C. C. Claiborne granted an executive pardon to a free Negro named Jean Louis Chesnaugh. A New

---

115. *Laws of Louisiana* (1841–1842), 15th Leg., 2nd Sess., 518.
116. *Ibid.*, Appendix O, L.
117. *Journal of the House of Representatives (1843)*, 17th Leg., 1st Sess., 41.
118. *Ibid.*, (1845), 17th Leg., 1st Sess., Appendix F.
119. *Laws of Louisiana* (1845), 17th Leg., 1st Sess., 28.

Orleans court had found the free Negro guilty of larceny and had sentenced him to "receive twenty stripes" and a term in prison. Because Chesnaugh had been described as in need of money the Governor granted the pardon.[120]

In 1852, Governor Joseph Walker requested that the state Senate confirm his action of granting reprieves to the free Negroes Scott and Thomas Powell. The former had been convicted of assault and battery against a White citizen and sentenced to a fine of $100 and six months in the penitentiary. The chief executive explained that his action was based on the fact the persons in question were needed at home to care for ageing and indigent parents.[121]

Although the legal status of free Negroes was defined and guaranteed by law and judicial decisions, many of their rights depended on the friendly attitude of White friends. Whenever there was peace in the community a friendly or permissive attitude prevailed. On the other hand, when the "peculiar institution" came under attack, feelings turned against the free Negro population. In the late 1850s such hostility developed towards this group that action was taken in some country parishes to circumscribe, and even entirely abolish, free Negro citizenship privileges.

An attempt to deprive the free Negro of what civil rights they had gained by January 1859, by a group of St. Landry Parish planters who met for the purpose of asking the Legislature to put into law several resolutions which would have had the effect of reducing free Negroes to the status of semi-slavery. These planters were greatly

---

120. Claiborne to Sheriff of County of Orleans, June 16, 1806, Rowland (ed.), *Official Letter Book of W. C. C. Claiborne*, III, 332.
121. *Official Journal of the Senate* (1852), 4th Leg., 1st Sess., 19.

disturbed over, among other things, the ownership of slaves by free persons of color, a circumstance which was considered as "the greatest evil attending free colored citizenship among us." The custom of holding property in "beings of their own color, flesh and blood," seemed to this group to be "repugnant to the laws of good society, good government, Nature and Nature's God." To allow free Negroes to own slaves was deemed a "reflection upon the dignity and majesty of God himself." The withdrawal of citizenship, in the opinion of the planters, was easy, for the "government that gave this right has the power to remove it by appropriate legislation."[122]

The St. Landry planters had apparently become frustrated by their failure in dealing with the free colored class, for the first resolution reveals their exasperation:

> Whereas the free colored population of this state in general, and of this Parish in particular, is principally composed of individuals too lazy to work and numbers of them live by stealing and other malpractices, and as punishment at hard labor is no check upon them since they are aware that they are better fed and clothed in prison than in the enjoyment of liberty, therefore the criminal laws against them now in force should be amended.[123]

Furthermore, it was recommended that any free persons of color convicted of any crime should be sold into slavery for life; that any persons of this class who sold liquor to slaves were to be considered as "contributing to the creation of an insurrection among the negroes" and likewise should be sold into bondage. As a salutary measure, the

---

122. Opelousas *Patriot*, February 5, 1859.
123. *Ibid.*, February 19, 1859.

St. Landry planters recommended that justices of the peace should be invested with the power to try free Negroes by the same rules of procedure as slaves. A final recommendation touching on the rights of free Negroes was the following, which concerned ownership of property:

> . . . that hereafter no free person of color shall purchase any slaves or acquire any title to slaves, nor shall they either as principal agent, clerk, buy or sell, either wholesale or retail, any spiritous liquors whatsoever.[124]

At the same time these proposals were made to the legislature, that body was considering an act to legalize the sale of free Negroes for non-payment of their debts.[125]

Yet, lawmakers exhibited far more tolerance and they refused to approve any of these measures which tended to deprive free colored persons of their already guaranteed rights under the law. The General Assembly did, however, attempt to placate militant White factions demanding restrictive measures, by passing an act to enable free persons of color to go into voluntary servitude. However, this was not a compulsory measure inasmuch as only such free Negroes who desired to do so could become slaves of white masters of their own choosing.[126]

Up to the end of the pre-Civil War period, free Negroes of Louisiana enjoyed certain privileges pertaining to civil rights seldom afforded persons of similar status in other states of the South. In Louisiana, a free Negro's testimony in a court of justice was good against a White person; he

---

124. *Ibid.*
125. *Ibid.*, January 29, 1859.
126. *Laws of Louisiana* (1859), 4th Leg., 2nd Sess., 214–215.

could purchase, sell and hold property, both real and personal in his own name; he was allowed to sign and execute any notarial act, deed, bill and other legal instruments. Yet, because he was denied legal suffrage, the right to run for public office and made the subject of discriminatory legislation because of his color, free Negroes can best be described as quasi-citizens of Louisiana during the ante-bellum period.

5

Economic Life of the Free Negro

Between you and I, they [free Negroes] are a miserable set of devils; they won't work. . . . During the most part of the year they are in a state of abject want, and then they are very humble. But during the berry season they make a little money, and while it lasts they are fat and saucy enough. We can't do anything with them; they won't work. There they are in their cabins as you see them—a poor, woe-begone set of vagabonds; a burden upon the community; of no use to themselves nor to anybody else.[1]

EVEN though this estimate of Canadian Negroes of the 1850s seems harsh, it was not markedly different from similar opinions expressed by scores of White Americans throughout the United States. With very few exceptions the non-slave Negroes were represented as a lazy class of pariahs wholly incapable of assuming responsible positions in the economic structure of America. Race

1. Excerpts from Sparrowgrass' "Month with the Blue Noses," quoted in the Greensburg (La.) *Imperial,* June 13, 1857.

prejudices and fierce economic rivalry accounted for much of this attitude despite the fact that free Negroes, like their White countrymen, varied widely in their economic condition.

On the whole, free Negroes in the South were economically better off, more ambitious, better trained, and consequently more able to secure a firm foothold in the economic life of the section. This fact is demonstrated by demands for their labors even by those who criticized them as vagabonds and indolent members of society.[2] In some Southern states, however, disciplinary measures designed to uphold slavery often operated as a hindrance to free Negroes' economic opportunities to make a living in certain fields. In North Carolina, for example, legislation was enacted to restrict their right to trade in certain articles or to peddle any goods beyond the limits of the county in which they resided without first securing a license from the local authorities.[3] Georgia legislation in 1806 called for binding out free persons of color found "roving the country in idleness and dissipation." By an act passed by the Legislature of Georgia in 1828, free Negroes were prohibited employment as typesetters in printing offices.[4]

In Louisiana, however, the economic rights of the free Negro population were less severely curtailed. Few restrictions were placed upon them in earning a livelihood and in competing with the White race in agricultural or industrial pursuits. It will be recalled that free Negroes

---

2. Carter Woodson (ed.), *Free Negro Heads of Families in the United States in 1830*, xxxiii.

3. John H. Franklin, *The Free Negro in North Carolina 1790–1860*, 131.

4. Woodson (ed.), *Free Negro Heads of Families in the United States in 1830*, xv.

had access to the courts of law whenever their property rights became endangered. They were also allowed to conclude legal transactions pertaining to business affairs in the same way as White citizens. Although free Negroes were excluded from certain occupations by custom as well as by law, they could freely engage in any form of agricultural pursuits.

The vast majority of the free colored population of the rural areas made a living from the soil, because they had been trained for such pursuits or in allied occupations. In fact thousands enjoyed prosperity and some even enjoyed the high-status occupation of Louisiana planter. The compendium of the United States census in 1850 shows that there were 242 free persons of color classified as large, medium or small planters.[5] Among this select group, a few owned sugar and cotton plantations, with slaveholdings, which not only rivaled but in some cases even surpassed the estates of their White neighbors. Although few in number, this group played no small part in the economic life of the state. Like their White counterparts, they were sometimes sophisticated and highly cultured, and being a conservative group they were extremely proud—at times, even haughty. As such the colored planters were in complete agreement with their White counterparts as to the necessity of maintaining both the economic and social patterns established to insure the domination of the state's slaveowners.

Among the large and prosperous planters was Andrew Durnford of "St. Rosalie" place, located in Plaquemines Parish south of New Orleans. By 1850 this Mulatto was ranked among the largest planters of his class in the state.

---

5. DeBow (comp.), *Compendium of the Seventh Census,* 81.

United States officials who audited his estate in the mid-century showed his assets came to $80,000, counting both real and personal possessions.[6] This brown-skinned aristocrat's work force consisted of 70 slaves of whom 35 were female and 35 male[7]—indeed a perfect matching of sexes and indicative of good planning and management.

Durnford's land holding in 1850 was such that it included 1200 improved and 1460 unimproved acres of land. His farm machinery was valued at $10,000. His livestock—which included 19 asses and mules, 30 milch cows, 30 working oxen, 100 other cattle, 25 sheep and two swine—was estimated at $2800. Under the careful and astute management of Durnford, the plantation produced 1000 bushels of Indian corn, $100 in orchard products, 50 pounds of butter, 40 tons of hay, 200 hogsheads of cane sugar, and 16,000 gallons of molasses.[8]

There were other free colored planters in Plaquemines Parish engaged in either sugar or rice planting, but none of them possessed estates surpassing the master of St. Rosalie plantation. A sampling of the census reports of that parish for 1850, shows twelve free Negroes whose holdings were valued in excess of $10,000 each. For example, Adolph Reggio, a 46-year-old Mulatto sugar planter, was owner of an estate valued at $70,000.[9] Reggio also owned 43 slaves to work his plantation.[10] Another colored planter named Charles Reggio had property holdings amounting to $18,000, while Constance Larch was

6. MS. United States Census Reports for 1850, Schedule I, Plaquemines Parish, Louisiana, VII.

7. *Ibid.*, Schedule II, IV.

8. *Ibid.*, Schedule IV.

9. *Ibid.*, Schedule I, VII.

10. *Ibid.*, Schedule II, IV.

owner of a rice plantation estimated at $25,000 in value.[11]
Plaquemines came to be called the "Empire Parish"—
and little wonder, for even James Williams, a Mulatto
wood-yard keeper, was able to amass property holdings
amounting to $6000 at that occupation.[12] No doubt he
found many ready customers for his product, from among
the colored and White sugar planters during the busy
sugar making season.

There were other colored planters in Louisiana and
prominent among this group was Jean Baptiste Meullion
of St. Landry Parish, who during his lifetime accumulated
considerable holdings in lands and slaves. Meullion was
born a slave on the German Coast about 1764, the son
of a White planter, Luis Augustin Meullion, and his
Mulatto slave, Maria Juana. In 1776, Jean Baptiste Meullion and his mother were emancipated on condition that
they remain as servants until the death of their former
owner.[13] Following the death of his father, Meullion
moved to St. Landry Parish and on March 25, 1796, married Celeste Donatto [spelled Donate in some records]
in the Catholic Church at the Spanish post of Opelousas.
Celeste Donatto brought to this union a dowry of ten
piastres, which amount was paid to Meullion by his
father-in-law on the wedding day.[14] This marriage into
the Donatto family proved profitable to the former slave,
for his father-in-law, Martin Donatto, was by 1830 listed
as the largest of the colored slaveowners in Louisiana.
At that date he owned 75 slaves.[15]

---

11. *Ibid.*, Schedule I, VII.
12. *Ibid.*
13. MS. Deed of Emancipation, February 21, 1776, Meullion Papers.
14. Marriage Contract, March 25, 1796, *ibid.*
15. Woodson (ed.), *Free Negro Owners of Slaves in the United States in 1830*, 8.

Meullion was a devout Catholic and frequently made generous contributions to that church. In 1826, he gave $50 towards the construction of a new church building at Opelousas. The following year the pious colored member made a similar donation.[16] When he died in 1840, the last rites of his church were performed for him in the building he had helped to construct. The receipt for these services indicates that Meullion had an expensive as well as an impressive funeral:

Received of Mr. Antoine Donate [Donatto] Meullion 35 piastres for requiem mass and interment of his father, J. Bte. Meullion, died February 17, 1840.[17]

The Meullion papers consist primarily of bills of sale for lands and slaves made to Jean Baptiste Meullion, which illustrate to some extent the scope of his activities as a planter. On October 22, 1803, for example, he bought from Elemencia Enfancina Hermano of New Orleans land located in St. Landry amounting to "five arpents front and 80 in depth" for the sum of 400 pesos. The conditions of the sale agreement were such that Meullion was to pay in two short-term installments, "200 pesos within three months, the other 200 pesos within six months" from the sale date. Again, in 1832, he added to his holdings in land when he purchased 840 arpents "lying in the Prairie Laurent fronting on Bayou Teche," St. Landry Parish, Louisiana. By the terms of this sale, the colored planter paid ten dollars in cash for each arpent of land.[18]

16. MS. Receipts for $50, July 14, 1826, May 5, 1827, Meullion Papers.
17. Receipt for Funeral Expenses, February 17, 1840, *ibid.*
18. Bill of Sale, August 15, 1832, *ibid.*

From the numerous bills of sale for slaves, Meullion seemed especially anxious to increase his holdings. He made purchases from White planters in St. Landry as well as from planters in Natchez, Mississippi. One such bill shows that in 1817 he bought four male slaves in Opelousas from White planters for sums amounting to $2000 in cash.[19] In the early winter of 1811, Meullion made a trip to Natchez to buy slaves at a sheriff's sale. While in the Mississippi city he bought three slaves, for which he paid the sum of $1000 each.[20] By 1830, this colored planter's slave property came to 52 Negroes, an amount which ranked him among the largest of Louisiana's free Negro slaveholders.

Meullion's cotton and sugar crops were handled in the main by New Orleans merchant factors. In 1834, for example, he disposed of his sugar crop of $1418.32 through a contract with Sauf and Company of New Orleans.[21] The year after the panic of 1837, Meullion was able to sell 41 bales of cotton for $19,348.60 to the commission merchants—Waterman, Burgel, and Company— of the port city.[22] Necessary supplies for operating the plantation were frequently purchased from local merchants. In Opelousas, for example, Meullion had an account with the firm of A. Dupre and Tinet Company, which extended for over a two-year period. His account for 1839, totaling almost $1000, included charges for such items as four yards of tulle, 177 pounds of coffee, two gallons of whiskey and 200 pounds of pork.[23]

19. Bills of Sale, January 28, March 14, 1817, *ibid.*
20. Bill of Sale, February 5, 1811, *ibid.*
21. MS. Receipt, October 18, 1834, Meullion Papers.
22. Receipt, August 8, 1838, *ibid.*
23. Statement of Account with A. Dupre and Tinet Company, March 1, July 11, 1839, *ibid.*

Meullion processed his cotton on his Prairie Laurent plantation. In 1807, he effected a deal with a White mechanic to repair his cotton gin and the terms of this agreement reveal the colored planter as a shrewd and capable businessman. The contract stipulated the following:

I James Lee bargin and agree with Baptiste Meullion to repair his Cotton gin on consideration thereof that if the gin does not run well to the satisfaction of Meullion, the said Lee gets nothing for his work. Furthermore, after the said Lee commences to work if he goes off and leaves it without sufficient reason and it is not finished he gets nothing for his work.[24]

Meullion's financial condition enabled him to borrow money easily when he needed it to expand. In 1833, he secured a loan for $5000 from the Bank of Louisiana, to be repaid, with a 10 percent carrying charge, within twelve months. The bank accepted 12 slaves and 54 arpents of land as security.

In St. Landry Parish, free Negro planters were fairly numerous by the end of the ante-bellum period. One of them, Augustin Donatto, a brother-in-law of Meullion, owned $68,600 in real and personal property in 1860. In the same year, another colored planter, Donate Gullory, was worth an estimated $33,790. Besides these two colored planters, there were 15 other free Negroes who owned more than $10,000 each in real and personal properties on the eve of the Civil War.[25]

There were several free colored families living in Iber-

---

24. Contract between James Lee and Jean Baptiste Meullion, December 8, 1807, *ibid.*

25. MS. *United States Census Reports for 1860*, Schedule I, St. Landry Parish, Louisiana, IX.

ville Parish, a rich sugar producing region of Louisiana, classified as planters. Foremost among this group was the Dubuclet family. The head of this family, Antoine Dubuclet, is perhaps the best example of Negro frugality, industry, and success in sugar planting. His property was valued at $206,400 in the 1860 census.[26] This shows an increase of $119,400 over his holdings in 1850.[27] With 95 slaves in 1860, Dubuclet was not only the largest free Negro slaveowner in Louisiana, but the richest of his class as well.[28] Moreover, this colored planter employed a White overseer named Francois Laurier,[29] and the plantation produced 472 hogsheads of sugar in 1861.[30]

Members of the Ricard family are another example of successful free colored planters in Iberville Parish. Madame Cyprien Ricard and her son, Pierre, were listed as owning considerable properties located on Bayou Goula. In 1850 they had a combined estate valued at $86,000.[31] Ten years later the estate, which was worked by 77 slaves,[32] was worth an estimated $204,000 in value.[33] The sugar crops produced by this planting family were very large. Beginning in 1844, Annandale, the name given to the Bayou Goula plantation, produced 325 hogsheads of sugar;[34] in 1845, 194 hogsheads were produced,[35] with

26. *Ibid.*, Iberville Parish, Louisiana, III.
27. *Ibid.*, 1850, II.
28. *Ibid.*, 1860, Schedule II, II.
29. *Ibid.*, Schedule I, III.
30. P. A. Champomier, *Statement of the Sugar Crop of Louisiana of 1861–62*, 10.
31. MS. United States Census Reports for 1850, Schedule I, Iberville Parish, Louisiana, II.
32. *Ibid.*, 1860, Schedule II, II.
33. *Ibid.*, Schedule I, III.
34. P. A. Champomier, *Statement of Sugar Made in Louisiana in 1844*, 2.
35. *Ibid.*, 1845–46, 6.

213 hogsheads in 1850,[36] 187 hogsheads in 1852,[37] and 508 hogsheads in 1853.[38]

When Pierre Ricard bought a sugar plantation at public auction for $240,600 in 1858, the editor of the local newspaper waxed exuberant over the purchase. He said, in part, "horay for the f.m.c.'s of Louisiana, it is something for Northern philanthropy and abolitionists to ponder upon—the fact of a Louisiana f.m.c. purchasing a sugar plantation for $240,600, and yet, this is only one of many such individuals in this State whose fortunes vary from the simple thousand to hundreds of thousands of dollars!" The enthusiastic editor went on to ask "where is the colored man in the North worth $100,000?" He doubted whether any Negro "worth $50,000" could be found in any of the free states of the North. "The truth is," the editor wrote, "a darkey in Louisiana, if he is of the right stripe of principle, can make more money than one of his own countrymen can make in the North."[39]

Although the editor no doubt exaggerated the possibilities for fortune-making, there were a number of colored planters in Pointe Coupee Parish each of whose holdings exceeded $10,000. LeFroix Decuire, for example, had $25,000 in properties in 1860. At the end of the antebellum period, 11 other colored planters of this parish owned more than $10,000 in real and personal properties.[40]

Among the most interesting of free Negro planters were those of the Cane River section in Natchitoches

---

36. *Ibid.*, *1850–51*, 9.
37. *Ibid.*, *1852–53*, 12.
38. *Ibid.*, *1853–54*, 11.
39. Plaquemines (La.) *Gazette and Sentinel*, June 19, 1858.
40. MS. United States Census Reports for 1860, Schedule I, Pointe Coupee Parish, Louisiana, IV.

Parish. Many of these individuals, like their counterparts in other sections of the state, had started with small holdings, and by thrift and business practice had managed to accumulate large properties in lands and slaves. They usually engaged in cotton planting and marketed this crop in the same manner as White planters of Louisiana. When the well-known traveler Frederick Law Olmsted passed through the area he observed that the Cane River settlement was made up almost entirely of free colored persons who were descended from the progeny of old French or Spanish planters and their Negro slaves. In fact, he was informed by the captain of the steamboat *Delman* that only "one pure-blooded white man" lived in this colored community.[41]

The observant Olmsted also noted that the houses of colored planters along Cane River were "large, handsome and comfortable" dwellings.[42] A White merchant on being questioned by Olmsted replied with an answer which refuted the general opinion that these colored planters were "a lazy, beastly set," who allowed their plantations to go to ruin. The merchant had found them to be instead "a healthy, honest and industrious" group who entertained their friends with the same "lavish hospitality" as White persons of similar economic standing. The stage driver to Alexandria, who made stops at colored plantations, expressed a similar opinion, adding that "although distant toward white people, once they know you [they are] a very gentlemen-like people."[43]

Outstanding among this group of planters was Jean

41. Olmsted, *A Journey in the Seaboard Slave States in the Years 1853–1854*, II, 286–287.
42. *Ibid.*
43. *Ibid.*, 288.

Baptiste Louis Metoyer. When the latter died in 1838, he left an estate of $112,760.95½ to his widow and grandchild. The estate included 30 slaves with a total value of $23,670 and real property appraised at $67,290.37½. Included in the succession was a list of household goods that indicates comfortable and luxurious living. For example, during the course of his life, Metoyer had enjoyed the use of the following: one barouche valued at $100; two looking glasses valued at $25.00; one mahogany armoire valued at $25.00; one bookcase valued at $50.00 and twelve silver forks and knives valued at $80.00. In addition to these items, there were a mahogany sofa, a dozen mahogany chairs, a sideboard, four cherry bedsteads and two tables.[44]

By 1850, other members of the Metoyer family had massed large property holdings. According to the census of that year, Jean Baptiste Metoyer owned 500 acres of improved land on which he raised 140 bales of cotton.[45] Metoyer also owned 38 slaves to work the land.[46] Another member of this planting family, named F. C. Metoyer, owned 1000 improved acres on which he produced 160 bales of cotton in 1850,[47] with a labor force of 26 slaves.[48] In 1860, eight other members of the Metoyer clan were listed as planters with properties amounting to over $15,000 in value.[49] A sampling of the same census brings to light that five other free Negro families each had hold-

44. MS. Succession of Jean Baptiste Metoyer, Natchitoches Parish Succession Records, Record No. 362, May 1, 1843.

45. MS. United States Census Reports for 1850, Schedule IV, Natchitoches Parish, Louisiana.

46. *Ibid.*, Schedule II, III.

47. *Ibid.*, Schedule IV.

48. *Ibid.*, Schedule II, III.

49. *Ibid.*, Schedule I, IV.

ings exceeding $15,000. In this group were such colored men bearing the names of Condis, Roques and Rachals.[50]

The free colored planters of Louisiana thus enjoyed an amount of affluence seldom found in either slave or free states of the union. Members of this group, fearing that their financial interests were just as much endangered as Whites by abolitionism, willingly offered their services to the Confederacy after the firing on Fort Sumter in 1861. In May of 1861, on learning that a free colored military unit had been organized in New Orleans, a group of Pointe Coupee free colored planters volunteered for military duty as home guards and their services were eagerly accepted by the police jury of that parish. This unit was given the privilege of electing its own officers, provided that such individuals were White citizens at least 21 years of age.[51] After receiving this authorization, they assembled at the False River courthouse, and elected a Colonel F. L. Claiborne as their commanding officer.[52] In a letter to a friend in Natchez, Mississippi, Claiborne wrote that he had formed a company of 80 colored planters made up of "the flower of that description in the State." He also expressed confidence that if there "be a battle at Washington City I shall speed my dragoon company of brave quadroons to the scene of war and shall contend for the honor of taking old Abe captive, and running up the Confederate flag on the dome of the Capitol."[53]

Another home guard unit composed of colored planters

---

50. *Ibid.*
51. MS. Pointe Coupee Parish Police Jury Minutes, Volume II, 1848–1862, 177.
52. Baton Rouge *Gazette and Comet,* May 11, 1861.
53. Pointe Coupee *Democrat,* May 16, 1851.

was organized in Natchitoches Parish. Under the name of Monet's Guards, this outfit was commanded by two "respectable white planters" of the parish. The colored guardsmen of Natchitoches were congratulated by the editor of the local newspaper for "being inspired with the same sentiments which moved their ancestors in 1814 and 1815 in wanting to defend their homes and property" against invasion.[54] Oral testimony gathered by E. Franklin Frazier from an "old colored resident" of Louisiana supports the idea suggested by these two instances, that many well-to-do colored freemen prized their distinctive economic position so strongly that they deplored any prospect that would endanger it. According to the testimony of this informant it was revealed that her:

> Grandma, when a widow, had refused to marry a man who had fought in the Union Army. She regarded him as responsible for losing her slaves. She consistently refused to salute the American flag. Once when she had to get a passport to go to New Orleans and was ordered to salute the American flag, she spat upon it and put it under her feet. She was not punished for this, either because she was a woman or because she was a beautiful woman. Until her death she regarded Abraham Lincoln as her enemy.[55]

Equally feared by this group of colored planters was the prospect of a general emancipation, which would submerge them in the great black mass of Negroes.

It should not be assumed that free Negro planters were ever in the majority. By far, most who engaged in agriculture were owners of small estates worth anywhere

---

54. Natchitoches *Union*, May 1, 1862.
55. Manuscript document, quoted in E. Franklin Frazier, *The Free Negro Family*, 36.

THE FREE NEGRO IN ANTE-BELLUM LOUISIANA • 214

from a few thousand to less than $50. Moreover, they made up only a small part of the total free Negro population. In 1850, for example, 158 free Negroes were listed as farmers.[56] Small farmers of the colored class were most numerous in Calcasieu, Jefferson, Lafayette, Lafourche, Rapides and St. Tammany parishes. They appear a self-sufficient group, relying principally on non-staple crops and occupying lands nestled among the great plantations.[57]

A typical small farmer was Gibson Perkins of Calcasieu Parish. He cultivated a farm of 21 acres and owned eight horses, four oxen, several head of cattle and three hogs. Perkins's chief crops in 1860 were corn and sweet potatoes, of which he had 300 and 200 bushels respectively. Soloman Drake of the same parish grew corn, sweet potatoes and sweet peas. His livestock included four horses, ten milch cows, four oxen and twelve hogs.[58] In somewhat similar circumstances were eight colored neighbors of Perkins and Drake, small farmers whose landholdings ranged in value from $400 to $1500.[59] A few free Negro farmers engaged in truck farming, with potatoes and other vegetables as cash crops. These individuals lived, for the most part, in parishes adjacent to New Orleans where there were opportunities to dispose of crops at advantageous prices in the city markets. M. Rilleux and S. Labonnier of Jefferson Parish were typical of this group.

---

56. DeBow (comp.), *Compendium of the Seventh Census*, 81.

57. See, Adolphe Henry and Victor Gerodias (comps.), *The Louisiana Coast Directory, of the Right and left banks of the Mississippi River, from its mouth to Baton Rouge. Also, of the Bayou Lafourche, with the distances from New Orleans. Accompanied by a full index. Compiled in the Spring of 1857, passim.*

58. MS. United States Census Reports for 1860, Schedule IV, Calcasieu Parish, Louisiana.

59. *Ibid.*, Schedule I, II.

On his 20-acre farm, Rilleux raised 200 bushels of corn, 100 bushels of Irish potatoes, 30 bushels of sweet potatoes; the total value of his market produce in 1860 amounted to $600. This colored farmer's livestock consisted of two horses, one mule and 57 head of cattle.[60] The cash value of Rilleux's farm was estimated at $3000 in the census returns just preceding the Civil War.[61] The census of 1860 shows that there were five other free colored gardeners in Jefferson Parish with holdings, though small, of a cash value in excess of $1000 each.[62]

Less fortunate than colored farm proprietors were the "one horse" free Negro farmers located in the several parishes of Louisiana. E. V. Lepine of Lafourche Parish, for example, owned land in 1860 valued at the sum of $700,[63] consisting of five improved and 29 unimproved acres. Lepine owned only one horse, but he was able to raise 800 pounds of rice on this small tract of land.[64]

Another such farmer, J. B. Read of St. Tammany Parish, owned $740 in real and personal estate.[65] This type of farmer could be found in most of the country parishes of Louisiana before the Civil War. Possessing small, but self-sufficing lands, worked in the main by themselves and their family, they were an independent lot and may properly be called the free Negro yeomanry. Like their White neighbors, who were producing food crops under similar conditions, they formed an essential part of the economic organization of Louisiana.

Opportunity for employment in agricultural tasks was

---

60. *Ibid.*, Schedule IV, Jefferson Parish.
61. *Ibid.*, Schedule I, III.
62. *Ibid.*
63. *Ibid.*, Lafourche Parish, IV.
64. *Ibid.*, Schedule IV.
65. *Ibid.*, St. Tammany Parish, Schedule I, X.

abundant in ante-bellum Louisiana. One position the free Negro held with some degree of success was that of overseer on large plantations. This occupation, moreover, had been opened to them by law. According to an act passed by the Territorial Assembly in 1806, all plantation owners had to employ either a White or free colored overseer or be fined the sum of $50 for every month elapsed without compliance.[66] By 1850, at least 25 free persons of color were employed as overseers on Louisiana plantations.[67] Although the majority of them were without land, occasionally one might manage to accumulate property. For example, in 1860, S. Pasedo of Pointe Coupee Parish was listed as owning property worth $6000.[68] Pasedo's circumstances were better than those of a White overseer named Frank Buchere, who was listed as possessing no property in the 1850 census.[69] Another example of a well-to-do free Negro overseer was Louis Metoyer of Natchitoches Parish whose real property in 1860 amounted to $3000.[70] The accumulation of wealth in real estate was no mean accomplishment for individuals employed as overseers because of the many occupational hazards associated with that position and the constant turnover in employment to which persons employed at that task were subjected in the ante-bellum South.

Free Negroes also held other jobs connected with agriculture in Louisiana. They could find employment in such skilled trades as coopers, wheelrights, blacksmiths and wagoners. Coopers were especially numerous in the

---

66. *Laws of the Territory of Orleans* (1806), 1st Leg., 2nd Sess., 304.
67. DeBow (comp.), *Compendium of the Seventh Census,* 81.
68. MS. United States Census Reports for 1850, Schedule I, Pointe Coupee Parish, Louisiana, VIII.
69. *Ibid.*
70. *Ibid.,* Natchitoches Parish.

sugar parishes, where the demand for barrels kept them busy during the sugar grinding season.[71]

During the ante-bellum period, the great majority of free Negroes living in the country parishes were property-less and were forced to earn a livelihood as farm laborers. Failure to own land, however, was not confined to free persons of color. A large part of the White population engaged in agricultural pursuits as laborers or farm tenants, and frequently owned no property. According to the historian, Roger Shugg, three out of five families living in Louisiana in 1860 owned no land. He found that the majority of them made a living as hired laborers, mechanics, boatmen, fishermen and woodcutters.[72] In 1850 there were 232 free Negroes[73] who gave their occupation as laborer, but since this number represented a small percentage of the total free colored population in the country parishes one is led to the conclusion that many failed to give correct occupations to census takers. Furthermore, it is more than likely that a sizeable number of free Negroes who gave their occupation as laborer found work on plantations and farms and may have been more properly classified as farm hands. Moreover, those who were listed as having no occupation may have been employed from time to time as farm laborers.

Besides the rivalry with White persons for farm jobs, free Negroes found themselves in great competition with slave labor. The presence of large numbers of slaves in Louisiana would seem to preclude any chance for free Negro employment, but the ever growing economic boom

---

71. See, for examples of free Negroes employed in the above mentioned occupations, *ibid.*, 1850, Schedule I, West Baton Rouge Parish, Iberville Parish and St. Charles Parish, I.

72. Roger W. Shugg, *Origins of Class Struggle in Louisiana,* 86.

73. DeBow (comp.), *Compendium of the Seventh Census,* 81.

caused by the demands for more cotton and sugar decreased this competition and free Negroes were frequently hired by White plantation owners. In some cases they worked as the only employees, but it was not uncommon for them to work as extra labor, side by side with slaves.

The combined work of free Negroes and slaves was common throughout the state during the ante-bellum period. The employment of the two together occurred on the plantations of several White persons in Concordia and St. Mary parishes. In 1840, for example, a planter named J. Ellis of Concordia, in addition to owning 17 slaves, had six free Negroes living on his plantation. There can be little doubt that such persons were employed by this landowner to supplement the slave laboring force.[74] Another planter, C. Borrel of St. Mary Parish, not only had 12 slaves but he also had 13 free persons of color living on his plantation in the same year.[75] There is at least one instance in which free Negroes comprised the entire laboring force on a plantation. This was the case of Patris Mendis, who had 22 male and female free persons of color living on her Assumption plantation in 1820.[76] The practice of hiring free Negroes as farm laborers was continued at late as 1850, for the census returns of that year indicate many such persons living on the plantations of White persons.[77]

Although this type of work was unskilled and the remuneration small, a not inconsiderable number of Negro

74. MS. United States Census Reports for 1840, Concordia Parish, Louisiana, II.
75. *Ibid.*, St. Mary Parish, I.
76. *Ibid.*, 1820, Assumption Parish, I.
77. See, for examples, *ibid.*, 1850, Schedule I, Bienville Parish, Terrebonne Parish and West Baton Rouge Parish, I, VIII.

farm hands managed to accumulate some personal wealth. This was especially true at the end of the period. For example, Evarist Dorzart, a middle-aged farm laborer of Avoyelles Parish, was one of the more fortunate. His personal estate in 1860 was valued at an estimated $500.[78]

Another farm laborer listed as owning $750 in personal estate was Isiah Ashworth of Calcasieu Parish.[79] Such individuals, however, were not in the majority, since most colored farm hands were listed as having personal possessions ranging in value from $50 down to nothing.

Whenever extra help was required for the harvest, slaveholders had recourse to free Negroes and poor Whites. This was especially true during the busy cane cutting season when the crop had to be gathered before the destructive frosts of late fall. One such demand for laborers was made known in an advertisement in the New Orleans *Picayune* in 1840, when a call was made for:

> Thirty white or black laborers are wanted to get in crop of sugar about 100 miles up the coast, to whom liberal wages will be given. None need apply but those of sober and industrious habits.[80]

Specific information concerning the wages of colored farm hands before 1850 is almost nonexistent. There are, however, scattered entries in plantation books indicating returns from such employment. A sugar planter named John H. Randolph of Iberville Parish, as a case in point, hired a free Negro named Ned Farm for twelve years, at a little over six dollars a month and keep for himself and

---

78. *Ibid.*, 1860, Avoyelles Parish, IV.
79. *Ibid.*, Calcasieu Parish, I.
80. October 18, 1840.

family. When Farm died in 1850, the White planter recorded in his plantation journal the following:

> Ned Farm a free man of color departed this life in March 1850. My indebtness to him for hires from January 1834 to January 1850 at $80.00 a year (after deducting all credits) amounts to $619.85 which he requested me to keep in trust for his wife Betsy and his three children . . . and to use my discretion in using it for them to the best advantage which I promise to do.[81]

For the next ten years Randolph faithfully made payments, at five percent yearly interest, to this free Negroe's family. The White planter never fully paid Farm's heirs, for in 1861 he recorded a balance of $416.22 due them.

In the urban areas of Louisiana, free Negroes possessing little or no special training found employment opportunities only in unskilled jobs. They served as common laborers, draymen, waiters, chimney-sweeps, railroad hands, cabmen, fishermen and hunters. Even though free Negroes were in competition with White persons for these unskilled tasks, they nevertheless enjoyed a shaky monopoly in such menial jobs as waiters and draymen. George Chew, for example, was kept busy enough as a drayman in Bayou Sara to accumulate a personal estate amounting to $1400 by 1860. His nearest competitor was C. Johnson, who was listed as owning $500 in personal property.[82] At least three colored freemen of Baton Rouge listed as draymen possessed more than $500 each in personal estates on the eve of the Civil War.[83]

---

81. MS. Plantation Journal of John H. Randolph, Randolph Papers.

82. MS. United States Census Reports for 1860, Schedule I, West Feliciana Parish, Louisiana, III.

83. *Ibid.*, East Baton Rouge, I.

Newspaper advertisements offering employment opportunities for waiters were frequently published in the New Orleans press during the 1850 decade. During the summer, large numbers were needed in the resort centers in the country parishes. This was the case in July 1853, when an advertisement appeared calling for: "15 or 20 likely colored waiters at a healthy watering place across the lake [Pontchartrain]."[84] When it was discovered that there was only one chimney sweep in Baton Rouge, an appeal was made through the columns of the local newspaper to the unemployed free colored men to apply for work in that capacity. This appeal was prompted by a number of fires caused by defective flues. However, little hope was expressed in the newspaper that free Negroes would seek such employment.[85]

The largest single concentration of the population in Louisiana was in the city of New Orleans. It was here that the White laborer was brought into competition with both slave and free Negro labor. Consequently, a great deal of jealousy and ill feeling broke out between the races and the situation worsened with the coming of immigrants. To help provide for such persons, city authorities passed a resolution in 1822 stating that in the future only White laborers would be employed by the municipal labor-managers.[86]

The competition for jobs became even keener in the 1840s with the coming of large numbers of Irish immigrant laborers. In a short time Irishmen had replaced

---

84. New Orleans *Daily Picayune,* July 3, 1853.
85. Baton Rouge *Gazette,* January 17, 1852.
86. MS. Ordinances and Resolutions of the City Council of New Orleans, January 1, 1822 to December 20, 1822, Session of November 22, 1822, 141.

free colored labor as servants and cab drivers. It was the opinion of one traveler that "nowhere is the jealousy felt by the Irish toward the Negroes more apparent" than in the city of New Orleans.[87]

Employment opportunities did change toward the end of the ante-bellum period as free Negroes again found work in menial tasks, which they had been previously squeezed out of by Irish immigrants. James R. Creecy on a visit to the Crescent City in the late 1850s noted that Irish workers were seldom employed by White persons except in cases of dire necessity. "The Negroes have decidedly the preference," he wrote, "and readily obtain much higher wages." Creecy went on to account for the loss of Irish supremacy in the menial jobs. It was his contention that the White proletariat had turned out to be "a reckless, abandoned, drunken, lying, dirty, wretches, who are more at home in the police offices than anywhere else."[88] Even if Creecy overstated, the fact existed that free Negroes and slaves were preferred over white Irishmen. As a case in point the *Picayune* in 1856 carried the following advertisement for Negro laborers only:

> 50 stout able negro laborers to work on the superstructure of the Orleans, Jackson and Great Northern Railroad, north of the line of Louisiana, in a healthy piney woods country. Employment will be given for the summer or balance of the year.[89]

---

87. Charles Lyell, *A Second Visit to the United States of North America*, II, 160–161.

88. James R. Creecy, *Scenes in the South and Other Miscellaneous Pieces*, 25.

89. May 30, 1856.

During the ante-bellum era free Negroes also held a rather large portion of jobs requiring skills. This was especially evident in the city of New Orleans where there was a great demand for skilled workers. By 1850, it has been estimated that about one half of the city's free colored males came under this category. In fact they outnumbered the Whites.[90] City freemen of color were accounted much better off than in New York City or Connecticut. New York, for example, had 60 free Negroes in such jobs—a ratio of approximately one of every 55 free Negroes. However in New Orleans, 165—or 1 in 11—were engaged in similar pursuits. The state of Connecticut counted only 20 skilled free Negroes, for a ratio of 1–100. Throughout Louisiana, on the other hand, the number was 185, or 6 in 12 of the whole free colored population.[91]

Among the 1792 free Negroes over fifteen years of age employed as skilled workmen in New Orleans in 1850 there were 355 carpenters, 278 masons, 156 cigarmakers, 92 shoemakers, 82 tailors, 64 merchants, 61 clerks and 52 mechanics in trades at which over 50 men worked. In still other skilled trades, at which 15 or more worked, were 43 coopers, 41 barbers, 37 boatmen, 28 painters, 25 cooks and 19 cabinet makers.[92] In the country parishes, although fewer skilled jobs were held by free Negro workmen, almost every community had its free colored carpenters, blacksmiths, merchants, mechanics and cigarmakers. In 1850, 346 persons of color were at work in 24 different skilled jobs in the country parishes. The distribution of these is seen in Table III.

---

90. Shugg, *Origins of Class Struggle in Louisiana*, 119.
91. DeBow (comp.), *Compendium of the Seventh Census*, 80–81.
92. *Ibid.*

TABLE III

Occupations of Free Negroes in Rural Louisiana—1850.[93]

Kind	Black	Mulatto	Total
Apprentices	1	6	7
Boxers	—	3	3
Blacksmiths	2	9	11
Boatmen	2	—	2
Brickmakers	—	1	1
Butchers	—	7	7
Cabinetmakers	1	4	5
Carpenters	18	148	166
Cigarmakers	1	12	13
Clerks	—	2	2
Cooks	11	1	12
Coopers	1	11	12
Doctors	1	1	2
Engineers	—	3	3
Mariners	1	11	12
Masons	3	44	47
Mechanics	1	5	6
Merchants	2	11	13
Painters	—	2	2
Sailmakers	1	3	4
Shoemakers	2	5	7
Stewards	2	—	2
Tailors	—	4	4
Teachers	1	2	3
Total	51	295	346

Ten years later, in 1860, the free colored employment situation is shown by a sampling of the census listing for free Negroes in East Baton Rouge Parish, the home of the state capitol. At least 26 free persons of color held skilled jobs which included eight carpenters, five cigarmakers, five butchers, four merchants, three bricklayers and one

93. *Ibid.*

minister.[94] The prosperity of this group was far from moderate for the average sum possessed by each of them was in excess of $1000 in personal and real properties. At least one colored carpenter, Eli Guidry, owned over $4000 in personal and real properties. Wealthiest of them all was Theophile Bertram, a 45-year-old Mulatto merchant who had an estate valued at $14,500.[95] At Donaldsonville, likewise, nine free colored men were classified as skilled workers employed as carpenters, bricklayers, coopers and house painters.[96] A similar occupational situation existed in the town of Opelousas.[97]

A goodly number of free Negroes made a living in various maritime occupations. As carpenters, seamen and riverboat engineers employment opportunities were better in the nine river and lake towns of the state. E. Farrance of Mandeville, for example, was listed as a ship carpenter and he was able to accumulate over $2000 at this trade. In the same town, C. H. Techon, a lake captain, was worth an estimated $3000 in the census preceding the Civil War.[98]

Free Negroes were frequently employed as engineers on steamboats. In 1843, during a period in which sentiment against free Negroes was at its height, a steamboat explosion occurred near Baton Rouge in which many passengers and the assistant engineer, who was a Negro, were killed. Certain citizens, assuming negligence on the part of the colored engineer, used this incident as the basis for an attack upon free Negro labor. The editor of the

---

94. MS. United States Census Reports for 1860, Schedule I, East Baton Rouge Parish, Louisiana, II.
95. *Ibid.*
96. *Ibid.*, Assumption Parish, I.
97. See, for examples, *Ibid.*, St. Landry Parish, IX.
98. *Ibid.*, St. Tammany Parish, X.

Baton Rouge paper in reporting the incident insinuated that the accident was caused by the Negro engineer and expressed hope that this "awful catastrophe will be a warning to our river captains to see that competent engineers are always present at their posts."[99] In defense of his late employee, the captain wrote a letter to the newspaper describing the Negro in question as "a capable and trustworthy man" and cleared him of all responsibility in the incident.[100]

Yet, there were drawbacks to this kind of occupation and many became objects of suspicion by those who thought the Negroes were abolitionist agents spreading their propaganda among slaves. Writing in the New York *Daily Tribune*, a Louisiana slaveowner complained that free Negro riverboat employees—and especially the stewards—were with a few exceptions abolitionists trained for work among the slaves. This writer claimed that one of her servants had been "enticed away by the colored steward of the steamship *Diana*." The complainant alleged she had irrefutable evidence that the steward in question had engaged in such activity for years and that she had in her "possession a card of his house in Chicago, where he receives his colored friends—they paying him well for his trouble—as a matter of course."[101]

Free Negro engineers also were held in high esteem, provided they did not work aboard steamboats that went into northern states. In at least once case, George Menard of Baton Rouge, was held in great respect by his White neighbors for his efforts to dig the first artesian well in the state. This enterprising colored man was described as "a

---

99. Baton Rouge *Gazette*, September 23, 1843.
100. *Ibid.*, October 7, 1843.
101. November 11, 1858.

character that deserves more than passing notice" for he had not only purchased his own freedom, but had made a trip to Alabama in order "to enter into the subject of artesian wells." It was proclaimed that if he would meet with success his name would be known "to posterity associated in this state with the successful introduction of artesian wells."[102]

The best known free colored inventor was Norbert Rillieux, who won the reputation of having made one of the most important contributions ever to the technical advancement of the sugar industry.[103] While a student in Paris during 1830–32, Rillieux discovered the multiple evaporation process of making sugar. On returning home in 1833, he set out to sell his method to Louisiana sugar planters. Meeting with small success and impeded by the 1837 panic the colored inventor offered to rent Andrew Durnford's plantation for $50,000 to experiment with his invention. The offer was turned down because the free Negro planter refused to surrender complete control over his slave work force. Rillieux countered with another proposition: he would build sugar refiners at his own expense and give Durnford a percentage of the returns of all sugar made by the Rillieux method. This offer also was declined without reason.[104] Nevertheless, the colored inventor managed to perfect his refining method and secure two patents. The first was issued in 1843 and the second in 1846. Several daring planters adopted his process and the sugar produced was enthusiastically proclaimed to be "the best double-refined sugar of our northern refineries."[105]

---

102. Baton Rouge *Gozette*, November 27, 1852.
103. J. Carlyle Sitterson, *Sugar Country, The Cane Sugar Industry in the South, 1753–1950*, 150.
104. *Ibid.*, 148.
105. *Ibid.*, 149–150.

Besides this invention, Rillieux also submitted plans for sewerage disposal systems for the city of New Orleans. However, this project was rejected without any explanation. As the prejudices against free colored people intensified during the 1850s Rillieux returned to France and found work as a headmaster of a Paris school. He held this position at the Ecole Centrale until his death in 1894.[106]

As was to be expected free Negro women found themselves forced to become breadwinners for their families. In this capacity many engaged in a great variety of both skilled and unskilled occupations. Since few skilled positions were open, the majority found employment in menial tasks. They worked most frequently as washerwomen, domestics, peddlers and lodging house keepers. For example, Filis Antoine of Baton Rouge took in washing to support her two children who were listed in 1860 as attending school.[107] Catherine Davis of Shreveport apparently found much demand for her services as a washerwoman, for she was worth an estimated $5000 in 1860.[108] Many free Negro women living in New Orleans made their living as washerwomen as evidenced by the large number of advertisements in the city press offering employment opportunities for such persons.[109]

Other colored women supported their families by peddling food products in the small towns of Louisiana. Manate Veazy, for example, sold coffee and cakes in St.

---

106. R. L. Desdunes, *Nos Hommes et Nôtre Histoire*, 102–103.

107. MS. United States Census Reports for 1860, Schedule I, East Baton Rouge Parish, Louisiana, I.

108. *Ibid.*, Caddo, II.

109. See, for examples, New Orleans *Daily Picayune*, October 2, 1840, February 20, 1841, September 2, 1858.

Martinville for the support of her five Mulatto children.[110] In St. James, Louise Donate made an adequate living for herself and husband as an ice cream peddler.[111] In order to support her six children, Anne Winchler sold milk in the streets of Bayou Sara; apparently business was good since she had a personal estate valued at over $600 in 1860.[112]

The Quadroon women of New Orleans apparently had a monopoly in renting rooms to "white gentlemen," and traveling salesmen. A colored hairdresser from the North named Eliza Potter described such places as located on "no mean street but side by side with some of the best mansions" of the city. She went on to say that "they are generally occupied by gentlemen, who take their meals at the St. Charles [Hotel] and sleep in these apartments" and it was never deemed improper for the same "gentlemen to take their families to these rooms."[113] All colored rooming houses did not bear the high reputation as those described by the chatty Eliza Potter. When E. John Ellis visited his son, who was studying law in New Orleans, he found him living in a rooming house kept by an "unsavery" free colored woman. According to student the arrangements did not "exactly suit the sugar plum" of his father's taste and the latter forced his son to seek other accommodations.[114]

A sampling of the 1860 census indicates that among the large owners at least four free women of color derived a

110. MS. United States Census Reports for 1860, Schedule I, St. Martin Parish, Louisiana, X.

111. *Ibid.*, St. James Parish, IX.

112. *Ibid.*, West Feliciana Parish, III.

113. Eliza Potter, *A Hairdresser's Experiences in High Life*, 160.

114. T. C. W. Ellis to Mother, February 24, 1857, Ellis Papers.

decent living in keeping rooming houses in the country parishes. The average wealth of this group, amounting to over $1000 each, testified to both their good reputation and their prosperity.[115] Not all colored landladies had good reputations nor did they enjoy the prosperity of those operating in New Orleans. In 1831, Anne Royall registered shock at the accommodations offered her by a colored-operated inn at Bayou Sara. The Royall woman angrily described the place and its manager as a rich Mulatto who owned several taverns and was "a great tyrant" toward her slaves. Miss Royall found the Mulatress to be "very insolent, and, I think, drank. It seems one Tague (an Irishman), smitten with her charms and her property, made love to her and it was returned, and they lived together as man and wife. She was the ugliest wench I ever saw, and, if possible he was uglier, so they were well matched."[116]

In the quest for a livelihood, free Negro women branched out into varied lines of business. In New Orleans, some were found engaged in prostitution. Judging from the numerous arrests reported in the newspapers, quite a few kept body and soul together in practicing the world's oldest profession. On July 29, 1851, for example a free woman of color named Suzanne was arrested for managing a house of assignation on St. Peter Street. All of the girls were listed as free colored and described as exposing themselves on the balcony "in little too much of that simple attire known as the Georgia costume."[117] In the late

---

115. MS. United States Census Reports for 1860, Schedule I, East Baton Rouge, Caddo, Lafayette parishes, I, II, III.

116. Anne Royall, *Southern Tour*, 87–98, quoted in U. B. Phillips, *American Negro Slavery*, 433.

117. New Orleans *Daily Picayune*, July 29, 1851.

spring of 1851, another large number of colored prostitutes were arrested for keeping houses of "ill repute." Among those booked at police headquarters were "Cecelia Clay, f.w.c., occupying No. 154 Conti street; Adele Grand, f.w.c., occupying 164 Conti street and Fanny Palfrey, f.w.c., occupying 89 Burgundy street."[118] Instances of prostitution on a grand scale were rare in the rural parishes, or at least here, unlike the city, there was a conspiracy of silence on the matter by the newspapers. There was, however, at least one report of a "house of ill fame" operated by two colored prostitutes in Lafayette Parish. It was reported that this place, which was located in an isolated section known as Prairie Marronne, was frequented by White hunters of the community.[119]

An appreciable number of colored women were employed in such semi-skilled trades as seamstresses, hairdressers, nurses, merchants and midwives. That many of them excelled in these fields is attested to by the substantial amounts of personal properties owned by such persons, as revealed by the 1860 census reports.[120] Free colored women were especially esteemed as practical nurses, and when yellow fever broke out their services were sought by both White and Black patients. Their usual fees amounted to about $10 a day but many served for nothing during times of epidemics.[121] During the Yellow fever epidemic of 1853 in Vermillionville, the services of free Negro nurses were eagerly enlisted. Although 60 persons succumbed to

---

118. *Ibid.*, April 30, 1851.

119. Barde, *Histoire des Comités de Vigilance aux Attakapas*, 225.

120. See, for example, MS. United States Census Report for 1860, Schedule I, Orleans, East Baton Rouge, Caddo, Rapides and St. Landry parishes, I, II, VI, IX.

121. William L. Robinson, *The Diary of a Samaritan by a Member of the Howard Association*, 239.

the dreaded disease, the colored nurses were nevertheless highly commended for an "admirable defense against the scourge."[122]

Free Negroes of both sexes were generally excluded from any of the professions. However there were a few colored men who managed to establish themselves in the practice of medicine after they had obtained degrees in European universities. Alexandre Chaumette, a native of New Orleans, was one such individual who had been awarded a doctor's degree in France. After graduation, this free Negro was assigned to a Paris hospital where he "acquired a vast experience." After completing his interneship, Chaumette returned to Louisiana with the intention of practicing medicine in New Orleans. After his return to Louisiana he passed the state medical tests and was legally permitted to practice his profession. Because of his "serious studies" and charity work among the poor of both races in Louisiana, this Black doctor was able to win the respect of the Medical Fraternity of New Orleans.[123]

In the country parishes at least two free Negro doctors were listed in the 1860 census. These two individuals were probably untrained and consequently did not achieve either respect or success in their vocations. One of them, Octave Fortier of St. Charles Parish, was in jail at the time of the 1860 census. The other, Pierre Allain, apparently was unable to build up a flourishing practice for he was propertyless on the eve of the Civil War.[124]

Inconceivable as it may appear, teachers enjoyed higher esteem than those free Negroes engaged in the practice

---

122. Barde, *Histoire des Comités de Vigilance aux Attakapas*, 308.
123. Desdunes, *Nos Hommes et Nôtre Histoire*, 106.
124. MS. United States Census Reports for 1860, Schedule I, St. Charles Parish, Louisiana, IX.

of medicine. One of the most respected was Armand Lanusse, the principal of the Couvent school for free persons of color in New Orleans. Included among his colleagues were such highly respected colored teachers as Joanni Questy, Constant Reynes and Joseph Vigseuix.[125] Among prosperous and esteemed teachers of the country parishes was F. C. Christrope of Natchitoches, who was worth an estimated $12,000 in personal and real properties. No doubt this schoolmaster supplemented his teaching duties with other engagements.[126]

Before the Civil War there were many free Negro entrepreneurs and small businessmen scattered throughout the state. Just as their White counterparts some were prosperous and others were on the edge of poverty. There was an amazing variety of trades in which colored men entered and made a fair living for themselves and their families. For example, a free man named Julius operated the only ferry across Red River at Grand Ecore in Avoyelles Parish. The colored ferryman charged twelve cents a passenger "in high and low water."[127] Victor Vincent owned a barber shop on Lafayette street in Baton Rouge, which was frequently patronized by the White citizens of the town.[128] In New Orleans many free colored men were tailors or owners of tailoring shops and enjoyed the patronage of many prominent families.[129]

Some free Negroes won considerable success in operating mercantile concerns in which a sizeable capital investment was required, and also business acumen. In Nat-

125. Desdunes, *Nos Hommes et Nôtre Histoire,* 30.
126. MS. United States Census Reports for 1860, Schedule I, Natchitoches Parish, Louisiana, IV.
127. Avoyelles Parish Police Jury Minutes, Volume I, 1821–1843, 101.
128. Baton Rouge *Gazette,* June 12, 1847.
129. Grace King, *New Orleans, the Place and the People,* 344–345.

chitoches Parish, a free Negro, named Oscar Dubreuil, operated a general store in which he did a credit business of over $25,000 during the two year period from 1856 to 1858. The colored merchant kept an account book for sales on credit and most of his customers were free Negro planters living in the Cane River community of Natchitoches Parish. His stock consisted of drygoods, groceries, medical supplies, cosmetics, alcoholic beverages and notions of various kinds. One of Dubreuil's largest accounts was that of J. F. Metoyer, who was indebted to the merchant for $69.32 on March 1, 1857, for purchases of such things as candy, shirts, hats and whiskey.[130] White persons also had accounts with the colored merchant. A certain Dr. J. Gilbert made purchases as "1 pot creme de perce" and "2 pounds of candy" in 1856.[131] By far Dubreuil's largest credit business was in the whiskey line. During Christmas week of 1856 he sold over 30 gallons of liquor on credit to various customers.[132]

There were other ways in which free Negroes might become wealthy. During the period before the Civil War some acquired real and personal properties of considerable value through inheritance from relatives and White parents. The Donatto family of St. Landry Parish is a case in point. Martin Donatto, one of the wealthiest colored freemen in Louisiana, died in 1848, leaving members of his family an estate valued at over $100,000. Included in the estate were 89 slaves and 4500 arpents of land, as well as notes and mortgages amounting to $46,000.[133] In 1854,

---

130. MS. [Oscar Dubreuil] Account Book, Isle de Breville, Natchitoches Parish, 1856–1858.
131. *Ibid.*
132. *Ibid.*
133. Phillips, *American Negro Slavery*, 434.

Jean Baptiste Metoyer of Natchitoches Parish left his wife, Suzette, an estate appraised at over $84,000. This property included 37 slaves, valued at $29,000.[134]

Considerable amounts of personal property were accumulated by free Negroes. It passed from deceased persons to members of their families and sometimes even to the general public by the action of administrators in the settlement of estates. Administrators' sales, and the accounts rendered to probate courts by such functionaries in the settlement of the estates of deceased persons, furnish information on this point. Several cases from Natchitoches Parish may be cited to illustrate a condition common to the whole state.

Among the many items left in the home of Joseph Augustin Metoyer, a colored planter, were the following: a framed mirror, a dozen pewter spoons, a dozen plates and other kitchen utensils. Aside from household articles, Metoyer left seven horses, six mules, two wagons, harnesses, saddles and bridles. The sale of this property brought the sum of $1498.05. Among the purchasers were some of his free Negro friends as well as his relatives. Thus, O. Lecour, a planter, bought a horse and bridle, while the chairs, mirror, spoons, dishes and other articles were sold to Metoyer's widow.[135]

Charles N. Roques, a cigarmaker, left such items of personal property as a pair of candle sticks, a box of books, a dozen plates, a shotgun, 55 pounds of tobacco, 200 cigars, and 25 quarts of whiskey.[136] A free Negress named Nancy

---

134. MS. Succession of Jean Baptiste Metoyer, Succession Book 24, Natchitoches Parish, No. 896, September 1, 1854.
135. MS. Succession of Joseph Augustin Metoyer, Natchitoches Parish Mortgage Book N., July 3, 1851.
136. MS. Succession of Charles N. Roques, Natchitoches Parish Succession Records, No. 897, October 2, 1854.

Cozine left a bedstead, a chest of drawers, a band box, a bonnet and one lot of clothes. The sale of these articles was necessary to pay the expenses of the colored woman's funeral.[137]

The legacies left to free persons of color by White persons accounted for a great deal of wealth and comfort. It was not unusual for White men to make bequests of large amounts of properties and monies to free Negro women who had been their concubines. For example, a planter named John Anderson freed his slave, Phoebe, and at the same time bequeathed to her 100 acres, four slaves and $1000 in cash.[138] In like manner, a certain Sinnott willed his slave son, Thomas, freedom and all his real and personal effects, with the provision that the estate be used for the benefit of his White wife during her lifetime. After the latter's death, Thomas was to come into full possession of the property.[139] In still another case, the slave girl, Jane, was left her freedom and money amounting to $200 by her White owner.[140]

As we have seen, slave ownership by free Negroes was not unique in Louisiana. The extent of free colored persons in this category may be seen by an analysis of their holdings in 1830. Among the 212 free colored slaveowners in the country parishes, 50 of them owned 10 or more slaves. In this group 25 possessed 20 to 75 slaves. With 75 slaves, Martin Donatto was the largest Negro slaveowner

---

137. MS. Succession of Nancy Cozine, Natchitoches Parish Succession Record, No. 143, September 10, 1839.

138. *Anderson's Executors v. Anderson's Heirs,* 10 La. 29 (March 1836). The will is quoted in this case.

139. *Succession of Sinnot,* 3 La. An. 175 (February, 1848).

140. *Bird, Executor v. Vail,* 9 La. An. 176 (March, 1854).

in rural Louisiana.[141] The majority, however, had only one, two or three slaves, and the number of petitions to manumit slave relatives suggest that many bondsmen were owned by their kinsmen for purposes of giving them freedom.[142] Slaveholding by free Negroes in New Orleans followed patterns similar to those of the country parishes. In the city for instance, 753 persons of color were slaveowners. Among this number, 25 owned ten or more slaves, while 112 owned from five to ten slaves. Again, the majority of them had only one or two slaves. Cecée McCarty, with 32 slaves in 1830, was the largest slaveowner in the city of New Orleans.[143]

The economic status of Louisiana's free colored population was superior by far to that of free Negroes in either other slave states or free states. In 1850, the total real estate owned by free Negroes in Louisiana was valued at $4,270,295. In New Orleans alone, free Negroes owned property worth $2,214,020 while those living in the country parishes owned property amounting to $2,056,275. In the same year, New York City's free Negro population owned real estate worth $109,310. In Barnwell, Beauford and Charleston, South Carolina, 58 colored property owners each owned property worth less than $100; the property of ten others was worth between $100 and $5000 each; and there were only two with real estate valued at between $5000 and $10,000 each.[144]

---

141. Woodson, (ed.), *Free Negro Owners of Slaves in the United States in 1830,* 6–8.

142. *Cf. supra,* 134–135.

143. Woodson (ed.), *Free Negro Owners of Slaves in the United States in 1830,* 9–15.

144. "The Free Black Population, North and South," *DeBows Review,* XXIII (1857), 217.

The total wealth of free Negroes living in several of the country parishes in 1860 amounted to considerable sums in personal and real estate. For example, Natchitoches Parish was first among the rural parishes in free Negro wealth amounting to over $750,000.[145] St. Landry Parish was second with about $640,000 belonging to free Negroes.[146] Pointe Coupee Parish can be rated third, with property owned by colored inhabitants coming to over $480,000,[147] and Plaquemines was fourth with wealth in excess of $330,000.[148] These amounts represent approximately one-fourth of the Parishes' wealth. Other valuations ranging from $100,000 to $200,000 also can be estimated as representative of about one-fourth the total value of wealth in the respective parishes of St. Mary, St. Martin, St. Tammany and East Baton Rouge.[149] Wealth of others range in value from about $13,000 in Ascension[150] to a low of $50 in Madison Parish.[151]

In the main the most important contribution of free Negroes to the economic well-being of Louisiana cannot be measured by the wealth accumulated by landed colored aristocrats and professionals. It would be more accurate and appropriate to say that ante-bellum Louisianians owed more to those who worked at the menial manual tasks than to the economic aristocrats. It was the former who did more to help run the state's economy and make life a bit easier for those of the privileged classes of both

---

145. MS. United States Census Reports for 1860, Schedule I, Natchitoches Parish, Louisiana, IV.
146. *Ibid.*, St. Landry Parish, IX.
147. *Ibid.*, Pointe Coupee Parish, IV.
148. *Ibid.*, Plaquemines Parish.
149. *Ibid.*, East Baton Rouge, St. Martin, St. Mary, and St. Tammany parishes, IX.
150. *Ibid.*, Ascension Parish, I.
151. *Ibid.*, Madison Parish, IV.

races. Yet both enjoyed a contemporary position in the economic community of the state which placed them among highest paid and most respected colored laboring class in America. This factor alone goes a long way toward explaining why schemes to deport free colored persons as a group met with such dismal failure.

6

The Free Negro in the Social Life of Louisiana

ALTHOUGH Louisiana's free Negroes enjoyed exceptional legal and economic privileges, their social status was just above the slave level. At every turn they were victims of social discrimination imposed on them by custom as well as law. The White majority in guarding their self-ordained master-class standing relegated free colored persons into a status resembling neither fish nor fowl nor red herring. There were reasons aplenty for this curious behavior. Foremost was the ever-present fear of racial equality, which became an obsession of many Whites throughout the ante-bellum period. Such fear found expression when America first took control of Louisiana with the passage of laws designed to impress an inferior social position upon the free colored persons.

In 1806 legislation required free persons of color to pay special respect to White persons. According to a law of that year, they were not allowed to insult or strike Whites under penalties of fine or imprisonment. Free Negroes

240

were not only obligated by this law to speak and answer Whites with respect, but they also were required never "to conceive themselves equal" in any way with persons of the Caucasian race.[1] In giving added strength to this measure, Governor Jacques Villeré asked the Legislature in 1816 for an amendment that would make attacks upon Whites an offense punishable by a fine of $100 and imprisonment for three months.[2] The request was honored by the lawmakers.

In their encounters with White citizens, free Negroes did not always render the expected deferential deportment required by legislative enactments. This was especially true when Negroes were required to defend themselves: more often than not clashes between the races were started by Whites. An incident of this nature took place in St. John the Baptist Parish in 1823, when a White citizen, Edmond A'Hern, swore that his wife had deserted him to live with a free Negro woman named Zairé, and that all his efforts to persuade her to return had met with failure. A'Hern further related that, late one afternoon, while he was "walking and musing upon the levee" near Zairé's house, to "seek some information concerning his wife" the Negress ordered him to leave, threatening that he would be "hit on the head with a piece of iron" if he did not. When he refused to leave, Zairé enlisted the aid of a White sailor who seized A'Hern by the neck and with the assistance of the colored woman attempted to lock him in a boat-house. Escaping from his captors, A'Hern retreated, "as fast as possible" pursued by his assailants who were armed with paddles. He then man-

---

1. *Laws of the Territory of Orleans* (1806), 1st Leg., 1st Sess., 189.
2. *Official Journal of the House of Representatives* (1818), 3rd Leg., 2nd Sess., 60.

aged to secure a stone and struck the sailor in the face. Whereupon, Zairé ran to her house and returned with a gun. At the sight of this "formidable weapon" A'Hern retreated to a nearby woods. He returned an hour later, accompanied by the parish judge, who preferred charges of assault and battery against the free Negress and her White assistant.[3]

In New Orleans, free Negroes frequently insulted White persons, and the newspapers there carried many items of such violations of the state law. When a free Negro named Britannio Washington was found guilty of insulting a White citizen in 1850, he was sentenced to pay a ten dollar fine or serve ten days in jail. The free Negro took the former alternative, with a promise never to repeat such an offense in the future.[4] In 1851, Sylve Jean, a free woman of color, was arrested for insulting a certain Frederick Lemonier, by calling him "a nasty Frenchman."[5]

Instances of assault and battery between the races became frequent in cases in which the free Negro was employed as the supervisor of a White man. For example, in 1858, Auguste Morris, a colored bricklayer, was arrested for striking a White hod carrier named Michael Crosby while the two were working on a construction job in New Orleans. According to Crosby, his Negro boss had insulted him, and in defense of his honor "clipped the darkey with his hand," whereupon Morris "returned the compliment with his trowel and hammer."[6]

Cases of disrespect and attack on White citizens were

---

3. MS. Deposition of Edmund A'Hern, May 23, 1823, St. John the Baptist Parish Records, 1786–1924.

4. New Orleans *Daily Delta,* June 16, 1850.

5. New Orleans *Daily Picayune,* August 13, 1851.

6. New Orleans *Daily Crescent,* October 7, 1858.

not entirely confined to adults. A case in point was that of a colored boy named Robert, who was arrested in 1850 for striking a little White girl with a broom while the two were playing together. The Negro boy's mother came to the defense of her son and was also arrested for calling the child's parent a bitch.[7] Altercations of this kind however were not so frequent as newspapers would have had their readers believe. In general free Negroes complied with the laws and customs and acted out the role of being deferential towards their White neighbors. They had to assume such a role for resistance would surely have brought on swift repression.

During the pre-Civil War years Louisiana free persons of color of either sex were specifically prohibited from marrying White persons. Any such union was never considered legal by state officials. In fact the most specific regulation pertaining to free Negroes and Whites was the law which pertained to intermarriage. According to the law:

> Free [White] persons and slaves are incapable of contracting marriage together; the celebration of such marriages is forbidden, and the marriage is void; there is the same incapacity and the same nullity with respect to marriage contracted by free white persons with free people of color.[8]

In considering a case involving the marriage of a free Negro woman and a White man, the Supreme Court of the state found no precedent to legalize the union. Instead, the high court held that all marriages of this nature were "absolute nullities" and that if such contracts were

---

7. New Orleans *Daily Delta*, October 1, 1850.
8. *Civil Code of the State of Louisiana, 1825*, 30.

made, "either party could disregard it and neither could derive any consequences of a lawful marriage."[9] In still another case, the justices decreed marriages between colored persons and White contracted in France or any other place for that matter, as null and void in Louisiana. Accordingly the court declared: "Whatever validity might be attached in France to marriages of this kind . . . it is plain that the Courts of Louisiana cannot give effect to these acts, without sanctioning an evasion of the laws, and setting at naught the deliberate policy of the State."[10]

On the rare occasions that a White man defied law and custom in order to marry a rich free colored woman, the man made himself subject to exclusion from White society. He would be forced either to live *"en retraite* or leave the country."[11] There was, however, at least one who chanced the scorn of his White neighbors and also that of the colored class when he married a free Negress with all the rites of the Roman Catholic church. This incident came to light in a letter of a free colored woman living in New Orleans to her aunt in Natchez, Mississippi. In 1848 Lavinia Miller wrote her kinswoman, Mrs. William Johnson, the following details of the gala event:

> Wanda is married to a white man last Saturday night Madame . . . was not at the wedding nor her sister kitty none but the family and not all of them. Her mother says that the man has been courting her eight years and she told me that they was going to Bay of St. Louis [Missis-

---

9. *Succession of Jean Michel Minvielle R. Domes v. L. Barjac, Executor, and Cora Lalande, (f.w.c.)*, 15 La. An. 343 (May 1860).

10. *J. M. Dupré v. The Executor of Boulard, (f.w.c.), et al.*, 10 La. An. 211 (May 1855).

11. C. D. Arfwedson, *The United States and Canada in 1832, 1833, and 1834*, II, 61.

sippi] to marry to, because they could not get lawful married here, that was to fool me but . . . they did not go there, they had the french priest to make the ceremony at the house without licons, now what you call that.[12]

In addition to state laws defining the social status for free Negroes, local units of government imposed regulations, which were concerned with the segregation of the races. One of many such ordinances was that passed by the municipal council of New Orleans on November 18, 1820. It authorized the Mayor to prevent free Negroes from occupying theatre boxes or seats usually reserved for Whites. A stiff fine was the penalty for the ordinance's violation.[13] Segregation was also required in public conveyances of Louisiana and separate railroad cars were set aside for the use of the colored class while traveling in the state. On one occasion, such an arrangement displeased a free Negro named Voltaire Vonvergne. In 1843, he and a party of friends insisted on riding in the coach reserved for Whites. When asked to leave, he refused and the car the colored party occupied was unfastened from the train. Vonvergne then "discharged a pistol shot" at the conductor but that official escaped injury and deputized some White passengers who proceeded to almost "beat to death" the colored man. Vonvergne was turned over to New Orleans officers to await trial for violating the segregation regulations of Louisiana.[14]

The social position of the free Negro in Louisiana was

12. MS. Lavinia Miller to Mrs. William Johnson, December 9, 1848, William Johnson Papers.

13. MS. Ordinances and Resolutions of the City Council of New Orleans, March 4, 1820 to March 17, 1821, Session of November 18, 1820, 150.

14. Baton Rouge *Gazette*, August 10, 1843.

further revealed by the pronouncement of leading public personalities. Such persons considered the free Negroes to be inferior simply because of their African blood.

Reflecting the feeling of his constituents on the subject, state Senator H. M. St. Paul of Orleans Parish was quite typical of those despising free Negroes as a group. On the occasion of a bill to legitimize the colored child of a White citizen of Avoyelles Parish in 1857, St. Paul seemed livid with rage and proceeded to issue a blast against all persons of mixed blood. In part he said that, "If out on a hunt, he might set and take refreshments at a free colored man's table, he would never shake hands with one of them because there was social contagion in the touch." He went on to express a personal opinion that an honest slave was entitled to more respect than the "rich debauches of either sex, surnamed a free person of color." The angry solon believed he represented personally "one of the superior Caucasian race" and as "one who had the interest and welfare of a family to watch over," must then do all that was possible to discourage any measure which would bring about "the blending of the races, which God himself had marked with such visible distinction." As he warmed to the occasion, the Senator snorted aloud "Oh! but we are told that some of them are rich—some of them are fair, scarce a characteristic of their African origin remaining. What if they Be?" he asked the attentive lawmakers. In an argument reminiscent of a latter day contention, St. Paul continued, "Does it therefore follow that we are to recognize their social equality, invite them to our homes, and give our children to them in marriage? Never! Never!" would he submit to such "indignity and humiliation." The irate Senator therefore moved that the bill in question be laid indefinitely on the table and he stated loudly "if the rules of the Senate permitted it he would move that it be thrown under the table." After several other legislators voiced similar sentiments, the bill to give legal status to the Avoyelles Parish colored child was withdrawn from the calendar.[15]

In many ways Louisiana's Whites shared the opinion of others in the South and in the United States in that they considered any person with a known trace of Negro blood as Negro, and, as such, inferior to White persons. Only 100 percent White ancestry would permit legal entrance to the White race. Although the free Negro population of Louisiana was mainly composed of Mulattoes[16] such persons could never hope to be assimilated into the White group. Even though a few with especially noticeable Caucasian complexions crossed the color line, such was not always practicable in a white-dominated society that zealously guarded its status. Successful incidents of crossings were therefore rare occasions indeed.

Since free colored persons were never deemed equal to Whites, they created a society of their own. Within this group class lines were just as tightly drawn as among the Whites: the lighter the color the higher the social position. Consequently, the Griffe looked down upon the pure Negro; the Mulatto regarded the Griffe as inferior and in turn was spurned by the Quadroon; while the Octoroon refused any or little social intercourse with those ethnically below himself. The various shades of color were often designated in both public and private documents as follows: A Griffe was the offspring of a Mulatto and a Negro: a Mulatto of a White and Negro: a Quadroon, of a White

---

15. *Official Journal of the Senate* (1857), 3rd Leg., 1st Sess., 8–9.

16. In 1860, 15,158 of the 18,647 free colored persons were Mulattoes. See, *Eighth Census of the United States, 1860,* 194.

and a Mulatto; and an Octoroon of a White and a Quadroon. For convenience's sake, the word Mulatto was commonly used to refer to all of these people of mixed blood,
regardless of the amount.[17]

Almost all travelers who left accounts of their experiences in Louisiana used extravagant language in describing women of the colored class. An English visitor, for example, represented them as the most beautiful he had
ever seen, "resembling in many respects, the higher order
of woman among the Hindoos, with . . . full, dark, liquid
eyes, lips of coral and teeth of pearl, and with long raven
locks of soft and glossy hair."[18] Another observer found
them "walking the streets with the air of donnas,"[19] and
a third pictured them as having "regular features—wavy
black hair—pale but healthy color [and], look like a
Jewess from southern Europe."[20]

A northern governess visiting Louisiana in the 1850s
gave one of the most detailed descriptions of one "yellow
lady" she met on a train approaching New Orleans. According to her observation the Mulatto appeared as follows:

> Her head was surmounted by an orange and scarlet plaid
> handkerchief bound about it Turkish-turban fashion. . . .
> She had in her ears a pair of gold earrings, as large as a
> half-dollar, plain and massive. She wore a necklace of gold
> beads, hanging from which was a cornelian cross . . . [and]
> upon her neck was a richly worked black lace scarf; her

---

17. See Olmsted, *A Journey in the Seaboard Slave States in the Years
1853–1854,* II, 583.
18. James S. Buckingham, *The Slave States of America,* I, 36.
19. [Joseph H. Ingraham], *The South-West by a Yankee,* I, 188–189.
20. James H. Croushore and Stanley T. Williams (eds.), John W.
DeForest, *A Volunteer's Adventures, A Union Captain's Record of the
Civil War,* 47–48.

dress was plain colored silk made in the costliest manner. Her olive hands, which had very tapering fingers, and remarkably oval nails, were covered with rings, chiefly plain gold ones. She had a pair of magnificent eyes, and a face of surprising and unlooked-for beauty. . . . In one hand she held a handsome parasol, and the other fondled a snow-white French poodle upon her lap, said poodle having the tips of its ears tied with knots of pink ribbon, and a collar of pink silk quilled . . . made like a ruff, while the ends of its tail was adorned with a bow of blue ribbon. . . .[21]

As was to be expected not all visitors to Louisiana found such women attractive. One of the few writers, who differed in his description of the quadroons was Thomas Hamilton. This English observer expressed keen disappointment when he found that they always seem to retain something of the Negro in their make-up, such as "the long heel—the wooly hair—the flat nose—the thick lips—or the peculiar form of the head."[22] Perhaps Hamilton was not fortunate to have seen the same apparition as had the Northern governess.

In such a peculiar system, the men of the colored class were generally kept in the background, and married women of their own color. By and large they won the reputation of being industrious and law-abiding persons. However, on occasion they would be seen at public gatherings escorting their mothers, sisters or wives, but they were never invited to Quadroon balls, and in their homes, when females had White visitors they seldom were seen or showed themselves.[23]

---

21. Joseph Holt Ingraham (ed.), *The Sunny South, or, The Southerner at Home Embracing Five Years Experience of a Northern Governess in the Land of the Sugar and the Fine Cotton*, 330.
22. Thomas Hamilton, *Men and Manners in America*, II, 206.
23. MS. Charles Gayarré, The Quadroons of Louisiana, Gayarré Papers.

Besides the legal family, there existed a distinctive form concubinage or *placage*[24]—a liaison between a White man and Mulatto or Quadroon woman. One visitor to New Orleans in reporting on such extra-legal relations considered it as a "very peculiar and characteristic result of the prejudices, vices, and customs of the various elements of color, class and nation, which has been brought together" in Louisiana.[25] As a matter of fact *placage* (literally a situation) developed into an institution because of the legal restrictions against intermarriage.

It was at free Negro balls where women of color concluded agreements to become mistresses of White men. The manner in which such liaisons were handled has been outlined by Frederick L. Olmsted as follows:

> When a man makes a declaration of love to a girl of this class she will admit or deny, as the case may be. . . . [If] she is favorably disposed, he will usually refer the applicant to her mother. The mother inquires, like the Countess of Kew, into the circumstances of the suitor; ascertains whether he is able to maintain a family; and, if satisfied with him, in these and other respects, requires of him security that he will support her daughter in a style suitable to the habits she has been bred to, and that if he should ever leave her, he will give her a certain sum for her future support, and a certain additional sum for each of the children she shall then have.[26]

---

24. Taken from the term *une placée*. It was usually applied to those women who make arrangements for sexual connections with White men. See Olmsted, *A Journey in the Seaboard Slave States in the Years 1853–1854*, II, 245.

25. *Ibid.*

26. *Ibid.*, 244.

Once the arrangement had been reached the *une placée* was entertained by her friends as a prospective bride and then she moved into her newly furnished home.[27] Free colored women who entered these "left-handed marriages" felt no guilt, nor were they ostracized from their fellow Negroes. Yet, if the women were to become promiscuous, the union would be broken and the woman would be treated as a prostitute. On the other hand, once the arrangement was ended by marriage of the White man the women became free to make another such arrangement.[28] Some liaisons lasted for life, and it frequently happened that White men maintained two households quite happily and conveniently. This was especially true if his lawful marriage was one which 19th-century people dubbed one of convenience. As has been shown, the attachment for free colored women was so strong in certain cases that White men left them property which insured financial security.

Quite predictably interracial sex relationship was not a practice only of upper class White men. Both rich and poor persons made alliances with women of color in all parts of Louisiana. For example, in 1817 a visitor to Louisiana reported one such union between a Pointe Coupee planter and a Mulatto woman. When this traveler had been forced to spend the night at the plantation of a certain Mr. Martin, he was surprised to discover that his host was living with a "Mulatto woman and their six children." He, however, noticed that the children were

---

27. George W. Featherstonhaugh, *Excursion Through the Slave States,* II, 269.

28. Thomas Ashe, *Travels in America Performed in the Year 1806,* 314–315.

not allowed to call Martin "Father" nor did he conde-
scend to address them as "my children."[29] A. A. Parker,
a Northern traveler on his way to Texas in the 1830s,
wrote of seeing a White tavern-owner near Alexandria,
living with a "black wife." Parker expressed some un-
pleasant feelings on witnessing "half a dozen halfbloods
running about the house." This sensitive traveler was
further distressed when he was served only bread and
meat by the miscegenious innkeeper.[30]

The manuscript census reports of 1860, in listing White
heads of families, further suggest the practice of liaisons
between White men of all ranks of society with free
women of color. For example, a White day laborer of
Avoyelles Parish named Jean Baptiste Lacombe, had a
25-year-old Mulattress and five Mulatto children listed
as living in his household. All the Mulattoes in question
bore the Lacombe name.[31] In Catahoula Parish, a White
planter named R. Lincicum was living with Annie Lincicum, a 35-year-old Black woman and six Mulatto children.[32] A 37-year-old White cooper named Henry Durerney of Jefferson Parish lived with "Mrs. Durerney," who
was listed as a Mulattress. There were no children listed
in this household.[33] G. Barton, a White policeman of New
Orleans, was head of a family composed of Française
Barton, a Mulattress, and five Mulatto children.[34] In Concordia Parish, a 60-year-old White woodchopper named

---

29. Felix Flugel (ed.), "Pages from a Journal of a Voyage Down
the Mississippi to New Orleans in 1817," *Louisiana Historical Quarterly*,
VII (1924), 423.

30. A. A. Parker, *A Trip to the West and Texas, 1834–1838*, 112.

31. MS. United States Census Reports for 1860, Schedule I, Avoyelles
Parish, Louisiana, I.

32. *Ibid.*, Catahoula Parish, II.

33. *Ibid.*, Jefferson Parish, III.

34. *Ibid.*, Orleans Parish, V.

Joseph Clemmins, had Mary Clemmins, a 50-year-old Black woman in his household, together with nine Mulatto children bearing the Clemmins name.[35]

As successive generations turned lighter with the infusion of White blood, resentment developed against the extra-legal relations among the White women of Louisiana. A writer in the New Orleans *Gazette,* under the signature of "Mother of a Family," complained of the insolence of Mulatto sweethearts of White men, who were in the habit of driving White women from the sidewalks. She called them "Heaven's last, worst gift" to White males. The writer went on to say that the purity of blood of the best families of Louisiana was threatened, because "so delicate and white has the mixture become! that it was actually being introduced among the wives and daughters of the citizens."[36]

It occasionally happened that White women separated from their husbands on the grounds of concubinage with free women of color. In 1826, for example, the wife of a Pointe Coupee planter named Margaret Decuire filed separation proceedings against her husband for infidelity. She charged him with having "bred with his domestic, Josephine, and had more regard for the mulattress than for her." According to evidence submitted by Madame Decuire, the Negress in question not only had a child by her husband, but the latter had boasted in public that his colored son would figure in Paris society. Furthermore, the planter had sent his illegitimate offspring to the French capital to be educated. Meanwhile, Josephine had continued to live with Decuire on the plantation until 1825, at which time he took his mistress to France to be

---

35. *Ibid.,* Concordia Parish, II.
36. Quoted in *Niles' Weekly Register,* XXIX (November 5, 1825), 160.

near their child. A few years later, they returned to Louisiana and the ardent Decuire established his colored family in "a fine house" in New Orleans. On the basis of this evidence, Madame Decuire was granted an instrument of separation along with the right to administer her property as "*une femme seule.*"[37]

In some cases, White women went a step further and divorced their husbands for living in concubinage with free women of color. For example, in 1835, a certain Mrs. Adams entered suit for divorce against her husband on the grounds of "open and avowed adultery" with a colored woman named Rose Metoyer. Adams was also accused of living at the home of his mistress. Presented with overwhelming evidence, the court granted the White woman a divorce.[38]

It occasionally happened that free Negro parents objected to their daughters entering into the *une placage* arrangement. One such objection came to public attention through a slander suit instituted by a Delphine Solet against her father for calling her "a thief and the most base and infamous person that ever lived," when she left home to live with a White man. The Lafourche Parish court awarded the maligned woman judgment and five dollars damages. The case was appealed to the Supreme Court of Louisiana and that body reversed the lower court's decision. In rendering the decision, Justice Martin stated: "It appears to us that the relation in which the parties stand to each other, renders it probable that in rebuking his daughter for her ill conduct the father was

---

37. *Labbe's Heirs v. Abat et al.*, 2 La. 553 (September 1831).
38. *Adams v. Hurst*, 9 La. 243 (December 1835).

under the influence of a sense of duty, rather than prompted by malice to injure her."[39]

Sex relationships between White women and free Negro men did not often come to public notice, but there were nevertheless instances of its practice. There were, however, some reports in the New Orleans press concerning the conduct of women living with free colored men. In 1855, a White woman named Antoinette Sondo, who was described as a "buxom flax-haired German girl," was arrested in her home for being "in too close an intimacy" with a "good looking Mulatto" named Green Evans. They were both jailed by the arresting officers.[40]

Perhaps one of the most sensational cases in the country parishes was the concubinage between two White sisters and a free Negro named Coco. This free man was variously described as a very handsome Negro with "a body of Hercules and with eyes as black as the moonless nights of Africa."[41] The scene of this scandal was in an isolated section of Lafayette Parish known as Prairie Marronne where Coco farmed to support his "two white eves" and their nineteen children.[42] Thus Coco was credited with introducing "Mormonism" into Louisiana. As the descendants of this union increased, and white settlers began to come into Prairie Marronne, Coco and his "tribe" were accused of committing every crime in the community. When a jeweler was killed, allegedly by one of Coco's children, a vigilante committee of white citizens was

---

39. *Delphine Solet f.p.c. v. Jean Bte. Solet f.p.c.*, 1 Rob. 339 (February 1842).
40. New Orleans *Bee*, June 30, 1855.
41. Barde, *Histoire des Comités de Vigilance aux Attakapas*, 219.
42. *Ibid.*, 223.

formed and expelled Coco and his large family.[43]

Free Negroes of both sexes made sexual alliances with slaves. Such conduct was nearly always condoned or ignored, and brought about no significant amount of indignation from the Whites. On the other hand, if such affairs became violent, the press focused attention upon them. In 1851, for example, a slave named Mary Jane was arrested for shooting her free colored lover because he was "showing undue attention to another dusty colored damsel." The press account surmised correctly that the slave woman was "a victim of that green-eyed monster—jealousy."[44] In yet another case, Alexander, a slave, attempted to kill his free Mulattress sweetheart when he shot her in the neck causing serious discomfort to the victim. "Love and jealousy," said the *Picayune*, "caused this rash act."[45]

Not all free persons of color entered a state of concubinage. Many of them got married and it was not uncommon for such persons to have their nuptials performed in the churches of Louisiana.[46] In fact, some marriages were conducted in the most proper and fashionable manner. A case in point is the following announcement to one free colored wedding in 1860:

I write to inform you of the marriage of my daughter, Maria Sophie Carlotte Bingaman to Mr. Felix Casanave. She will be married at the St. Louis Cathedral on the

43. *Ibid.*, 242.
44. New Orleans *Daily Picayune*, August 17, 1851.
45. July 29, 1851.
46. See, for example, MS. First Book of Marriages of Negroes and Mulattoes of the Parish of St. Louis in the City of New Orleans, 1777–1830. During this period, 930 free Negroes were married in the St. Louis Cathedral.

evening of the 30th April, 1860. As we will have but a family wedding we have issued no invitations, but will send your family a piece of her wedding cake.[47]

Religion played an important role in the social life of the free Negro population. The majority belonged to the Roman Catholic church, and accordingly had the obligation of attending Sunday mass as well as on holy days of obligation. Many were members of the same congregations as Whites and in some cases contributed to the support of this denomination with generous donations of money. In 1841, the free colored people of New Orleans contributed funds for the construction of St. Augustine Church, and afterwards rented about half of the pews. Seating accommodations were also provided for slaves in the aisles of this church.[48] In Natchitoches Parish, a free colored planter named Augustin Metoyer deeded a plot of ground for the construction of a Catholic church near his plantation on Cane River. This church was used by both White and Negro members.[49]

Many free Negro Catholics were very devout members of their respective congregations. Harriet Martineau, the English sojourner to the United States from 1834 to 1836, tells of witnessing the pious actions of New Orleans persons of this class. She was impressed on noticing an old colored woman in St. Louis Cathedral "telling her beads as if her life depended on the task." Her estimation was

47. MS. M. E. Bingaman to Mr. William Johnson, April 21, 1860, William Johnson Papers.

48. MS. Notes on St. Augustine's Church.

49. J. A. Baumgartner, "Isle Brevelle," quoted in Annie Lee West-Stahl, "The Free Negro in Ante-Bellum Louisiana," *Louisiana Historical Quarterly* XXV (1942), 362.

less than flattering regarding an old Mulatto man whom she wrote followed "with stupid eyes the evolutions of the priest" at mass.[50]

The devotion of one colored Catholic named Martil Ferdinand Liotau was so strong that he gave himself over to verse. Under the title of "The Impression," which apostrophized the St. Louis Cathedral in the following way:

O thou, temple devine, thou final abode,
Of beloved men whom the people still lament,
And who, sensing all thy woes,
Perhaps also weep with us from the depths of their graves,
Thou who didst see me a child within they very walls,
Receive upon my forehead the symbols of baptism;
Alas! Have I grown to see thee on this day,
Deserted, perhaps forever abandoned![51]

Perhaps the most positive achievement in the religious life of Catholic free Negro women was the founding of the Congregation of the Sisters of the Holy Family in New Orleans in 1842. At first, these colored nuns rendered social services to poor persons, but gradually expanded their duties to include the teaching of catechism and sewing to free colored children and adults of New Orleans.[52] In 1851, this religious order was given formal recognition by the ecclesiastical authorities and allowed to don a distinctive habit of black.[53] Once approved by the Church, the colored nuns became active in the edu-

---

50. Harriet Martineau, *Retrospect of Western Travel,* I, 259.

51. Armand Lanusse (ed.), *Les Cenelles, Choix de Poesies Indigenes,* 162–103.

52. Sister Mary Frances Borgia, "A History of the Congregation of the Sisters of the Holy Family of New Orleans," B.A. thesis, Xavier University of New Orleans, Louisiana, 11–12.

53. *Ibid.,* 13–14.

cation of young women of color. The order also continued to give refuge and aid to orphan girls and infirm old colored persons.[54]

Many free Negroes of Louisiana were also members of various Protestant denominations. Segregation for religious worship was generally the pattern for such persons in most of the Protestant churches and often even separate buildings were established by the White members for the use of Negroes. In making such arrangements, free Negroes were provided opportunities to exercise leadership in the religious life of their community. For example, the Episcopalian Bishop L. L. Polk made arrangements with the French Protestant Church of St. Thomas in New Orleans to provide religious instruction for free persons of color. According to an agreement made in 1855, services for colored Episcopalians were conducted in the afternoon "of each Lord's day" in St. Thomas church. Significantly, they were permitted to choose their pastor only with the approval of the bishop of the diocese.[55] In the following year, C. H. Williamson, who had been in charge of the colored congregation, reported on the advancements of his charges as especially rewarding.[56] In Baton Rouge free Negroes were members of St. James Episcopal Church, where they were provided with special seating accommodations.[57]

The Louisiana conference of the Methodist Episcopal

---

54. Joseph Bogaerts, *Convent of the Holy Family, Golden Jubilee of the Sisters of the Holy Family,* 7.

55. *Journal of the Proceedings of the Seventeenth Convention of the Protestant Episcopal Church in the Diocese of Louisiana, which Assembled in St. Paul's Church, in the City of New Orleans, on Friday, May 11, A.D. 1855,* 22.

56. *Ibid., Eighteenth Convention, May 15, A.D. 1856.*

57. Baton Rouge *Gazette,* May 15, 1847.

church, South, provided three chapels for colored Methodists of New Orleans. These were Soule, Wesley and Winans, and each chapel was administered by free colored pastors. Religious services were conducted every Sunday in these chapels at 10 A.M. and at 3:30 P.M. A Sunday school met at 9 A.M.[58]

Negro Methodists were enthusiastic in religious functions. In 1855, for example, the pastors of the three colored chapels were presented by their congregations with a complete outfit of clothing for their "fidelity in Filling Sunday appointments." The presentation was described as "tastedly done by a committee of themselves."[59] On another occasion the "colored ladies of Winans Chapel held a fair to raise money for missionary purposes. All citizens regardless of color were "respectfully invited to attend" this fair.[60]

In Louisiana several free Negro preachers of the Protestant persuasion enjoyed wide-spread respect for their leadership and work in their respective communities. It was a free Negro who received credit for establishing the first Baptist Church in Louisiana. This man was the minister Joseph Willis of whom Baptist historian William Paxton wrote: "The History of the Louisiana Baptist Church could not be written without the mention of this brother."[61]

Willis was born in South Carolina about 1762 of free colored parents and received a grade school education.[62] In 1798 he showed up in Southwest Mississippi, where he

58. New Orleans *Semi-Weekly Creole*, November 22, 1854.
59. *Ibid.*, October 27, 1855.
60. New Orleans *Daily Picayune*, December 20, 1856.
61. William E. Paxson, *A History of the Baptist of Louisiana, from the Earliest Times to the Present*, 515.
62. *Ibid.*

associated himself with a White preacher named Richard Curtis in establishing a church at Natchez. In 1804, he came to Louisiana and preached at Vermillionville and Plaquemines Brule. Both his color and his faith posed severe problems and he returned to Mississippi.[63] However, he reentered the following year and settled on Bayou Chicot in St. Landry Parish. There he began to convert both White and Black people. Because Willis was not an ordained minister at this time, he elicited the assistance of a local Methodist minister in baptizing converts. In 1810, he went back to Mississippi for ordination, but was refused with the explanation that "the Church of Christ might suffer reproach owing to the status" of the Negro preacher.[64] Willis's White friends urged him to get the backing of his small Bayou Chicot followers and present their recommendations at the next meeting of the Mississippi Baptist Association. By 1812, he formed a congregation at Chicot into a church and at their urging Willis was ordained a minister of the gospel. This church, which Willis named Calvary was the first Baptist congregation in Louisiana west of the Mississippi River.[65]

Joseph Willis was an extraordinary personality and seemingly favorably received by white Baptist during the early days of his mission. In fact, he apparently concentrated his spiritual efforts on Whites to the neglect of his own race. "Father Willis," as he was affectionately named, traveled widely in his efforts to organize churches in various parts of the state. In 1816, he organized one in Cheneyville in Rapides Parish and another at Hickory Flat.

63. *Ibid.*, 139–140.
64. William Hicks, *History of Louisiana Negro Baptists from 1804 to 1914*, 18.
65. Paxson, *A History of the Baptists of Louisiana*, 142.

Two years later, on October 31, 1818, the Louisiana Baptist Association was organized out of churches founded by this free Negro minister. Willis was elected its first moderator and served in that capacity on several other occasions.[66] He was frequently invited to deliver the opening sermon at these annual meetings and on one occasion, in 1834, it was reported that: "It was truly affecting to hear him speak of his churches as his children; and with all the affection of a father alluded to some schisms and divisions [doctrinal] that had arisen in the past, and to warn them against a repetition of anything of this kind in the future. When speaking of some becoming extinct he shed tears and surely the heart was hard that could not be melted by the manifestations of such affection, for he wept not alone."[67]

In 1833, Joseph Willis led a group of free Negroes from the Bayou Chicot church to Rapides Parish where he founded Occupy Church on Ten Mile Creek. As he passed through the country, he made some keen observations of conditions among the people. He was impressed by the fact that "slaves were introduced into the country by the thousands. . . . The forest was being leveled and farms extended . . . and people generally so absorbed in making money that they seemed to be infatuated; and one [like himself] who suffered religion to interfere in the least was pronounced a fanatic. Hence it required a degree of moral courage to come out publicly as a follower of Jesus."[68]

When Willis became so enfeebled by age that he could not efficiently serve his Occupy congregation, the Louis-

---

66. *Ibid.,* 171, 175.
67. *Ibid.,* 188.
68. *Ibid.,* 150–151.

iana Baptist Association ordained his grandson, Daniel H. Willis, in 1849, as assistant pastor of the Ten Mile church.[69] Willis, however, continued to preach and establish churches in the western part of Rapides Parish. Despite the fact Willis was a Negro, the Louisiana Baptist Association held him in high esteem. The respect and admiration which members of this group had for their colored founder was expressed in their desire to care for him in his old age. Accordingly, in 1843, the Association went on record that "it was their privilege to aid Joseph Willis who had grown old and needy."[70] Upon his death on September 14, 1854, Willis was buried in the cemetery of Occupy church. Years later Thomas Rand, Jr., as the clerk of the state Baptist Association praised Willis for having crossed the Mississippi River before Louisiana had become a part of the United States. The clerk also pointed out that the colored man had suffered great hardships in preaching a Protestant faith to hostile listeners. In Rand's own words, this preacher spent fifty years "in season and out of season, preaching, exhorting and instructing; regarding not his property, his health, or even his life, if he might be the means of turning sinners to Christ."[71] Indeed, Joseph Willis merited the title of the Baptist "apostle of the Opelousas."

Another free Negro minister who figured prominently in the founding of the Baptist Church in Louisiana was Henry Adams. In 1837, in company with a group of White migrants from South Carolina, Adams settled in the northern parish of Bienville where they established Mount

69. *Ibid.*, 616–617.
70. *Ibid.*, 197.
71. John Pickney Durham and John S. Ramond (eds.), *Baptist Builders in Louisiana*, 15.

Lebanon community. When a church was organized here in 1837, Adams, an ordained minister, was elected the first pastor. He was described as "a man of some education, who was very much respected in the community." This free Negro preacher served Mount Lebanon church until 1839 and then moved to Kentucky where he became pastor of the First Colored Baptist Church of Louisville. Adams served in that capacity until his death in 1872.[72]

Although these free Negro ministers were mainly concerned with White congregations, a few colored preachers devoted their entire attention to the spiritual welfare of Louisiana's slaves and free persons of color. John Jones, for example, was a free Negro preacher in Shreveport who was ordained by a White Baptist presbytery of that city to care for the religious needs of the Negro population.[73] He was affectionately called "John the Baptist" by both White and Negro residents of Shreveport and was said to exercise a greater influence on the colored population than police officers.[74] This colored minister was held in such high esteem that he was often invited to preach to large congregations of White Baptists of Shreveport.[75] In New Orleans, Asa C. Goldbury and Robert Steptow, were two free colored Baptist ministers who received aid from White congregations in establishing churches for the colored population. Goldbury and Steptow were primarily concerned with missionary work among the Negro population of the port city.[76]

The practice of Voodooism, which emphasizes ritual

72. William Cathcart (ed.), *The Baptist Encyclopaedia*, I, 615.
73. *Ibid.*, 595.
74. Hicks, *History of Louisiana Negro Baptists*, 179.
75. Paxton, *History of the Baptists of Louisiana*, 361.
76. *Ibid.*, 24, 26.

and secrecy, had widespread appeal to Louisiana's free Negro population and even for some White devotees. Its informal structure allowed limitless opportunities for Voodoo leaders to acquire handsome profits and followers and at the same time to enjoy high social prestige in the colored communities. This cult was doubtlessly practiced from the beginning of the colonial period, but it was given greater impetus with the coming of both slave and free Negroes from the West Indian islands.[77]

Voodoo attracted a surprising number of Whites, and both the press and pulpit focused much attention on the activities of high priestesses when such persons were apprehended by the police. For instance on July 15, 1850, a city newspaper reported a raid on one ceremony in which slaves were present. During the trial a free colored priestess named Betsy Toledano claimed the right to hold Voodoo services on the grounds of the constitutional guarantee of freedom of religion.

In outlining Voodoo's origin Betsy pointed out that it was of African origin and that her version of the religion had been passed on to her by her grandmother. She continued to explain certain objects used in a ceremony. Concerning a necklace she wore was said to be able to cause rain; a bag of flint and sand pebbles were safeguards against lightning. Other objects were explained as powerful enough to prevent certain diseases or bring about the love of one person for another. Although this priestess's right of religious practice was not denied, her right to permit slaves to attend was a violation of the law, and she was fined.[78]

Newspaper columns on Voodoo ceremonies suggested

77. Grace King, *New Orleans, the Place and the People,* 241.
78. New Orleans *Daily Delta,* July 31, 1850.

that the African religion also had White followers. In 1850, police broke up a meeting of Whites and Negroes engaged in Voodoo worship at the house of a free colored priest named Fostin. Some of the women were found entirely or nearly nude; all were dancing around an idol in the center of the room. Among those White women present were married persons and others who belonged to prominent families of the city.[79]

Free Negroes of Louisiana were given a wide latitude by state authorities when it came to religious beliefs. The only time both White individuals and authorities voiced any concern was when religious services contained slaves and such meetings were not supervised by so-called responsible White persons. The master race often registered fear that free persons of color might use religion as a ruse to cause slaves to become discontented with their lot. As a result certain alarmed White citizens called the public's attention to the dangers of mixed assemblies through the use of letters to newspaper editors. Under the signature of "A Citizen," one complainant sent a letter to the Baton Rouge press in 1833 stating that a free colored preacher was exercising "a very hurtful influence over the weak-minded slaves of the town." The letter writer pointed out that he for one had felt the influence of the Negro preacher "in the mental alienation of a valuable slave." For this reason he thought it wise to expose the "mischief to the proper authorities and warn my fellow citizens against the continuance of such evil practices."[80]

The White citizens of Opelousas were less apprehensive about assemblies of Negroes for religious purposes. In 1841, the press there considered the matter in a more

---

79. New Orleans *True Delta*, June 29, 1850.
80. Baton Rouge *Gazette*, September 28, 1832.

satirical vein when it reported only "bountiful outpouring of ardent spirits" at one such meeting.[81] In New Orleans, on the other hand, free Negroes and slaves were often arrested for conducting informal religious meetings. For example, in 1846 a group of twelve free Negroes and slaves were arrested for holding religious services in a building just beyond the city limits. In commending the authorities for doing their duty, the press stated that there were already enough legal places of worship open to Negro people.[82]

Up to 1850, free Negroes had no religious restrictions placed on them by the Legislature. In that year they were prohibited from forming any corporation for either religious purposes or secret associations such as lodges and clubs.[83] Furthermore, the measure declared null and void all previous associations which had been organized with legislative approval. In 1858, the City Council of New Orleans sanctioned an ordinance that made it mandatory for all free Negro churches to be under the supervision of White churches. However, these two regulations were contested before the Supreme Court of the state in 1860 by a group of free colored persons, who had incorporated three African Methodist Episcopal churches under the corporation laws of Louisiana before the passage of the 1850 statute. The high court in sustaining both laws declared that since "the African race are strangers to our Constitution, they are the subject of special exceptional legislation" and therefore the two regulations in litigation were "within the police administration" of both state and

---

81. Opelousas *Enquirer*, quoted in Baton Rouge *Gazette*, August 21, 1841.
82. New Orleans *Daily Delta*, June 12, 1846.
83. *Laws of Louisiana* (1850), 3rd Leg., 1st Sess., 179.

city governments.[84] Unquestionably the previously liberal Court began following the opinions of the majority of Whites and even showed hostility regarding religious freedom to free Negroes.

Education played a large role in the social life of free Negroes, but at no time were they permitted to enroll in White schools of the state. However, Negroes devised various methods to supply educational opportunities for their children. For example, the apprenticeship system was sometimes used by parents as a functional method of education. In addition to teaching a trade this system sometimes included a modicum of training in the fundamentals of reading and writing. A case in point was an agreement made by a free Negress named Millie Heating in apprenticing her son to a White merchant of Baton Rouge. According to the terms of the contract, executed in 1811, Will Clark in exchange for services "as he saw fit for five years" agreed to supply the colored woman's son with the necessities of life and "to learn him to read and write."[85]

The most important school providing practical educational advantages for indigent colored children was the New Orleans *Institution Catholique des Orphelins Indigents*. Familiarly known as the Couvent school, it was founded in 1847 with funds provided in the will of a free colored woman named Madame Bernard Couvent for the purpose of educating poor free Negroes. It was under the supervision of a free colored men's association, which was empowered to regulate the discipline, education, health and religious instruction of the students. When the pupils

---

84. *African M.E. Church v. New Orleans,* 15 La. An. 442 (June 1860).
85. *Archives of the Spanish Government of West Florida, 1783–1812,* XIX, 370.

reached a certain age, they were apprenticed to "learn a useful trade."[86] This eleemosynary institution was aided by Aristide Mary, a wealthy free man of color, who bequeathed the sum of $5000 for its support. Thomy Lafon, another well-to-do free Negro of New Orleans, made sizeable donations for the maintenance of this colored institution. Even the state of Louisiana made appropriations for its upkeep. In 1854, for example, $2000 from public funds were earmarked for the support of Couvent school. The Joint Committee on Charitable Institutions of the General Assembly recommended this amount "after a careful scrutiny of the establishment" satisfied them that "it was conducted in a proper manner."[87]

Education facilities for wealthy free colored persons were offered in parochial and private schools established for the exclusive use of elite children. In St. Landry Parish, many of the colored planters sent their children to the Grimble Bell school for free Negroes at Washington, Louisiana. This institution offered instruction on the primary and secondary levels, and it usually enrolled about 125 students. The teaching staff consisted of four instructors who used the Lancastrian method of teaching. Students attending the school were, as a rule, charged $15 a month for board and tuition. The subjects taught were common to most academies of the nineteenth century, which included reading, writing, arithmetic, history, geography, bookkeeping, English, French and Latin. This institution continued its work for a number of years but was forced to close in the late 1850s because of the grow-

---

86. Alice Durbar-Nelson, "People of Color in Louisiana," *The Journal of Negro History*, II (1917), 66.

87. *Journal of the House of Representatives* (1854), 2nd Leg., 1st Sess., 108.

ing hostility towards free Negroes in St. Landry Parish. After the Grimble Bell school closed, many of the students were sent to private institutions in New Orleans.[88]

In Pointe Coupee Parish, many colored planters employed private tutors to educate their children. Classes were often conducted in special buildings constructed on the plantation; in other cases tutors instructed their charges in the homes of their employers. For more than fifty years such educational facilities were maintained in this manner.[89]

The education of free Negroes in Natchitoches Parish was fostered by the Catholic church and it included, in addition to religious instruction, training in the rudiments of learning. A four-room schoolhouse was built on Cane River. One room served as a chapel where the priest from Cloutierville said mass once or twice a month and instructed the colored children in religion. The rest of the structure was occupied by two Sisters of the Cross who taught catechism and the three R's to girls. The boys were taught by the visiting priest. Instruction was always given in French and for the most part never exceeded the primary level.[90]

In New Orleans the Ursuline nuns operated a school for colored children from 1831 to 1838 in a building on the grounds of St. Augustine Church. However, the Ursulines turned the operation of this school to the Carmelite nuns in 1838 because they were financially unable to care for both their White and colored students. Soon after taking

---

88. Nathan Willey, "Education of the Colored Population of Louisiana," *Harper's New Monthly Magazine*, XXXIII (1866), 248.

89. *Ibid.*, 249.

90. Baumgartner, "Isle Breville," quoted in Stahl, "The Free Negro in Ante-Bellum Louisiana," *Louisiana Historical Quarterly*, XXV (1942), 360.

over St. Augustine school, the Carmelites added a school for Whites, yet they did not abandon the Negro children and continued teaching them in a separate part of the school building.[91] Many of the colored students were from the wealthy families and paid a high price for their education.[92]

Besides parochial schools, there were private institutions set up in New Orleans that catered to free colored students. As early as 1813, a G. Dorfeuilles operated a school for the children of "the prudent colored people" of the Crescent City as well as for those from throughout Louisiana. When the school opened it had twenty students.[93] The prevailing philosophy and curriculum of at least one such school can be seen in the following advertisement announcing the opening of an Academy for free colored students in 1844:

> School for young people of color. The families of color often complain of not having schools where their sons may be raised in the principles of religion. We are pleased to be able to let them know that a school where they will be able, with instruction, to obtain for their children the knowledge of religious principles. It is the establishment of M. Peter . . . a man remarkably talented and trained to teach. He knows how to inspire in children love of work and study and [he] applies desireable principles of religion and morals. Branches taught are reading, writing, arithmetic, history, geography, accountings, English, French, Greek and Latin.[94]

91. Roger Baudier, *History of the Catholic Church in Louisiana*, 364–365.
92. B. M. Norman, *Norman's New Orleans and Environs*, 105.
93. Betty Porter, "The History of Negro Education in Louisiana," *Louisiana Historical Quarterly*, XXV (1942), 735.
94. New Orleans *Le Propagateur Catholique*, Mai 4, 1844.

That free Negroes enjoyed especially good educational opportunities is best illustrated in the 1850 census figures. In that year attendance records showed that 1008 free colored students were enrolled in New Orleans educational institutions. In the country parishes, 211 were listed as attending schools.[95] It is quite conceivable, however, that among those listed as attending New Orleans schools were the children of the well-to-do colored families of the country parishes.

Free Negroes of Louisiana were sometimes aided by White persons in acquiring an education. In 1803, for example, a certain William Marshall of Baton Rouge, after bequeathing freedom to his slave, Peggy, and her daughter, Isabella, stipulated the following in his will:

> I bequeath to Isabella $1,000 to be put out at interest . . . to defray the expenses of her education and maintenance. . . . It is my Will and desire that she shall be taught to Read and Write, Arithmetic and to sew. . . . Whereas my negro woman Peggy is now pregnant, if the child shall prove to be a Mulatto, I give it its freedom immediately after my decease, [and] I also bequeath to said Child $1,000 to be put out at interest . . . until it becomes of age. . . . It is my Will . . . that it shall be taught to read and Write, Arithmetic, and to sew if a female, and if a male to be taught a mechanical trade.[96]

The solicitous White man also left his colored family cattle and lands, but to insure legality for such bequests, the largest portion of his estate went to his brother and sister of Georgia.

---

95. *Seventh Census of the United States, 1850,* 479.
96. *Archives of the Spanish Government of West Florida, 1783–1812,* VIII, 409.

Some free Negroes were educated in Northern institutions and such persons were usually furnished the necessary financial assistance and influence of White friends. One such arrangement, for instance, was made for the son of Andrew Durnford, the free colored planter and intimate friend of John McDonogh. As the godfather of Thomas Durnford, McDonogh took such an interest in young Durnford that he made arrangements to send him to Lafayette College in Easton, Pennsylvania.[97]

A considerable number of wealthy free colored children obtained expensive educations in France or other European nations. In fact, it has been estimated that about 2000 were educated in Paris alone.[98] Although most of these were males a few girls went abroad for the sole purpose of matriculating in European schools. Prominent among the males educated at Paris were Camille Thierry, Pierre Dalcour and M. B. Valcour.[99] Valcour, as an example, had received a liberal arts education in Paris where he won a reputation as an especially diligent Latin and Greek scholar. It was said that he was knowledgable in the works of Horace and Virgil and when receiving a collection of poems from his Paris instructor wrote a verse in his mentor's honor entitled *Epitre a Constant Lepouze.*[100]

There were others who received French educations. In 1857, a New Orleans group of free colored people raised the necessary funds to send the colored musician, Ed-

97. James T. Edwards (ed.), *Some Interesting Papers of John McDonogh, Chiefly Concerning the Louisiana Purchase and the Liberian Colonization,* 53.

98. Willey, "Education of the Colored Population of Louisiana," *Harper's New Monthly Magazine,* XXXIII (1866), 246–247.

99. Desdunes, *Nos Hommes et Nôtre Histoire,* 44.

100. *Ibid.,* 55.

mond Dede, to France for a musical education. These funds made possible his entry into the Paris Conservatory of Music where he studied string instruments. Following his graduation Dede accepted the post of conductor of L'Alcazar Orchestra in Bordeau.[101]

Free Negro women had approximately the same educational opportunities as that of their White sisters. It was not considered important that young ladies of either race should be trained beyond the bare fundamentals. Such was the spirit of the 19th century and women were shamelessly neglected in both private and public schools of Louisiana. Yet there were a few free Negro women who broke through the prejudices and received some training abroad. Leading the list of those educated in France was Louisa Lamotte, who later became the principal of a school for young women in Abbeville, France. This free Negress also taught in several Paris schools. Prior to her death in 1907 she was honored with the Academic Palm by the prestigious French Academy.[102]

The various activities of free persons of color included much more than the mundane feats of making a living, getting an education and practicing a particular religion. There were many hours devoted to recreation and enjoying the companionship of their friends and relatives. Among the leading forms of entertainment was dancing. Free Negroes of every rank found much pleasure in all kinds of balls, which were given for and by the free Negroes. Among the most common were the public balls for free colored women and White men of New Orleans. Aside from concluding concubinage agreements at these

---

101. Charles B. Roussève, *The Negro in Louisiana,* 52.
102. Desdunes, *Nos Hommes et Nôtre Histoire,* 137.

dances, many Whites frequented them merely to dance. Certain nights of the week were set aside by the managers of public dance halls for Negro balls.[103]

Tourists were always introduced to these entertainments as they were considered not only curious spectacles, but amusements par excellence in the Crescent City. Edward Sullivan was one visitor who vividly described his gay experiences at one of these dances. This author wrote of the graceful dancing of the women: "They danced one figure, somewhat resembling the Spanish fandango, without castanets, and I never saw more perfect dancing. . . ." Sullivan went on to describe the etiquette required of all patrons: "At the entrance you pay one-half dollar [and] you are required to leave your implements, by which is meant your bowie-knives and revolvers; and you leave them as you would your overcoat on going into the opera."[104]

Another contemporary noticed that the clientele at one colored ball he attended was made up "of some men past middle age (fathers and grandfathers) but the majority were young men that seemed to be either French or Spanish." He also called attention to the fact that colored women danced the waltz slower than "Northern Belles" and presumably prolonged the pleasure since it "took longer to get around the room."[105]

Other visitors were equally impressed by free Negro

103. See, for example, New Orleans *Daily Picayune,* May 24, 1849. Advertisement in this issue indicated that quadroon balls were held at the Louisiana Ball Room on Thursday, Friday and Saturday nights; while those for White couples only were held on Wednesday and Saturday nights.

104. Edward Sullivan, *Rambles and Scrambles in North and South America,* 223–224.

105. John E. Semmes (ed.), *John H. B. Latrobe and His Times, 1803–1891,* 315.

balls. In 1857, a young law student at the University of Louisiana named Thomas Ellis wrote his parents: "We had a negro ball here Saturday Night, and of all the times I ever saw, that was one to be remembered." As if to convince his parents of the seriousness of his purpose in New Orleans, the letter writer added the following postscript: "I wish my times was out and I had my sheepskin and was at home."[106]

Colored balls became so popular that one member of the Legislature charged his colleagues with neglecting their duties to attend such affairs. According to his argument, as long as the Legislature continued to meet in New Orleans, the people of Louisiana would have to pay four times more than necessary for legislation because "the committees after adjournment, instead of applying themselves to the preparation of reports . . . go sauntering about the city . . . visiting quateroon balls . . . or to places which shall be nameless."[107]

There were also objections based on moral grounds. The editor of the *Semi-Weekly Creole* condemned such places as "breeding grounds for crime where youth of all ages are corrupted by association with women of color." He called on the authorities to do something about this "lamentable state of affairs."[108] Other newspapers of the city echoed similar sentiments and singled out those dances which were frequented by slaves and White persons of unsavory reputation as especially detrimental to public safety.[109] Yet, if such places obeyed regulations

---

106. Thomas C. W. Ellis to E. John Ellis, January 27, 1857, Ellis Papers.

107. Baton Rouge *Gazette*, March 19, 1831.

108. May 3, 1851.

109. See, New Orleans *Daily Picayune*, September 16, 1851, April 27, 1852.

and paid required license fees together with prohibiting attendance by slaves, the authorities left them alone.[110]

Another kind of dance was that given in the homes of well-to-do free Negro families. One such affair staged in 1857 by a New Orleans colored family illustrated that unpleasantness could happen as it often did at White home-dances. According to the account of this gala affair, Emma Hoggatt tells of one male reveler, who was either hacked at something or intoxicated; he suddenly left his partner and in leaving almost knocked her to the floor. In the best deportment of Southern belles of the day Miss Hoggatt turned toward the churlish guest saying "I am astonished at you," and later told a kinswoman who was his date for the evening, that she could not "excuse him" for such conduct. A family quarrel followed and Emma Hoggatt became so angry that she left home and rented a room from one of her colored friends in another part of New Orleans.[111]

Still another contemporary found dances of this nature riotous affairs frequented by bandits and White men of questionable reputation. Alexandre Barde, in his account of a family dance given by the free Negro Coco at his Prairie Marronne home, wrote that "on hearing the violins one would die of apoplexy." "The Dancers," continued the critical Barde, "all cried and screech like witches. Barde also wrote that Coco was seated between his "white wives" presiding over the fete with the gravity of "an emperor of India occasionally shouting aloud 'Amuse yourselves children!'" This writer was so irritated at such

110. Fees ranging from $5.00 to $25.00 were required for public free colored balls. See Donatien Augustin (ed.), *A General Digest of the Ordinances and Resolutions of the Corporation of New Orleans*, 373, 375.

111. MS. Emma Hoggatt to Mrs. William Johnson, May 16, 1857, Johnson Papers.

proceedings that he compared it to the Court of Miracles in Victor Hugo's novel *The Hunchback of Notre Dame*.[112]

Free Negroes enjoyed playgoing. They were allowed to attend the various theatres of New Orleans and in other places of the state where special sections of the buildings were reserved for the exclusive use of free colored persons and slaves. Special boxes were set aside for the use of wealthy colored families in the larger theatres of the city of New Orleans.[113]

Two free persons of color enjoyed widespread popularity as performers and composers in ante-bellum Louisiana. Although they never gave public performances on the stage, they nevertheless were received in the homes of White citizens. One of them, Victor Eugene Macarty, flourished about 1854 and was considered extremely gifted as a pianist, and in constant demand as a purveyor of music of all kinds of social gatherings of White persons. Another Negro composer was Basile J. Bares who apparently flourished in popularity about 1856. His *Valse des Carnival* was published in New Orleans and received favorable public notice in the press. This musician also wrote several popular dance numbers and was considered quite an elegant performer on the piano. He was educated in Paris and continued to play and compose for several years after the Civil War.[114]

Overwhelming evidence points to the fact that the most popular form of amusement was gambling in all of its

---

112. Barde, *Histoire des Comités Vigilance aux Attakapas*, 227–228.

113. See, for example, the advertisement of the St. Charles Theatre in which the second and third tiers were reserved for the use of free colored persons and slaves respectively. New Orleans *Daily Picayune*, October 22, 1857.

114. John S. Kendall, "New Orleans Musicians of Long Ago," *Louisiana Historical Quarterly*, XXI (1948), 135.

varied forms. It was especially common in New Orleans, and despite laws prohibiting it, Whites, free Negroes and slaves quite often gambled together whenever the opportunity presented itself. Newspapers carried scores of accounts describing raids and arrests for violations of gambling laws. For example, on May 23, 1859, seven slaves and a free man of color were arrested for playing "picayune chuck-a-luck to the tune of root hog or die" in a house on Religious street. "The culprits," wrote the reporting journalists, "will have to take a chance at 'high die' with the Recorder today."[115]

White citizens were often caught gaming with Negroes, and in some cases they operated gambling dens for the convenience of such persons. In an editorial entitled "Negro Gambling Dens" the *Picayune* pointed out that certain "unprincipled white men" were operating gambling places where free Negroes and slaves gathered for the express purpose of betting the proceeds of stolen property. The editor called the public's attention to the fact that such conduct "corrupted the servile population and it was high time that the authorities put a stop to this nuisance."[116]

Social intercourse between free persons of color and slaves was ever regarded as a threat to the established social order. The anti-free-Negro forces never seemed to tire of repeating the timeworn phrase that such association was "fraught with serious mischief." The *Bee* editorialized in 1853 that any assemblies in which slaves and free Negroes were present resulted in the former being "taught to despise the commands of their legitimate pro-

---

115. New Orleans *Daily Crescent,* May 23, 1859.
116. August 1, 1857.

tectors, the white man, and they [therefore] become insolent to the highest degree, and a nuisance in every well
regulated family."[117]

In the last decades of the ante-bellum period the press
devoted much space to reports of the gathering of slaves
and free Negroes. There was almost mass paranoia as the
articles and letters to the press reflected fears of insurrection and civil war between the races. For example, in
1846, three free Negroes and 36 slaves were arrested for
celebrating New Year's Eve in contravention of existing
law. Each reveler was fined $50 and these fines were ear-
marked for the White public school library fund.[118] "A
large haul of darkies" was made in 1856 while attending
"a colored ladies fair" which was being staged for the
charitable fund of the colored Methodist church. Some 43
slaves and free Negroes were arrested for not having
passes or free papers. According to the article, there was
"a rapid stampede of the nice young men and aged" men
when the police burst upon the scene.[119]

It occasionally happened—and probably more often than
the records show—that free Negroes gave aid to runaway
slaves. There was considerable risk in this practice, and
as the abolitionists increased their fulminations so did the
risk; consequently, few were willing to gamble their
lives in behalf of their brothers in bondage. In fact, free
Negroes were not always kind toward the slave population or their own for that matter. Actually they had the
reputation of being more cruel than White slaveowners.[120]

---

117. December 16, 1853.
118. New Orleans *Daily Delta*, January 3, 1846.
119. New Orleans *Bee*, April 7, 1856.
120. Calvin D. Wilson, "Black Masters, a Side-light on Slavery,"
The North American Review, CLCCI (1905), 685–686.

In 1845, for example, John Edwington, a free man of color, was placed on trial for beating his slave Rachel "in a savage manner." According to the newspaper account, had it not been for the intervention of his White neighbor, Edwington would have killed the slave in question.[121] A free colored woman named Kate Parker was arrested in 1857 for "nearly beating her slave to death with a cowhide."[122] In another account of this incident, it was revealed that the free Negress had only recently been freed from slavery by a sugar planter, who had given her the slave in question at the time of the emancipation.[123]

At least one slave belonging to a free person of color became a fugitive to escape cruel treatment at the hands of his master. The fugitive was found aboard the steamer *Dewitt Clinton* in Ascension Parish and was described as having "lash marks on the breast and iron rings on both legs." When captured, this slave told the authorities that he belonged to Nelson Fauché, a free man of color living in New Orleans. He also expressed the desire "to remain where he was."[124]

The ubiquitous Olmsted records the views of one slave in regard to free colored masters. According to this slave "dey is very bad masters, sar, I'd rather be a servant to any man in de world, dan to a brack man." He went on to say that, "If I was sold to a brack man, I'd drown myself. I would dat—I'd drown myself; dough I shouldn't like to do that nudder; but I wouldn't be sold to a colored master for anything."[125]

---

121. New Orleans *Daily Delta*, November 26, 1845.
122. New Orleans *Daily Picayune*, October 15, 1857.
123. New Orleans *Daily Crescent*, October 2, 1837.
124. Donaldsonville (La.) *Le Vigilant*, February 7, 1849.
125. Olmsted, *The Cotton Kingdom,* I, 336–337.

On the other hand, social relationships between well-to-do colored planters and White planters were usually cordial. When coming into contact with each other for business or other purposes both parties exhibited the amenities characteristic of the 19th century. The historian Gayarré has testified to the mutual respect won by at least two free Negro planters. Once, riding on a steamboat, a White planter struck up a conversation with a cultured Mulatto grower. When dinnertime arrived, a solitary table was set aside for the latter. Moved by the colored man's quiet acceptance, the White man went to him with a friend: "We desire you to dine with us." The free colored man expressed his appreciation for their hospitality, but declined as his presence at their table, even though acceptable to them, might displease the other passengers.[126]

The same historian recounts another incident in which a White planter while traveling in the country found it necessary to stop and rest at the plantation of a free Negro acquaintance. What followed merits full consideration:

The white Creole said 'I come to tax your hospitality.' 'Never shall a tax be paid mor willingly' was the prompt reply. 'I hope I am not too late for dinner.' 'For you sir, it is never too late at my house for anything you may desire.' A command was given; cook and butler made their preparations and dinner was announced. The guest noticed but one seat and one plate at the table. He exclaimed: 'What am I to dine alone?' 'I regret sir that I cannot join you, but have already dined.' My friend answered his guest with a good natured smile on his lips, 'Permit me on this occasion

---

126. Charles E. Gayarré, The Quadroons of Louisiana, Gayarré Papers.

to doubt your word, and to assure you that I shall order my carriage immediately and leave, without touching a mouthful of this apertising menu, unless you share it with me.' The host was too much of a Chesterfield not to dine a second time, if courtesy or a guest required it.[127]

Just as the Whites, Louisiana free Negroes created organizations of both social and benevolent objectives and derived much benefit from both types. Negro benevolent secret clubs greatly resembled the Masonic and other orders current among Whites. One of the first to come into existence was the Colored Female Benevolent Society of Louisiana, founded in 1846 at New Orleans. The aim of these ladies was the "suppression of vice and inculcation of virtue among the colored class—to relieve the sick and bury the dead—to alleviate the distress of the Widows" and help the orphans of the state's free persons of color.[128]

Louisiana legislation and the force of custom specifically relegated the free Negroes within its borders to an inferior social status and were based primarily upon the idea that such persons were never and could never be equal to White persons just because of their Negro ancestry. Thus excluded from any outward social intercourse with the "master race" free Negroes formed a society of their own. This structure bore many similarities to the White social pyramid. It was a graded society with the top possessing the greatest amount of visible White blood and the bottom almost always blacker in color. Colored aristocrats dressed, thought, and in many ways acted as haughty as

---

127. *Ibid.*
128. W. H. Rainey (comp.), *Mygatt and Company* (New Orleans city) *Directory for 1857*, 28.

their White counterparts towards the "lowly," but they could never hope to cross the color line and become peers of the White ruling class. However, neither the Negro aristocrats nor their White counterparts formed the majority element in Louisiana.

The most significant and edifying aspect of free Negro social life was in the areas of religion and education. Here, opportunity for self-expression, leadership, self-improvement and satisfaction of private equality with Whites was possible. This was, moreover, the only way in which equality became a reality. In spite of the great handicaps imposed upon free colored people the vast majority preferred their Louisiana homes and rejected the prospect of living either abroad or in the North. Indeed free Negroes had become so Americanized—or better Louisianized—that they accommodated themselves to the status imposed on them by Whites, and no amount of intimidation would force them into a mass exodus.

7

An Undesirable Population

THE presence of free Negroes of the mildest disposition irritated most Louisiana Whites. Their very existence was even more irritating to slaveowners whose fears grew into unrequited hatred as the decade preceding the Civil War witnessed an ever-growing intensification of the Anti-slavery crusade. The wildest kind of rumors involving free Negroes were accounted as truth, and no amount of evidence that such were only old wives tales seem to have quieted or allayed the suspicions of that section of the White population bent on extermination of the free colored people. Such hostility came early in the history of Louisiana, when schemes came into being to colonize the "undesirable population" in other parts of the world. For a time colonization gripped White policymakers as the surest means of ridding the state of Negroes not classified as slaves. These projects waxed hot and cold, and towards the end of the era White extremists resorted to violence and intimidation as "the only way" of ridding the state of free persons of color. Like other methods this too failed, as the state's citizens turned to more pressing

285

problems—that of blending into the Confederate States and surviving during the Civil War.

The Colonization of free Negroes first began as the product of private enterprise. Among the first of such schemes was the one offered by a retired Mexican officer named Nicholas Drouette. In 1834 this enterprising free Mulatto conceived the idea of settling 500 free colored residents of New Orleans on lands in the Mexican province of Texas. After several meetings with Texas authorities the project was rejected because the prospective colonists were artisans and deemed unsuitable for agricultural work. In a letter to the Mexican Foreign Minister, Texas Governor Almonte also pointed out that White Texans harbored a deep antipathy towards free Negroes and that any addition of that population would therefore not be a wise move.[1]

Yet, for the most part Mexican government officials encouraged those free Negroes possessing agricultural skills. In fact such immigration received a high priority and authorities offered land and tools together with full rights of citizenship as inducements for free Negroes to come into Mexican territory. Although existing records do not indicate the numbers who availed themselves of this privilege at least one Louisiana free Negro, Filip Elua, settled on lands near San Antonio. Here he prospered selling sugar cane, cotton and sweet potatoes.[2] Elua was representative of a small and daring number of colored migrants going into Texas. The outbreak of revolution, and

---

1. Harold Schoen, "The Free Negro in the Republic of Texas," *The Southwestern Historical Quarterly*, XXXIX (1937), 305.

2. Benjamin Lundy, *The Life, Travels and Opinions of Benjamin Lundy, Including His Journeys to Texas and Mexico; with a Sketch of Contemporary Events, and a Notice of the Revolution in Hayti*, 54–55, quoted in *ibid.*, 298.

subsequent hostility towards the free Negro class by the Texas Republic, prevented any widespread movement of these people from Louisiana.[3]

Another individual colonizing enterprise was undertaken by a Presbyterian minister named William King, who had manumitted his slaves in Louisiana and moved them to a colony, under his supervision, near Buxton, Canada. Here King taught them agricultural and mechanical trades in addition to providing for their spiritual welfare. When the colony was visited by two members of the British Parliament in 1858, King's experiment was considered by this delegation to be "highly successful."[4]

Because of high costs, individual efforts for removing a large body of Louisiana's free persons of color were insignificant in effecting its purpose. The great expense involved in transporting large numbers of emigrants required a capital outlay greatly in excess of that possessed by individual enterprise. Moreover, a favorable public opinion was necessary, along with a campaign to induce free Negroes themselves to emigrate out of the state. Quite understandably, Louisianians then turned to the American Colonization Society, which had been founded in 1817, to solve the problem of transporting free Negroes from the United States to Africa.

It was fortuitous that the Reverend Robert S. Finley organized a branch of the national society in New Orleans on December 18, 1831. The name taken was the Louisiana State Colonization Society.[5] At the January 16, 1832, assembly, Alexander Porter, a wealthy St. Mary Parish

3. *Cf. supra*, 97.
4. "Colored Settlement in Canada," *The African Repository and Colonial Journal*, XXXIV (1858), 30.
5. "State Society of Louisiana," *ibid.*, VIII (1832), 59.

Planter, was elected president of the state organization. Equally prominent officers included General E. W. Ripley of West Feliciana, Benjamin Winchester of St. James, Henry A. Bullard of Rapides, Colonel Daniel Edmunds of St. Landry, W. H. Ireland and Judge James Workman of New Orleans.[6] Members of the society held high hopes for a successful future, as can be seen in the following remarks made at the first meeting:

> We have now the names of Mr. Dominique Bouligny (late U. S. Senator) . . . and the Secretary of State Thomas F. McCaleb. In addition there are twelve members of the Senate and twenty-five members of the House of Representatives, all amounting to nearly one hundred (members). We have had considerable number of copies of the constitution in French and English printed. With regard to money, we have considered that as a secondary consideration here at present, it will follow in good time.[7]

The society immediately began an intensive propaganda campaign to attract members and the support of auxiliary organizations throughout Louisiana. By 1838 a Young Men's Colonization Society had come into being in New Orleans. In speaking to this group Robert S. Finley proclaimed that the main aims of the organization were to help the parent society in "carrying civilization and the light of Christian religion into a land hitherto in utter darkness. . . ." Finley stoutly maintained that sending free Negroes to Liberia would have the added advantage of opening "to the civilized world, the resources of a country

6. *Ibid.*
7. *Ibid.*, 62.

rich in every product of nature."[8] Women, too, came forward in 1839 to form auxiliaries and encouragement pledging "to aid the cause of colonization, education and Christianity in Africa."[9] As an additional means by which to attract supporters, the Louisiana organization adopted a plan in 1843 to supply the official magazine, *The African Repository*, free of charge to all ministers, editors, legislators and judges of the state.[10]

In promoting more local support for the movement, the state organization purchased a tract of land in Liberia for the exclusive use of Louisiana's free colored population. It cost $4000 in 1836 and was formally dubbed "Louisiana in Liberia."[11] The next year the state society allocated $20,000 a year for the support of this colony.[12] The project caused trouble with the national organization and in 1840 Louisiana and Mississippi jointly left the American Colonization Society. Yet within two years Louisiana returned to the parent organization and was given the special privilege of spending its funds for the support of the Liberian colony.[13]

While the movement for deportation of free Negroes received a more or less sympathetic reception in the Crescent City, a less than enthusiastic viewpoint characterized the sentiment in the rural parishes. When Robert S. Finley

---

8. "Meeting of Young Men's Colonization Society in First Presbyterian Church," *ibid.*, XIV (1938), 94.

9. "Letter from Secretary of Louisiana Colonization Society (Robert R. Gurley)," June 22, 1839, *ibid.*, XV (1939), 195–196.

10. "Louisiana Colonization Society," *ibid.*, XIX (1843), 161.

11. "Mr. R. R. Gurley's Report to Board of Managers of American Colonization Society," *ibid.*, XII (1836), 332.

12. "Letter from Mr. R. S. Finley dated Natchez, February 22, 1837," *ibid.*, XIII (1837).

13. "Louisiana State Colonization Society," *ibid.*, XIII (1842), 50.

tried to organize in Baton Rouge in 1840, he was arrested for speaking "as to excite insubordination among the slaves."[14] At a court hearing the suspect tried to explain that such a society was to send only free Negroes to Africa and was in no way associated with any Northern abolitionist organizations. Several witnesses spoke in his behalf, pointing out that Dr. Finley represented "a worthy cause."[15]

Although Finley was declared innocent he never succeeded in forming an auxiliary colonization association in Baton Rouge or in any other place in rural Louisiana. The Society was regarded by the mass of Whites with either apathy or as one that was tainted with abolitionism.[16] For example, in 1849 the national society found it necessary to circulate a letter in Louisiana disclaiming any connection whatsoever with abolitionists and went on to explain that: "Our concern is entirely with the free blacks, and with that portion of them chiefly who are or who may become useful colonists."[17]

Despite suspiciousness and outright hostility, contributions for the support of the Liberian colonization scheme came primarily from ministers, editors and a few interested planters scattered over the state. In 1852, for example, funds collected in the country parishes—including subscriptions for *The African Repository*, church donations and individual offerings—amounted to $1631.[18] The

14. Baton Rouge *Gazette*, November 14, 21, 1840.

15. *Ibid.*, December 19, 1840.

16. "Annual Report of the American Colonization Society," *The African Repository and Colonial Journal*, XII (1846), 39.

17. "Circular to the Friends of African Colonization in the State of Louisiana," *ibid.*, XXV (1849), 4–5.

18. "Louisiana Colonization Society," *ibid.*, XXVIII (1852), 160.

monetary contributions from interested persons in St. Mary Parish alone totalled $362.25 in 1855.[19]

It occasionally happened that a few wealthy citizens made sizeable donations in lands and cash. For example, in 1836, a Carroll Parish planter named Hasten M. Childers bequeather about $30,000 to the American Colonization Society.[20] After liberating all his slaves on condition that they emigrate to Liberia, a New Orleans citizen named W. H. Ireland left the Society a sum of money amounting to $18,500.[21] Another city resident, Maunsel White, donated "a valuable lot in the city . . . worth $250" to the Colonization Society.[22]

In an elaborate scheme for raising funds, the national organization, at the suggestion of Gerrit Smith, devised a plan to award life membership to all those pledging $100 a year for ten years. Among the earliest subscribers to the so-called Smith plan was the Louisiana millionaire John McDonogh, who became an ardent supporter of colonization. He often made donations, such as the one in 1840 in which he gave $50 worth of books for the high school library in Liberia.[23]

This stingy scotsman also devised a complex system of manumitting his own slaves in order to send them to Liberia. The slaves were to purchase their own freedom with money earned on Saturday afternoons. Males were paid 62½ cents and women 50 cent a day during the summer months. In the winter, when there was more leisure

19. *Ibid.*, XXXI (1855), 255.
20. "Providence in Carrol County, Louisiana," *ibid.*, XII (1836), 334.
21. "Mr. Ireland's Legacy to American Colonization Society," *ibid.*, XII (1836), 333.
22. "Col. M. White of New Orleans," *ibid.*, XII (1835), 202.
23. "John McDonogh," *ibid.*, XVI (1840), 168.

time, men were able to earn 50 cents a day and the women 37½ cents. When the stipulated amount fixed by Mc-Donogh had been saved, the slave paid the price of his evaluation and was granted freedom. As soon as it was practicable the freed man had to leave for Africa.[24]

The city press especially favored the idea of colonizing free Negroes out of Louisiana. The New Orleans *Delta* led all other newspapers in advocating emigration to Liberia. In 1845, when a group of free Negroes departed, the editor wrote: "Let them go where by industry, they may assume a social and political position which they can never hope to attain here."[25] Five years later, the same paper invited free Negroes to pioneer in Africa just as young White men of America were doing in the western part of the United States. It was a "Go to Africa Young Man" campaign, and it lasted for several months. By pioneering it was explained they would not only better their own lot, but at the same time contribute to "the civilizing of the Dark Continent."[26] Many editions contained pleas for funds for supporting this most "worthy of causes of sending free Negroes to Africa."[27]

Equally in sympathy with the colonization project were members of the Legislature. Most lawmakers had come to the conclusion that this was the best means of getting rid of free colored persons without resorting to doubtful legal acts of expulsion.

In 1831, a committee of the General Assembly considered a proposition to appropriate sufficient funds for the

---

24. *A Letter of John McDonogh on African Colonization: Addressed to the Editors of the New Orleans Commercial Bulletin,* n.p.
25. October 28, 1845.
26. August 31, 1850.
27. *Ibid.*

transportation of free Negroes to Africa. In an effort to win approval to spend such funds, the majority of the committee resorted to their favorite pro-slavery clichés. They proceeded to describe free persons of color as "an indolent depraved caste which laws and public opinion had placed an impossible chasm betwixt them and white persons." Even Thomas Jefferson was quoted as an advocate of removing free Negroes from the United States for the sake of public order. It was further the committee's contention that expulsion could be accomplished "cheaply . . . at $20 a head," and it strongly urged that funds be made available as soon as possible. The committee also asked that federal aid be solicited in helping Louisiana get rid of its free colored persons. In justifying federal assistance it was pointed out that the national government had given aid in removing Indians and by the same token the government should help Louisiana get rid of its free Negro population.[28]

Charles Gayarré, the chairman of the committee's minority issued a strong rebuttal insisting that free Negroes would refuse to go to Africa. In part he reported the following:

Your Committee may be persuaded that the colored people of most of our sister states . . . deserve the expression . . . [of] a degraded case of the most baneful influence in society. . . . But thank God, among the children of Louisiana there does not exist such a race of men. Your Committee cannot conceive the expectation that a colored man, born in Louisiana, will break so many ties . . . to cross the ocean and settle among men whose origins, whose language,

28. *Journal of the House of Representatives* (1831), 10th Leg., 1st Sess., 80–82.

and whose manners are so different from his own. A colored man of French origin, born in Louisiana would not voluntary go to Liberia even if it had pleased the Almighty to transform that favored spot into a paradise. Africa is a word which will always sound harsh in his ears and he will shrink from the very utterance of that hateful name. This may sound strange to the stranger but not to a long resident of Louisiana.[29]

Gayarré closed with a reminder to the lawmakers that asking federal aid was a dangerous thing since it was in opposition to the Southern view of states' rights. Actually Gayarré spoke the true sentiments held by the majority of Louisiana free Negroes and consequently foretold the doom of all colonization purposals.

The Legislature did attempt to award financial assistance to the Colonization Society. In 1852, for example, following the approval of the manumission law requiring slave owners who emancipated slaves to send them to Africa, the House of Representatives adopted a resolution urging Louisiana members in Congress to "use their best exertions to promote the success of that great enterprise."[30] The next year, a Senate bill imposed a tax on free persons of color "for the purpose of raising a fund to provide for the transportation to Liberia all those free Negroes who desire to move."[31] This measure was, however, tabled by the lower chamber of the General Assembly.[32] During the 1854 session the Senate again approved a similar bill which proposed to set up a Colonization

29. *Ibid.*, 83–84.
30. *Journal of the House of Representatives* (1852), 4th Leg., 1st Sess., 127.
31. *Journal of the Senate* (1853), 1st Leg., 1st Sess., 153.
32. *Journal of the House of Representatives* (1853), 1st Leg., 1st Sess., 231.

Board that would govern the transportation of free Negroes to Africa. The scheme would have been financed
by levying a one dollar tax on each free colored adult to
defray transportation expenses,[33] but this measure failed
also to win the approval of the House.

The Louisiana Colonization Society failed in its primary
purposes. It was unable to persuade either the federal or
state governments to give financial support, and the
contributions of members proved sufficient for such a
tremendously expensive enterprise. It also was weak-
ened by internal dissensions when it embarked on a
separate career in 1849. More important, however, the
society was never warmly supported by slaveholders and
thus contributed very little toward decreasing the large
number of free Negroes in the state. Louisiana's free Negroes themselves failed to show any great enthusiasm
for returning to Africa. In face, as Gayarré had predicted,
the majority of them unalterably opposed the scheme. In
the final analysis only a small number of free Negroes left
Louisiana for their "African fatherland." During the period
1831–1860, the state organization was able to send only
309 free colored emigrants from Louisiana.[34] More reveal-
ing is the fact that during those decades the only sizeable
contingent leaving the state were the 81 who left in 1842
and the 56 who left in 1851.[35] Then too, the majority of
these were slaves who had been recently freed by their
owners provided they emigrate to Liberia.

Besides the Liberian scheme, there were spokesmen
who touted the idea of colonizing free Negroes in Latin

---

33. *Journal of the Senate* (1854), 2nd Leg., 1st Sess., 63.
34. "Table of Emigrants," *The African Repository and Colonial
Journel*, XLIII (1867), 117.
35. *Ibid.*

America. Again Mexico came up as a possible place for settlement. To effect this end, the Legislature was urged to enlist the help of other Southern states in purchasing lands from the Mexican government. The federal government was requested to assume part of the burden of such negotiations, since states could not constitutionally make any treaties with foreign powers. The title to the land was to be fully guaranteed to colored colonists, provided they agreed to renounce their American citizenship and become Mexican citizens. In promoting the project, Mexico was depicted as especially advantageous for free Negroes; the soil and climate being adaptable "to their natures." Moreover, it was contended that within a few years amalgamation with the Mexican people would take place and thus "obliterate their origin."[36]

Although the plan never materialized, free Negroes, on their own initiative, moved from Louisiana into the southern republic. In the summer of 1857, a small party from St. Landry Parish settled on lands they had bought near Vera Cruz, on the Popolopan River. This group concentrated their efforts to the cultivation of Indian corn, and were so successful that they wrote their friends in Louisiana, describing the advantages "held out to them in Mexico." It was also pointed out that in Mexico "they were not subjected to the inequalities from caste as they were in their homes." The representations of these pioneers induced several other free Negro families of Louisiana to try their fortunes in Mexico.[37] Among this group were members of the industrious Donatto family who were reported to have carried with them "a considerable for-

36. Baton Rouge *Weekly Gazetter and Comet*, February 2, 1857.
37. Vera Cruz *Mexican Extraordinary*, July 30, 1857 quoted in *National Intelligencer*, August 20, 1857.

tune and technical equipment which promised to make the experiment a success."[38]

Whether these colonists remained in their adopted land is uncertain since their Mexican neighbors looked upon such a population with strong suspicion. *The Mexican Extraordinary* in opposing the colony pointed out that although they had "diligently and successfully cultivated maize, in view of the history of Santo Domingo and Jamaica and the nature of the African, the project augurs but poorly of the future for Mexico."[39]

The efforts at removal of free persons of color by legislative action and colonization had failed up to the 1850s, primarily because of lack of popular support. From the previous chapters it must seem obvious that the Whites and the free colored population lived in the same society without too much friction. The ever increasing tempo of the abolition crusade and the fear of free Negro and slave revolt excited the Whites into an extreme frame of mind. White citizens of Louisiana determined to rid the state of this class by intimidation and violence. In some communities they initiated a veritable reign of terror which in many ways resembled the Ku Klux Klan and other intimidating organizations. Both desirable and undesirable free Negroes were beaten or driven out of the state by night riding armed bands of White men. One of the most blatant examples of extra-legal community action occurred in the southwestern parishes of Louisiana. That region, generally called by its aboriginal name of Attakapas, embraced the parishes of St. Landry, Calcasieu, St. Martin, St. Mary, Lafayette and Vermillion. Here, where the free

---

38. Barde, *Histoire des Comités de Vigilance aux Attakapas*, 337.

39. Vera Cruz *Mexican Extraordinary*, July 30, 1857, quoted in New Orleans *Daily Picayune*, August 12, 1857.

colored element was most numerous in the rural areas, there developed the main centers of hostility towards the latter class. In a series of meetings between January 1859 and 1860, the citizens of these communities formed vigilante committees and waged a campaign to drive free Negroes out of the state.

This lawlessness was first preceded by a villification campaign against the free colored population in the local press. In 1859, for example, the Opelousas *Patriot*, the leading journal promoting violent action, wrote that rumors of the formation of vigilantes had induced many free Negroes "to quit the country and seek homes more congenial to their feelings." In an open letter to the free colored population of the Attakapas region, the editor advised the rest of this class to do likewise. He said, in urging them to take this action:

> The enjoyment of your natural rights and privileges may be found in your native country—Africa or in Hayti, or in one of the West Indies Islands. . . . You cannot live in the United States with the white man in peace, you cannot ever hope to approach anything like an equality with him, this idea on your part would be repugnant to the laws of natural reason, nature, and nature's God. We advise you to flee the society of the white man voluntarily before you are compelled to do so by his irrevocable decrees. Take a fair price for your lands and we will insure you speedy purchasers. We speak advisedly and know that your places . . . will be quickly filled by good moral and respectable white families from a neighboring state. This is the element we desire—this is the kind of population we want—all white citizens and their slaves—no free colored citizens in our midst. Then we may look for the dawn of better society,

better government and more general prosperity among us as white citizens.[40]

As the first step to bring about "the dawn of a better society" vigilante committees were organized, ostensibly, to purge the state of undesirable free Negroes as well as certain White men of questionable reputation. Under the banner of "war against vagabonds, perjurers, murderers, bandits, and arsonists" the private citizens took action.[41] Another of the aims of this group was to prevent slave insurrections and immoral conduct between White men and free colored women. These White citizens blamed the weakness of the law in allowing such disorder to take place in their communities and singled out the grand juries of the respective parishes as especially derelict in performing their duties.[42]

The vigilantes therefore adopted a kind of "criminal code," which called for banishment for first offenses against the peace of the community, whipping for the second and hanging for a third offense.[43] Free Negroes of respectable reputation were promised immunity, but they too were urged to leave for their own good as well as that of St. Landry's society. It was with a note of relief that many of the colored class had decided to leave that Attakapas region and migrate to Haiti before violent measures could be taken against them.[44] For the "idle and debauchee among the free Negroes," the vigilantes declared a war to the death.[45]

---

40. Opelousas *Patriot*, August 6, 1859.
41. Barde, *Histoire des Comités de Vigilance aux Attakapas*, 10.
42. *Ibid.*, 16.
43. *Ibid.*, 26.
44. *Ibid.*, 337–338.
45. *Ibid.*, 236.

This movement was initiated by a Major Aurellen St. Julien in Lafayette parish in the spring of 1859 under the fear of free Negro and slave revolt. Riding by night this planter and his band of vigilantes sought out recalcitrant free Negroes and White men allegedly guilty of infractions of the "criminal code." They were especially watchful for Whites living in concubinage with free colored women. On one occasion the Lafayette Parish Vigilantes whipped a White man named Auguste Gudbeer and his free Mulattress mistress, and they gave the unfortunate couple eight days to leave the parish.[46] In another night raid this committee of citizens thrashed and banished a slave named Don Louis and his free Negress wife, Marie la Polanaise, for allegedly being implicated in robberies and murders which had been recently committed in Lafayette Parish.[47] Several slaves and a free Negro named Alfred Oril were given the same treatment for stealing cattle.[48] St. Julien always preceded these punishments with a "drumhead" trial, and while the sentence was being meted out, he lectured the unfortunate victim on the error of his ways.

In Vermillionville, a committee led by ex-Governor Alfred Mouton, exiled three free colored prostitutes. At the same time "an order of exile" was signed against another woman of color for entering "in public relations with the slave of Madame P. Saumier."[49] The movement begun in Lafayette spread like "prairie fire" to other parishes of the Attakapas country. The citizens of St. Martin, St. Landry and Calcasieu parishes likewise formed

46. *Ibid.*, 59, 216.
47. *Ibid.*, 66.
48. *Ibid.*, 72–73.
49. *Ibid.*, 335–336.

vigilante committees and proceeded to intimidate free
Negroes as well as White persons in the area. In St. Martin, for example, the vigilantes raided "a bandits nest"
near the town of St. Martinville and apprehended a large
number of alleged bandits of both races. The latter were
first whipped and then banished from the parish.[50]

The climax of this movement came on September 3,
1859, when the vigilantes of Attakapas assembled at
Bayou Queue Tortue in Lafayette Parish and wiped out a
colony of White men and free Negro "criminals." Some of
the latter were killed in the battle and the remainder were
given the usual treatment of whipping and banishment
out of the state.[51] This action prompted Governor Robert
Wickliff to visit the disturbed area, and after a series of
conferences with the various vigilante chiefs, commanded
them to commit no further violence.[52] The Governor was
unable, however, to persuade them to disband and the
committees operated, although without the previous violence, until 1860. In that year as a last gesture of hostility
towards free Negroes, the St. Landry committee went on
record "to prevent as far as they can legally do so the
presence of free persons of color at all political discussions,
debates or speeches during the presidential canvass of
1860."[53]

The vigilantes were successful in their purpose to some
degree. Many free Negroes from the southwestern parishes
fled their homes and sought asylum out of the United
States. The majority of those who left went to New Orleans to await transportation to the Republic of Haiti.

50. *Ibid.*, 135.
51. *Ibid., passim,* 383–401.
52. Baton Rouge *Advocate,* quoted in *ibid.,* 407–408.
53. Opelousas *Courier,* September 8, 1860.

Among the first group to arrive in the Crescent City in 1859 were over 100 free Negroes from St. Landry Parish, comprising planters, storekeepers, merchants and farmers. A similar number also arrived from other parishes in which the committees operated.[54]

At the same time free Negroes were being victimized by intimidation, Emperor Soulouque of Haiti appointed a free man of color named P. E. Desdunes as agent to Louisiana to promote the emigration of the harrassed people to his island kingdom. Desdunes offered them not only free transportation to Haiti, but political and social equality as well. Soon after this colored agent made arrangements to send a contingent of free Negroes to Haiti, a revolution deposed Soulouque and a republic was established under the leadership of Fabre Geffrard. The latter, however, continued the policy of encouraging colored immigration from Louisiana, and in receipt of his invitation, 150 free persons of color left the port of New Orleans in May 1859, for the island republic.[55] The movement continued, and one New Orleans paper gleefully reported that 195 from St. Landry and East Baton Rouge parishes had left for Haiti in June of 1859.

The departure of the Baton Rouge group, however, was looked upon with some regret by George Pike, the editor of the *Gazette and Comet.* He blamed "blacklegs" in the state legislature with their "bar-room oratory" for initiating "uncalled-for legislation designed to intimidate the respectable native free colored population of Louisiana." The editor was referring to a bill under consideration which would enslave all free Negroes who refused to

---

54. MS. Register of Free Persons of Color Entitled to Remain in the State, Mayor's Office, New Orleans, 1859–1861.

55. Opelousas *Courier,* June 14, 1859.

leave the state after a specified date. Commenting further on the proposition, Pike accused the lawmaker of "arguing to themselves if they can frame a bill, bearing more odiously upon this class than the last bill, and make buncomb speeches of the subject . . . which their flat-headed constituents will account them as faithful watch dogs on the tower of liberty, and give them proper advancement." Pike could find no cause for alarm concerning the native colored population on the grounds that such persons "know the position they occupy in our society," and while he approved of laws restricting immigration from other states, he considered it a "mad and mistaken policy to pass oppressive and arbitrary enactment against the native colored population." Such action was pointed out as unjustified since history showed them true to Louisiana and ready "to take the front line in case of invasion and receive the first fire from her enemies."[56]

Before the end of the summer of 1859, a sizeable contingent of the Haitian emigrants returned to Louisiana. After speaking ill of the group in general, the New Orleans *Crescent* pointed out rather ironically that those who returned could never be content in any other place than Louisiana.[57]

Still, free colored persons continued to arrive in New Orleans from the Attakapas country to await transshipment to Haiti. Early in 1860, a group of 81 of them left that port aboard the *Laurel*, destined for Port-au-Prince. They were described as "cultivators well versed with agriculture." Some were brickmakers, blacksmiths, wheelwrights and carpenters. Others were described as "pro-

---

56. Baton Rouge *Daily Gazette and Comet*, April 19, 1859.
57. July 4, 1859.

ficient weavers of that stuff called Attakapas cottanade"
which was in great demand as cheap cloth for slave
clothes. One emigrant was described as being worth
$50,000, which he carried with him to Haiti. This group's
departure was deemed one of the most important ever
to leave Louisiana because of the great amount of capital
they took with them. Some concern was manifested because of the withdrawal from the state, but in the interests of the slave society and the "integrity of our institutions" the reporting newspaper wished them: "God
speed with the hope they better themselves and relieve
us from the painful task of maintaining the proper equi-
librium between them and whites, their superiors, on
one side, and the slaves, their inferiors, on the other."[58]

The intense hatred of free Negroes as a class grew more
intense during the last two years of the ante-bellum period. Such came as a direct result of the growing fear of
the Northern attacks on slavery, but even more animosity
was generated because of that old bugbear that free Negroes were physical reminders to slaves that they too
could and should be free. To others the presence of Negroes not in a state of slavery was an unnatural thing—
a contradiction to every premise of the pro-slavery philosophy. And there were the less fortunate Louisianians
who looked upon their free Negro compatriots as their
worst and most damaging competitors for menial jobs of
the state. There were some few who just hated anyone
or anything tainted with Negro blood—the genuine rac-
ists and the pathologically maladjusted who wished nothing but harm for the objects of their unreasoning hatred.

Mirroring almost all these points of view was the editor

---

58. New Orleans *Daily Picayune*, January 15, 1860.

of the Opelousas *Patriot* when he called attention to the fact that free Negroes could not be tolerated on the grounds that "involuntary servitude to the white man is the only normal condition of the Negro and his natural relation to life." In this journalist's opinion only slaves could find "happiness and contribute more to the progress of civilization than free Negroes who were found in a state of unnatural freedom."[59] In an article published in *De-Bow's Review*, A. Featherman echoed like sentiments and went on to add that: "the only dangerous element, which must ultimately destroy the harmony and compactness of Southern society is the free Negro." He therefore pleaded with Southern policy-makers to effect stringent measures for expelling free Negroes from "our borders."[60]

Other writers focused their blasts against Negroes of any status on the grounds of racial and biological inferiority. It had long been the prevailing opinion among many Southerners that Negroes constituted the world's most inferior race of beings and were infinitely inferior to Whites in all respects, but especially in regards to intelligence, moral standards and physiology. They were deemed to be about on the level of the lower animals of the earth. Dr. Samuel Cartwright of New Orleans wrote in reflecting this viewpoint. He also spoke at length in attempting to prove his thesis on the subject. For example, in a speech before the Louisiana Medical Convention of 1851 he frankly stated that Negroes were inferior to Whites mainly because of their dark color. It was his contention that a darker color than Caucasian persons could even be detected in Negroes' "muscles, tendons, and in all fluid and

---

59. July 17, 1858.
60. A. Featherman, "Our Position and that of Our Enemies," *DeBow's Review*, XXXI (1861), 27.

secretions of their bodies." Even the brain and nerves were seriously described as "tinctured with a shade of prevailing darkness."[61] This man of medicine also advanced the idea that all Negroes were an inferior race because they were under a "satanic influence" as revealed in the practice of Voodooism. One White man armed with a whip, he maintained, could easily intimidate such persons. Cartwright implied that this was possible because White persons were immune from the worship of the devil.[62]

Dr. Josiah C. Nott of Mobile, Alabama, was of equal influence in shaping opinion regarding the "biological inferiority" of Negroes as a race. This physician held that the "cranial conformation" of Negroes distinguished them from all other species of man. He pointed out that the whole group "craniologically" were characterized by "prognothous jaws, narrow elongated forms, receding foreheads, larger posterior development, and small internal capacity."[63] Nott claimed he was following Louis Agassiz of Harvard University when he asserted that the brain of an adult Negro never reaches the size of "the Caucasian in boyhood; and bears . . . a marked resemblance to the brain of the Orang-outan."[64] In cataloguing women of the Negro race, Nott advanced the thesis that their mam-

---

61. Dr. Samuel A. Cartwright, "Diseases and Peculiarities of the Negro Race," *ibid.*, IV (1851), 65.

62. Cartwright, "Negro Freedom an Impossibility," *ibid.*, XXX (1861), 650, 658.

63. J. C. Nott, and George R. Gliddon, *Types of Mankind; or, Ethnological Researches, Based upon the Ancient Monuments, Paintings, Sculptures, and Crania of Races, and upon their Natural, Geographical, Philological, and Biblical History: illustrated by selections from the inedited paper of Samuel George Morton, M.D., and by additional contributions from Prof. L. Agassiz, L.L.D.; W. Usher, M.D.; and Prof. H. S. Patterson, M.D.,* 430.

64. *Ibid.,* 415.

maries are more conical, the areolae much larger, and the abdomen projects as a hemisphere."[65] All of these features ostensibly rendered the female Negro as inferior to that of White women.

These and other arguments had as their sole purpose that of proving the Negro to be inferior and that their only normal state was therefore that of slavery. Free Negroes were an abomination and should either be reduced to slavery or expelled from the entire nation. Among the authors who received a sympathetic hearing on such matters was the Virginian Edmund Ruffin. This militant defender of slavery and sworn enemy of free Negroes published scores of articles in Louisiana's newspapers and magazines. In 1858, Ruffin wrote that free Negroes in all parts of the United States were considered as "a nuisance and noted for ignorance, laziness, improvidence and vicious insults," and should be expelled, at any cost, from the country. He failed, however, to suggest where these people were to go if such an action was adopted by the governing authorities. Although Ruffin admitted that a very few free Negroes had managed to acquire wealth, the likelihood of their children falling back into a "state of barbarism was ever possible because of the peculiar characteristics of the race." He went on to explain the failure of the Liberian colonization scheme by the fact that Negroes had a strong aversion to being governed by their own race or to live where there were no White people.[66]

Writing on the subject of Negro failure at self-government in Haiti W. W. Wright proclaimed that: "The fruits

---

65. *Ibid.*
66. Edmund Ruffin, "Equality of the Races—Haytian and British Experiments," *ibid.*, XXV (1858), 129–131.

of freedom in that island since 1804 has been revolution, massacres, misrule, irreligion, ignorance, immorality, indolence, neglect of agriculture and, indeed, an actual renewal of slavery under another shape." This author singled out Haitian mothers as especially devoid of moral principles since they commonly deserted their children "to grow up as they pleased, the victims of wayward poison and of conduct without restraint." Wright concluded his article with a quotation from de Gobineau's *The Inequality of Human Races,* which in fact was the general sentiment in the South regarding Haiti: "Their Supreme felicity is idleness; their Supreme reason murder."[67]

The New Orleans *Bee* also shared these views and hammered the point that nowhere were free Negroes capable of governing themselves.[68] The colored class also was declared to be totally devoid of the qualities necessary for self-government on the grounds that they were "naturally, habitually, and constitutionally lazy." Without direction and the compulsion to work from "the superior race they would soon lapse into a state of barbarism and crime."[69]

Such arguments printed in the periodicals and press of the state soon found expression in renewed demands for legislation which would once and for all rid Louisiana of its free colored population. The pro-slavery leaders increased their efforts to achieve this goal when the General Assembly failed to pass a total exclusion bill in the 1859 session.[70] Undaunted, the anti-free Negro forces then

67. W. W. Wright, "Free Negroes in Hayti," *DeBow's Review,* XXVII (1859), 531, 538, 549.
68. February 9, 1856.
69. Monroe (La.), *Register,* April 12, 1860.
70. *Cf. supra,* 114–116.

bombarded the Legislature for action on this matter. They stressed the point that free Negroes were a constant menace to slavery, solely because they spread abolitionism in Louisiana. According to an editorial in the Opelousas *Patriot* if laws were not made to expel "this really anomalous class of persons," they will continue to exercise a "pernicious and corrupting influence upon the slaves."[71] The New Orleans *Bee* added that even though free Negroes were better off in the South than in the North, they should be expelled because such people were "dangerous companions to the slaves." To prove this contention the editor wrote that the free Negro "gets drunk, debauches our slaves, and preaches insubordination to them."[72] The *Picayune* stoutly maintained that the state government had the right to protect its citizens by expelling this "debauching, drunken, insolent group whose main object was to tamper with slaves and thereby make them discontented."[73]

Speaking for the entire state of Louisiana, the Monroe *Register* predicted that if "this mongrel race" were not removed they will "pollute the name of our fair State with their worthless carcasses and pave the way to indolence, dissipation and vice" among all peoples of Louisiana.[74]

To further buttress their arguments, Louisiana proslavery leaders pointed out how other states were taking steps for ridding themselves of their free color population. After the Harper's Ferry incident in 1859, the neighboring state of Mississippi passed a law requiring all free

71. July 23, 1859.
72. October 10, 1859.
73. January 17, 1859.
74. April 12, 1860.

Negroes to leave within a certain period of time. This measure was held up as "worthy of imitation for the Louisiana legislature."[75] The editor of the leading paper in Alexandria favored the Mississippi law, but he placed some qualification upon his endorsement. He contended that the expelled free Negroes would undoubtedly come to Louisiana and therefore increase an already large body of unwanted people. Instead of suddenly expelling such persons, the editor suggested that every free Negro in Mississippi, and Louisiana as well, be required to select some competent White person as a guardian who would have control over their wards such as a master has over his slaves. If this plan should prove a failure, then take steps to expel the whole class.[76]

Most of the press gave its unqualified approval of the actions of Missouri, Alabama, Arkansas and other states in expelling the hated free Negro. For example, in 1859 the Arkansas Legislature approved a bill requiring all free Negroes in that state to leave by January 1, 1860, or become slaves for life. This measure was hailed as worthy of emulation in Louisiana and it was justified on the grounds that "desperate diseases require desperate and powerful remedies."[77]

In a long article in the *Patriot*, the most violent anti-free Negro organ in Louisiana, that paper reviewed anti-free Negro movements all over the nation. It pointed out that not only had the slaveholding states taken measures to rid themselves of free Negroes, but New York and Ohio were also seriously considering similar measures. The editor then dedicated himself and his

---

75. New Orleans *Daily Picayune*, November 16, 1859.
76. Alexandria (La.), *Democrat*, December 7, 1859.
77. Opelousas *Patriot*, July 16, 1859.

paper to keep this "pressing matter" before the people of Louisiana until the end had been accomplished: "The complete removal of free Negroes from the sovereign state of Louisiana."[78] One editor of the influential newspaper in Monroe advocated the removal of free Negroes by giving them proper warning to leave in a given length of time or be sold into a lifetime of servitude. It was further suggested that they be sent North "to rest in the bosom of those who worship them by day and night." The writer justified this move on the following grounds:

> There is no telling but what there is kindred relationship existing between them [free Negroes] and their Northern admirers. At least we have no doubt but that some of them would make model husbands and wives for their sons and daughters. No doubt they would be welcomly received by their fanatical friends. As far as we of the South, we deem it an act of self-preservation to relieve ourselves of these worthless creatures, and the sooner it is done the better.[79]

Thus, the articulate element in Louisiana were made conscious of the fact that it was lagging behind other states in the enactment of stringent legislation affecting free Negroes.

Such writings as these, reflecting the opinion of many Louisianians, clearly indicate that in a pro-slavery society of Louisiana free Negroes were considered an anomalous group which must be expelled for the public welfare. They were not, however, entirely friendless; occasionally editors of newspapers wrote in their behalf. For example, on several occasions, George Pike, the editor of the Baton

---

78. *Ibid.*, July 16, 1859.
79. Monroe *Register*, April 12, 1860.

Rouge *Gazette and Comet,* protested the generalizations indulged in by Louisiana newspaper editors concerning the depravity of native-born free Negroes. He asked for evidence which would "point out the particular evil or evils complained of" by his fellow journalists. This request was made by Pike so that "ordinary justice could be meted out for the class concerned." In the opinion of this editor, the native free colored population was "an orderly and well behaved class which acted as a restraint upon the slaves and in no way excited the servile population to insurrection and insubordination."[80]

On another occasion, Pike published a long article from the New Orleans *True Delta* reciting that paper's objection to legislative intimidation of native colored persons. Protesting such proposals to reenslave them, this article reviewed the contributions and propriety of free colored persons and went on record to oppose any "cruel, arbitrary and unusual legislation" then pending before the General Assembly.[81] At least one White citizen approved the stand taken by Pike and the *True Delta.* Under the signature "notes" this citizen contended that native-born colored persons could not be legally expelled since they were "almost aboriginal and have been indulgently entertained by the Constitution and laws of Louisiana and they are precautioned in the Treaty of Cession."[82] Writing in November 4, 1859, in what was his last reference to the matter, Pike pointed out that it was significant that free Negroes in Virginia during "the excitement at Harper's Ferry offered their services to the authorities to put

---

80. Baton Rouge *Gazette and Comet,* May 6, 1859.
81. New Orleans *True Delta,* March 16, 1859, quoted in *ibid.,* April 27, 1859.
82. *Ibid.,* May 4, 1859.

down John Brown's diabolical scheme."[83] Such was the acme of good citizenship.

The pro-slavery campaign was much too strong for any one or group to buck. Undoubtedly there were many more than came to the surface who championed the free Negro cause, but such persons preferred silence in an atmosphere which might trigger violence against their persons. Yet, it is significant that in the face of overwhelming demands for removal of the "undesirable" class the Legislature did not seem sufficiently concerned to pass expulsion measures. The extreme anti-free colored forces were apparently too radical for the majority of Louisiana's White citizens.

While the expulsion demands raged there were also propositions to confiscate properties belonging to free colored citizens. Less radical proposals called for legislation to prohibit free colored persons from giving testimony against Whites in the courts.[84] These unreasonable measures also failed to win legislative approval. Doubtless such failed because many fair-minded lawmakers reasoned that the same strictures could be used against White persons at some future date. Then too, the Purchase Treaty of 1803 doubtlessly influenced more legal-minded lawmakers from violating the provision that granted to all Louisianians "the enjoyment of all the rights, advantages and immunities of citizens of the United States."[85] When expulsion failed to materialize, the state's policy-makers turned their attention of reducing free Negro into volun-

---

83. *Ibid.*, November 6, 1859.

84. For list of such acts, see Baton Rouge *Gazette and Comet*, April 27, 1859.

85. Cession Treaty, April 30, 1803, in Henry S. Commanger (ed.), *Documents of American History*, I, 191.

tary slavery. The first step in this direction came in 1859 when an act passed allowing any free Negro to choose a master and become a life-time slave.[86] Such was as far as the General Assembly was willing to go in answering the demand of those who would eliminate native free colored population or deprive them of certain civil rights which had been theirs since the beginning of the American period. It was at this point that the White citizens took matters into their own hands and attempted to rid the state of free Negroes through violent means. This method also failed in its immediate purpose.

Even though efforts at reducing the number of free Negroes failed, White attitudes of hatred deepened as the pre-Civil War period drew to a close. Much of the animosity stemmed from both real and imagined evidence and articulate Whites demanded immediate action. The hovering spirit of hatred and fear of Negroes in general brought on demands for stricter enforcement of laws against any of that race who would make common cause with the militant anti-slavery forces. When extremists failed to bring on legal expulsion measures they resorted to violence, but even this method failed to obtain the desired ends. As for the free Negroes personally, a few weary of the constant pressures against them took the hard way out and migrated to other lands. The majority, however, stayed on hoping that the future would be kinder than their miserable present. The weak voice of defenders of the much maligned race was but a will-o-the-wisp in an over excited atmosphere. Yet during the entire reactionary years, native-born free Negroes continued to enjoy economic and certain civil rights which had always

86. *Cf. supra,* 149.

been their privilege. At least one incontestable fact remained, over 18,000 free Negroes stayed in Louisiana. It was their home too and no amount of wild ranting or threats of violence could intimidate or force these American citizens from their homeland.

Bibliography

MANUSCRIPTS:
LETTERS, DIARIES, ORGANIZATIONAL

Brown (James) Papers, 1764–1811. Department of Archives, Louisiana State University.

[Dubreuil, Oscar], Account Book, 1856–58, Isle de Breville, Natchitoches Parish. Department of Archives, Louisiana State University.

Durnford, Andrew, Plantation Record Book of Andrew Durnford, April, 1840 to July, 1868. Archives, Howard-Tilton Memorial Library, Tulane University.

Ellis (E. John, Thomas C. W., and Family) Papers, 1829–1860. Department of Archives, Louisiana State University.

First Book of Marriages of Negroes and Mulattoes in the Parish of St. Louis in the City of New Orleans, 1777–1830. St. Louis Cathedral Archives, New Orleans.

Gayarré (Charles E.) Papers, 1720–1895. Department of Archives, Louisiana State University.

Johnson (William T., and Family) Papers, 1793–1860. Department of Archives, Louisiana State University.

Marriage Register of St. Louis Cathedral, July 1, 1720 to December 4, 1730. St. Louis Cathedral Archives, New Orleans.

Meullion (Family) Papers, 1776–1860. Department of Archives, Louisiana State University.

Notes on St. Augustine Church and School. Rectory, St. Augustine Church of New Orleans.

Randolph (John H.) Papers, 1822–1860. Department of Archives, Louisiana State University.

Weeks (David, and Family) Papers, 1782–1860. Department of Archives, Louisiana State University.

MISCELLANEOUS DOCUMENTS

A *Letter of John McDonogh, on African Colonization: addressed to the editors of the New-Orleans Commercial Bulletin.* New Orleans: Commercial Bulletin Office, 1842.

Commager, Henry S., *Documents of American History*, 2 vols., New York: Appleton-Century-Crofts, Inc., 1949.

Journal of the Proceedings of the Eighteenth Convention of the Protestant Episcopal Church in the Diocese of Louisiana, which assembled in St. Paul's Church, in the City of New Orleans, on May 15, A.D. 1856. New Orleans: B. M. Norman, 1856.

Journal of the Proceedings of the Seventeenth Convention of the Protestant Episcopal Church in the Diocese of Louisiana, which assembled in St. Paul's Church, in the City of New Orleans, on Friday, May 11, A.D. 1855. New Orleans: B. M. Norman, 1855.

[Robinson, William L.] *Diary of a Samaritan, By a Member of the Howard Association of New Orleans.* New York: Harper and Brothers, 1860.

Sinclair, Henri de (editor), *Journal Letters of Joseph Delfau de Pontalba to his wife Jeanne Françoise le Breton des Charmeaux.* Works Progress Administration, Survey of Federal Archives in Louisiana. New Orleans: Typescript in Department of Archives, Louisiana State University, 1939.

The By-Laws and Constitution of the Union Band Society of New Orleans, Organized July 22, 1860, Love, Union, Peace. New Orleans: Printed 201 Chartres near St. Ann, n.d.

Works Progress Administration, Survey of the Federal Archives in Louisiana, *County-Parish Boundaries in Louisiana.* New Orleans: Typescript in Department of Archives, Louisiana State University, 1939.

MANUSCRIPTS: GOVERNMENT DOCUMENTS

Colonial

New Orleans City Records, 1790–1799. Department of Archives, Louisiana State University.

Works Progress Administration, *Survey of the Federal Archives in Louisiana, Alphabetical and Chronological Digest of the Acts and Deliberations of the Cabildo, 1769–1803,* 10 vols. New Orleans: Typescript in Department of Archives, Louisiana State University, 1939.

———, *Archives of the Spanish Government of West Florida, 1783–1812,* 19 vols. Baton Rouge: Typescript in Department of Archives, Louisiana State University, 1939.

———, *Despatches of the Spanish Governors of Louisiana,* 25 vols. New Orleans: Typescript in Department of Archives, Louisiana State University, 1939.

Federal

United States Census Reports for 1820, Louisiana Population, Assumption Parish, I. Microfilm in Louisiana State University Library.

United States Census Reports for 1840, Louisiana Population, Concordia and St. Mary Parish, I, II. Microfilm in Louisiana State University Library.

United States Census Reports for 1850, Schedule IV, Agricultural Production, Calcasieu, Jefferson, Lafourche, Natchitoches, Plaquemines parishes, Louisiana. Microfilm in Louisiana State University Library.

———, Schedule I, Free Inhabitants, Bienville, Iberville, Plaquemines, Pointe Coupee, St. Landry, Terrebonne, West

Baton Rouge parishes, Louisiana, I–IX. Microfilm in Louisiana State University Library.

———, Schedule II, Slave Inhabitants, Iberville, Natchitoches, Plaquemines parishes, Louisiana, II–IV. Microfilm in Louisiana State University Library.

United States Census Reports for 1860, Schedule I, Free Inhabitants, Ascension, Assumption, Avoyelles, Caddo, Calcasieu, Catahoula, Concordia, East Baton Rouge, Iberville, Jefferson, Lafayette, Lafourche, Madison, Natchitoches, Orleans, Pointe Coupee, Rapides, St. Charles, St. James, St. Landry, St. Martin, St. Tammany, West Feliciana parishes, I–X. Microfilm in Louisiana State University Library.

State

Register of Free Colored Persons Entitled to Remain in the State. Mayor's Office, 1840–1857, 1856–1859, 1859–1861, 1861–1864. City Archives, New Orleans Public Library.

Parish

Ascension Parish Police Jury Minutes, Volume I, 1837–1856. Ascension Parish courthouse, Donaldsonville, Louisiana. *Works Progress Administration Historical Records Survey*, handscript copy in Department of Archives, Louisiana State University.

Avoyelles Parish Alienations Book F, No. 2401. Will of William Inrufty, October 5, 1827. Avoyelles Parish courthouse, Marksville, Louisiana.

Avoyelles Parish Police Jury Minutes, Volume I, 1821–1843, II, 1843–1852. Avoyelles Parish courthouse, Marksville, Louisiana. *Works Progress Administration, Historical Records Survey*, handscript copy in Department of Archives, Louisiana State University.

Calcasieu Parish Police Jury Minutes, Volume A, 1840–1846, Volume 1847–1856. Calcasieu Parish courthouse, Lake Charles, Louisiana. *Works Progress Administration, His-*

torical Records Survey, handscript copy in Department of Archives, Louisiana State University.

East Baton Rouge Parish Police Jury Minutes, Volume I, 1847–1868. East Baton Rouge Parish Courthouse, Baton Rouge, Louisiana. *Works Progress Administration, Historical Records Survey,* handscript copy in Department of Archives, Louisiana State University.

East Baton Rouge Parish Probate Records, Record No. 382. Succession of Margaret Bird, April 1, 1854. East Baton Rouge Parish courthouse, Baton Rouge, Louisiana.

Iberville Parish Police Jury Minutes, Volume I, 1850–1862. Iberville Parish courthouse, Plaquemine, Louisiana. *Works Progress Administration, Historical Records Survey,* handscript copy in Department of Archives, Louisiana State University.

Iberville Parish Succession Records, Record No. 85. Succession of Joseph Erwin, April 14, 1829. Iberville Parish courthouse, Plaquemine, Louisiana.

Jefferson Parish Police Jury Minutes, Volume I, 1834–1843. Jefferson Parish courthouse, Gretna, Louisiana.

Lafayette Parish Police Jury Minutes, Volume I, 1823–1857. Lafayette Parish courthouse, Lafayette, Louisiana. *Works Progress Administration, Historical Records Survey,* handscript copy in Department of Archives, Louisiana State University.

Lafourche Parish Police Jury Minutes, Volume I, 1841–1852, Volume II, 1852–1862. Lafourche Parish courthouse, Thibodoux, Louisiana. *Works Progress Administration, Historical Records Survey,* handscript copy in Department of Archives, Louisiana State University.

Natchitoches Parish Mortgage Book N. Succession of Joseph Augustin Metoyer, July 3, 1851. Natchitoches Parish courthouse, Natchitoches, Louisiana.

Natchitoches Parish Succession Records, Record No. 143. Succession of Nancy Cozine, September 10, 1839. Natchitoches Parish courthouse, Natchitoches, Louisiana.

———, Record No. 895. Succession of Jean Baptiste Augustin Metoyer, September 1, 1854. Natchitoches Parish Courthouse, Natchitoches, Louisiana.

———, Record No. 362. Succession of Jean Baptiste Metoyer, May 1, 1843. Natchitoches Parish courthouse, Natchitoches, Louisiana.

———, Record No. 897. Succession of Charles N. Roques, October 2, 1854. Natchitoches Parish courthouse, Natchitoches, Louisiana.

———, Record No. 2. Succession of William Sutherland, October 1, 1817. Natchitoches Parish courthouse, Natchitoches, Louisiana.

Orleans Parish Will Books, I–XIII (1805–1860). Orleans Parish civil courthouse, New Orleans, Louisiana.

Pointe Coupee Parish Police Jury Minutes, Volume I, 1829–1840, Volume II, 1840–1848, Volume III, 1848–1862. Pointe Coupee Parish courthouse, New Roads, Louisiana. *Works Progress Administration, Historical Record Survey*, handscript copy in Department of Archives, Louisiana State University.

St. James Parish Police Jury Minutes, Volume 1849–1855. St. James Parish courthouse, Convent, Louisiana. *Works Progress Administration, Historical Records Survey*, handscript copy in Department of Archives, Louisiana State University.

St. John the Baptist Parish Collection, 1786–1860. Department of Archives, Louisiana State University.

St. John the Baptist Parish Police Jury Minutes, Volume 1814–1817, Volume 1834–1837, Volume 1837–1849, Volume 1849–1882. St. John the Baptist Parish courthouse, Edgard, Louisiana. *Works Progress Administration, Historical Records Survey*, handscript copy in Department of Archives, Louisiana State University.

St. Martin Parish Police Jury Minutes, Volume I, 1843–1855. St. Martin Parish courthouse, St. Martinville, Louisiana. *Works Progress Administration, Historical Records Survey,* handscript copy in Department of Archives, Louisiana State University.

West Feliciana Parish Police Jury Minutes, Volume I, 1840–1855. West Feliciana Parish courthouse, St. Francisville, Louisiana. *Works Progress Administration, Historical Records Survey,* handscript copy in Department of Archives, Louisiana State University.

Municipal

Documents of the City Council of New Orleans, 1823–1835, Record Book # 4084. Typescript in Cabildo Museum Library, New Orleans, Louisiana.

Mayor's Messages to the City Council of New Orleans, 1812–1813. Message of Mayor Nicholas Girod, November 14, 1812. City Archives, New Orleans Public Library.

New Orleans City Records, 1840–1850, Department of Archives, Louisiana State University.

Proceedings of the City Council of New Orleans, November 30, 1803 to March 29, 1805. City Archives, New Orleans Public Library.

Ordinances and Resolutions of the City Council of New Orleans, 1805–1815, 1816–1821, 1822, 1830. City Archives, New Orleans Public Library.

OFFICIAL GOVERNMENT DOCUMENTS: COLONIAL, FEDERAL, STATE, PARISH AND MUNICIPAL

Alcott, Edward R. and Spofford, Henry M. (editors), *The Louisiana Magistrate, and Parish Officer's Guide Containing Copious Forms and Instructions for Justices of the Peace, Administrators, Executors, Clerks, Sheriffs, Constables, Coroners, and Business Men in General, Together with the Constitution of Louisiana and of the United States.* New Orleans: J. S. and C. Adams, 1848.

Appendix to an Account of Louisiana, Being an Abstract of Documents in the Offices of the Department of State, and of the Treasury. Philadelphia: Printed for Thomas Jefferson, 1803.

Augustin, Donatien, *A General Digest of the Ordinances and Resolutions of the Corporation of New Orleans.* New Orleans: Jerome Bayon, 1831.

Carter, Clarence E. (editor), *The Territorial Papers of the United States,* 14 vols., IX, *The Territory of Orleans, 1803–1812.* Washington, D. C.: Government Printing Office, 1940.

Catterall, Helen T. (editor), *Judicial Cases Concerning American Slavery and the Negro,* 5 vols., III, *Cases from the Courts of Georgia, Florida, Alabama, Mississippi, and Louisiana.* Washington, D. C.: Carnegie Institute of Washington, 1932.

Civil Code of the State of Louisiana. New Orleans: J. C. De Romes, 1825.

Compiled Edition of the Civil Codes of Louisiana. Baton Rouge: Louisiana Law Institute, 1940.

Constitution of the State of Louisiana for 1852. New Orleans: By authority, 1853.

Constitutions of Louisiana of 1812, '45 and '52, also the Constitution of the United States with Amendments, Articles of Confederation and the Declaration of Independence. New Orleans: n. p., 1861.

Cruzat, Heloise H. (translator), "Records of the Superior Council of Louisiana," *Louisiana Historical Quarterly,* III–XXII (1920–1939).

———, "A Murder Case Tried in New Orleans in 1773," *Louisiana Historical Quarterly,* XXII (1939), 623–641.

———, "Cabildo Archives—French Period," *Louisiana Historical Quarterly,* III and IV (1920–1921), 551–569, 361–368.

Cummings, John (compiler), *Negro Population, 1790–1915.* Washington, D. C.: Government Printing Office, 1918.

Dart, Henry P. and Porteous, Laura L. (translators), "Trial of Mary Glass for Murder, 1780," *Louisiana Historical Quarterly,* VI (1923), 591–654.

DeBow, J. D. B. (compiler), *Statistical View of the United States. Embracing its Territory, Population—White, Free Colored, and Slave—Moral and Social Condition, Industry, Property, and Revenue; the Detailed Statistics of Cities, Towns, and Counties; Being a Compendium of the Seventh Census; to which are added the results of every previous census, beginning with 1790, in comparative tables, with explanatory and illustrative notes, based upon the schedules and other official sources of information.* Washington, D. C.: Beverly Tucker, 1854.

Journals of the House of Representatives of the State of Louisiana, 1818, 1831, 1841–1842, 1843, 1845, 1846, 1852, 1853, 1854, 1855, 1856, 1860.

Journals of the Senate of the State of Louisiana, 1852, 1853, 1854, 1857.

Kinnaird, Lawrence (editor), *Spain in the Mississippi Valley, 1765–1794,* 3 vols., *Annual Report of the American Historical Association, 1945.* Washington, D. C.,: Government Printing Office, 1949.

Laws of Louisiana, 1812, 1812–1813, 1815, 1816, 1816–1817, 1819, 1823, 1824–1825, 1826, 1827, 1830, 1831, 1832, 1838, 1841–1842, 1842, 1843, 1845 1846, 1847, 1848, 1850, 1852, 1853, 1855, 1857, 1859.

Laws of the Territory of Orleans, 1806, 1807, 1808, 1810, 1811.

Le Code Noir, ou Recueil des Reglemens rendus jusqu'a présent. Concernant le Gouvernement, l'Administration de la Justice, la Police, la Discipline & la Commerce des Negres dans les Colonies Françoises. Et les Conseils Compagnies establit a ce Sujet. Paris: Prault, Imprimeur-Librarie, 1767.

Lislet, L. Moreau and Carleton, Henry (translators), *The Laws of Las Siete Partidas Which are still in Force in the State of Louisiana,* 2 vols. New Orleans: James M. Daraker, 1820.

Louisiana Legislative Documents, 1857, 1858.

Lugano, G. (translator), "Records of the Superior Council

of Louisiana," *Louisiana Historical Quarterly*, XXIII–XXVI (1940–1943).

Martin, François X., *Term Reports of Cases argued and determined in the Superior Court of the Territory of Orleans* [1809–1823]. 12 vols. New Orleans, 1854.

——, *Louisiana Term Reports or Cases argued and determined in the Supreme Court of that State*, 8 vols., New Orleans, 1823–1830.

Morgan, Thomas G. (editor), *Civil Code of the State of Louisiana; with the Statutory Amendments, from 1825 to 1853, Inclusive.* New Orleans: J. B. Steel, 1853

Official Journal of the Convention to Form a New Constitution for the State of Louisiana, 1852. New Orleans: Printed at the Crescent Office, 1852.

Official Report of Debates in the Louisiana Constitutional Convention, 1844–1845. New Orleans: Besanson, Ferguson and Company, 1845.

Peirce, Levi, Taylor, Miles, and King, William W. (editors), *The Consolidation and Revision of the Statutes of a General Nature.* New Orleans: Printed by the *Bee*, 1852.

Porteous, Laura L. (translator), "Index to the Spanish Judicial Records of Louisiana," *Louisiana Historical Quarterly*, VI–XXXI (1923–1949).

——, "Trial of Pablo Rocheblave Before Governor Unzaga, 1771," *Louisiana Historical Quarterly*, VIII (1925), 372–381.

——, "Torture in Spanish Criminal Procedure in Louisiana, 1771," *Louisiana Historical Quarterly*, VIII (1925), 5–23.

Price, William (translator), "Abstracts of French and Spanish Documents Concerning the Early History of Louisiana," *Louisiana Historical Quarterly*, I (1918), 224–257.

Reports of Cases argued and determined in the Supreme Court of Louisiana, 52 vols., New Orleans, 1846–1900.

Reports of Cases argued and determined in the Supreme court of the State of Louisiana, 19 vols., New Orleans, 1831–1841.

Robertson, Meritt M. (compiler), *Reports of Cases argued and determined in the Supreme Court of Louisiana*, 12 vols., New Orleans, 1842–1846.

Rowland, Dunbar (editor), *Official Letter Books of W. C. C. Claiborne, 1801–1816*, 6 vols. Jackson, Mississippi: State Department of Archives and History, 1917.

Samford, D. B. (editor), *Police Jury Code of the Parish of East Feliciana, Louisiana, Containing a Digest of the State Laws, Relative to Police Juries, and also a Digest of the Ordinances of the Parish of East Feliciana, Having the Force of Laws, Up to May 1, 1859, Inclusive*. Clinton, Louisiana: G. Wilson Reese, 1859.

The Eighth Census of the United States, 1860. Washington, D. C.: Government Printing Office, 1864.

The Fifth Census of the United States, 1830. Washington, D. C.: Duff Green, 1832.

The Fourth Census of the United States, 1820. Washington, D. C.: Gales and Seaton, 1821.

The Seventh Census of the United States, 1850. Washington, D. C.: Robert Armstrong, 1853.

The Sixth Census of the United States, 1840. Washington, D. C.: Thomas Allen, 1841.

The Third Census of the United States, 1810. Washington, D. C.: n.p., 1811.

Woodson, Carter G. (compiler and editor), *Free Negro Owners of Slaves in the United States in 1830 together with Absentee Ownership of Slaves in the United States in 1830*. Washington, D. C.: The Association for the Study of Negro Life and History, 1924.

————, *Free Negro Heads of Families in the United States in 1830*. Washington, D. C.: The Association for the Study of Negro Life and History, 1925.

NEWSPAPERS: LOUISIANA

Alexandria
Alexandria *Democrat,* December 7, 1859.
Baton Rouge
Baton Rouge *Gazette,* 1827–1852.
Baton Rouge *Daily Comet,* October 29, 1852.
Baton Rouge *Gazette and Comet,* May 11, 1861.
Baton Rouge *Daily Gazette and Comet,* 1857–1859.

Benton
Benton *Bossier Banner,* 1859–1860.
Donaldsonville
Le Vigilant, February 7, 1849.
False River
Pointe Coupee Democrat, May 18, 1861.
Franklin
Franklin *Planters Banner,* 1853–1854.
Greensburg
Greensburg *Imperial,* June 13, 1857.

Monroe
Monroe *Register,* April 12, 1860.
Natchitoches
Natchitoches *Union,* May 1, 1862.

New Orleans
New Orleans *Bee,* 1850–1859.
New Orleans *Daily Crescent,* 1855–1859.
New Orleans *Daily Delta,* 1847–1860.
New Orleans *Daily Picayune,* 1837–1860.
New Orleans *Friend of the Laws and Commercial Journal,*
    May 22, 1820.
New Orleans *Le Propagateur Catholique,* May 4, 1844.
New Orleans *Orleans Gazette and Commercial Advertiser,*
    February 6, 1817.

New Orleans *Semi-Weekly Creole*, 1851-1855.
New Orleans *True Delta*, 1850–1854.
New Orleans *Weekly Delta*, July 19, 1853.
New Orleans *Weekly Picayune*, November 1, 1841.

Opelousas
Opelousas *Courier*, 1856–1859.
Opelousas *Patriot*, 1856–1859.

Plaquemine
Plaquemine *Gazette and Sentinel*, June 19, 1858.

West Baton Rouge
West Baton Rouge *Capitolian Vis-A-Vis*, September 29, 1852.
West Baton Rouge *Sugar Planter*, 1857-1858.

Out of State Newspapers
New York *Daily Tribune*, November 11, 1858.
Washington (D. C.) *National Intelligencer*, August 20, 1857.

OTHER PERIODICALS: CONTEMPORARY AND SECONDARY

"Annual Report of American Colonization Society," *The African Repository and Colonial Journal*, XXXII (1846), 39.
Cartwright, Dr. Samuel A., "Diseases and Peculiarities of the Negro Race," *DeBow's Review*, IV (1851), 64–69.
———, "Negro Freedom an Impossibility," *DeBow's Review*, XXX (1861), 648–659.
"Circular to the Friends of African Colonization in the State of Louisiana," *The African Repository and Colonial Journal*, XXV (1849), 3–7.
"Colonel Maunsel White of New Orleans," *The African Repository and Colonial Journal*, XII (1836), 202.
"Colored Settlement in Canada," *The African Repository and Colonial Journal*, XXXIV (1858), 30.

"Contributions," *The African Repository and Colonial Journal,* XVI (1840), XXXI (1855), 80, 144, 255.

Cruzat, J. W. (translator), "The Defenses of New Orleans in 1797," *Publications of the Louisiana Historical Society,* I (1896), 34–38.

Cusacks, Gaspar (editor), "Bernardo de Galvez's Diary of the Operations Against Pensacola, May 13, 1781," *Louisiana Historical Quarterly,* I (1917), 44–85.

Dart, Henry P., "Episodes of Life in Colonial Louisiana," *Louisiana Historical Quarterly,* VI (1923), 35–46.

deGournay, P. F., "The F. M. C.'s of Louisiana," *Lippincott's Monthly Magazine* (Philadelphia), LIII (1894), 511–517.

"Dr. John Sibley of Natchitoches, 1757– 1837," *Louisiana Historical Quarterly,* X (1927), 467–508.

Dunbar-Nelson, Alice, "People of Color in Louisiana," *Journal of Negro History,* I (1916), 361–376.

"Emancipation at the South-Tolerance of Louisiana," *The African Repository and Colonial Journal,* XXII (1856), 275–276.

Featherman, A., "Our Position and that of Our Enemies," *DeBow's Review,* XXXI (1861), 27–32.

Flugel, Felix (editor), "Pages From a Journal of a Voyage Down the Mississippi to New Orleans in 1817," *Louisiana Historical Quarterly,* VII (1924), 414–441.

Greer, James K., "Louisiana Politics, 1845–1861, "*Louisiana Historical Quarterly,* XIII (1930), 67–116.

Harrison, Fairfax (editor), "The Viginians on the Ohio and the Mississippi, 1742," *Louisiana Historical Quarterly,* V (1922), 316–333.

Kendall, John S., "New Orleans Musicians of Long Ago," *Louisiana Historical Quarterly,* XXXI (1948), 130–149.

Kneeland, Dr. Samuel, "The Hybrid Races of Animals and Men," *DeBow's Review,* XIX (1855), 535–539.

"Letter from Secretary of Louisiana Colonization Society, June 22, 1839," *The African Repository and Colonial Journal,* XV (1839), 195–196.

Liljegren, Ernest R., "Jacobinism in Spanish Louisiana, 1792–1797," *Louisiana Historical Quarterly*, XXII (1939), 47–98.

"Louisiana Colonization Society, State Society for Louisiana," *The African Repository and Colonial Journal*, VIII (1832), 59.

"Louisiana Colonization Society," *The African Repository and Colonial Journal*, XII (1836), 192–193; XIV (1838), 11–12, 126, 147; XVIII (1842), 50; XIX (1843), 161.

"Louisiana Legislature," *The African Repository and Colonial Journal*, VI (1830), 29.

"Meeting of Young Men's Colonization Society in Presbyterian Church," *The African Respository and Colonial Journal*, XIV 1836), 94.

"Mr. Ireland's Legacy to American Colonization Society," *The African Repository and Colonial Journal*, XII (1836), 333.

"New Orleans *Daily Crescent*," *The African Repository and Colonial Journal*, XXVI (1850), 148.

Niles' Weekly Register (Baltimore), XXIX (November 5, 1825), 160.

Porter, Betty, "The History of Negro Education in Louisiana," *Louisiana Historical Quarterly*, XXV (1942), 728–821.

Price, William (translator), "Sidelights on Louisiana History," *Louisiana Historical Quarterly*, I (1918), 87–153.

Prichard, Walter, "A Tourist's Description of Louisiana in 1860," *Louisiana Historical Quarterly*, XXI (1938), 1110–1214.

"Prospects in Louisiana," *The African Repository and Colonial Journal*, VIII (1832), 62.

"Providence in Carrol County Louisiana," *The African Repository and Colonial Journal*, XII (1836), 334.

"Report from Agent Robert S. Finley, December 20, 1831," *The African Repository and Colonial Journal*, VII (1831), 345.

Robertson, Frances, "The Will of General Philemon Thomas," *Proceedings of the Historical Society of East and West Baton Rouge*, II (1918), 26–27.

Ruffin, Edmund, "Equality of the Races—Haytian and British Experiments," *DeBow's Review*, XXV (1858), 27–38.

"Secretary of Louisiana Colonization Society," *The African Repository and Colonial Journal*, VIII (1832), 286.

Shoen, Harold, "The Free Negro in the Republic of Texas," *The Southwestern Historical Quarterly*, XXXIX (1936), 292–309; XL (1936–1937), 85–114.

Smither, Nelle, "A History of the English Theatre at New Orleans, 1806–1860," *Louisiana Historical Quarterly*, XXVIII (1945), 85–572.

West-Stahl, Annie L., "The Free Negro in Ante-Bellum Louisiana," *Louisiana Historical Quarterly*, XXV (1942), 301–396.

Willey, Nathan, "Education of the Colored Population of Louisiana," *Harper's New Monthly Magazine* (New York), XXXIII (1866), 246–250.

Wilson, Calvin D., "Black Masters: A Side-Light on Slavery," *The North American Review* (New York), CLXXXI (1905), 685–698.

"Table of Emigrants," *The African Repository and Colonial Journal*, XLIII (1867), 109–118.

Wright, W. W., "Free Negroes in Hayti," *DeBow's Review*, XXVII (1859), 526–549.

———, "Free Negro Rule," *DeBow's Review*, XXVIII (1860), 440–460.

———, "Free Negroes in the Northern United States," *DeBow's Review*, XXVIII (1860), 573–581.

CONTEMPORARY TRAVEL BOOKS

Arfwedson, C. D., *The United States and Canada in 1832, 1833, and 1834*, 2 vols. London: Richard Bentley, 1834.

Ashe, Thomas, *Travels in America Performed in the Year 1806, for the Purpose of Exploring the Rivers Alleghany, Monongahela, Ohio, and Mississippi, and Ascertaining the Produce and Conditions of Their Banks and Vicinity*. London: Phillips, 1809.

Atwater, Rev. H. Cowles, *Incidents of a Southern Tour or the South as Seen with Northern Eyes*. Boston: J. P. Magee, 1857.

Buckingham, James S., *The Slave States of America*, 2 vols. London: Fisher, Son, and Company, 1842.

Creecy, James R., *Scenes in the South and Other Miscellaneous Pieces*. Washington, D. C.,: Thomas McGill, 1860.

Croushore, James H., and Williams, Stanley T. (editors), DeForest, John W., *A Volunteer's Adventures, A Union Captain's Record of the Civil War*. New Haven, Connecticut: Yale University Press, 1946.

DuLac, M. Perrin, *Travels through the Two Louisianas and among the Savage Nations of the Missouri; in the United States, along the Ohio, and the adjacent Provinces, in 1801, 1802, and 1803*. London: Richard Phillips, 1807.

Duvallon, Berquin, *Vue de la Colonie Espagnole du Mississipi, ou des Provinces de Louisiane et Floride Occidentale, en l'année 1802*. Paris: l'Imprimerie Expeditive, 1803.

Featherstonhaugh, George W., *Excursion Through the Slave States*, 2 vols. London: John Murray, 1844.

Hamilton, Thomas, *Men and Manners in America*, 2 vols. Edinburgh: W. Blackwood, 1833.

Ingraham, Joseph H. (editor), *The Sunny South; or, the Southerner at Home, Embracing Five Years Experience of a Northern Governess in the Land of the Sugar and the Cotton*. Philadelphia: G. S. Evans, 1860.

[Ingraham, Joseph H.], *The South-West. By a Yankee*, 2 vols. New York: Harper and Brothers, 1835.

Loziérs, Baudry des, *Second Voyage a La Louisiane, faisent suit au premier de l'auteur de 1794 a 1798*. Paris: Charles Imprimeur, 1803.

Lyell, Sir Charles, *A Second Visit to the United States of North America*, 2 vols. New York: Harper and Brothers, 1849.

Martineau, Harriet, *Society in America*, 2 vols. Paris: A. and W. Galignani and Company, 1837.

————, *Retrospect of Western Travel*, 3 vols. New York: Harper and Brothers, 1838.

Norman, B. M. (editor), *New Orleans and Environs*. New Orleans, B. M. Norman, 1845.

Olmsted, Frederick L., *A Journey in the Seabord Slave States in the Years 1853–1854, with remarks as to their economy*, 2 vols. New York: G. P. Putnam's and Sons, 1904.

————, *The Cotton Kingdom*, 2 vols. New York: Mason Brothers, 1861.

Parker, A. A., *Trip to the West and Texas, 1834–1835*. Concord, New Hampshire: White and Fisher, 1835.

Potter, Eliza, *A Hairdresser's Experience in High Life*. Cincinnati, Ohio: Published for the Author, 1859.

Robertson, James A. (editor), *Louisiana Under the Rule of Spain, France, and the United States, 1785–1807. Social, Economic and Political Conditions of the Territory Represented in the Louisiana Purchase as Portrayed in hitherto Unpublished Contemporary Accounts by Doctor Paul Alliot and various Spanish, French, English, and American Officials*, 2 vols. Cleveland, Ohio: Arthur H. Clark Company, 1911.

Semmes, John E. (editor), *John H. B. Latrobe and His Times, 1803–1891*. Baltimore, Maryland: Norman, Remington, Company, 1917.

Shippe, Lester B. (editor), *Bishop Whipple's Southern Diary, 1843–1844*. Minneapolis: University of Minnesota Press, 1937.

Stuart, James, *Three Years in North America*, 2 vols. New York: J. and J. Harper, 1833.

Sullivan, Edward, *Rambles and Scrambles in North and South America*. London: Richard Bentley, 1853.

PAMPHLETS AND DIRECTORIES

Bogaerts, Rev. Joseph, *Convent of the Holy Family; Golden Jubilee of the Sisters of the Holy Family.* New Orleans; n.p., 1892.

Cathcart, William (editor), *The Baptist Encyclopaedia, A Dictionary of the Doctrines, Ordinances, Usage, Confessions of Faith, Sufferings, Labors, and Successes, and of the Central History of the Baptist Denomination in all Lands with Numerous Biographical Sketches of Distinguished American and Foreign Baptist, and a Supplement,* 2 vols. Philadelphia: Louis H. Everts, 1881.

Champomier, P. A., *Statement of the Sugar Crop of Louisiana.* [1844–1861] New Orleans: Cook, Young, and Company, 1844–1861.

Henry, Adolphe and Gerodias, Victor, *The Louisiana Coast Directory, of the right and left banks of the Mississippi River, from its mouth to Baton Rouge, Also, of the Bayou Lafourche, with the distances from New Orleans. Accompanied by a full index. Compiled in the Spring of 1857, from actual measurement and personal canvassing.* New Orleans: E. C. Warton, 1857.

Rainey, W. H. (compiler), *A Mygatt and Company's* [New Orleans] *Directory for 1857.* New Orleans: L. Pesson and B. Simon, 1857.

Walker, David, *Walker's Appeal in Four Articles Together with a Preamble to the Colored Citizens of the World. But in Particular and Very Expressly to those of the United States of America.* Boston: n.p. 1830.

CONTEMPORARY BOOKS

Barde, Alexandre, *Histoire des Comités de Vigilance aux Attakapas.* Saint-Jean-Baptiste, Louisiane: *Meschacebe et de l'Avant-Coureur,* 1816.

Hosmer, H. L., *Adela, The Octoroon*, Columbus, Ohio: Follett, Foster, and Company, 1860.

Lanusse, Armand (compiler), *Les Cenelles. Choix de Poesies indigenes*. Nouvelle Orleans: H. Lauve et Compagnie, 1845.

Nott, Josiah C., and Gliddon, George R., *Types of Mankind: or, Ethnological Researches, Based Upon the Ancient Monuments, Paintings, Sculptures, and Crania of Races, and upon their Natural, Geographical, Philological, and Biblical History: illustrated by selections from the inedited papers of Samuel George Morton, M. D., and by additional contributions from Prof. L. Agassiz, L. L. D.,; W. Usher, M. D.; and Prof. H. S. Patterson, M. D.* Philadelphia: Lippincott, Grambo and Company, 1854.

SPECIAL MONOGRAPHS

Baudier, Roger, *The Catholic Church in Louisiana*. New Orleans: A. W. Hyatt Company, 1939.

Burson, Caroline M., *The Stewardship of Don Esteban Miro, 1782–1792*. New Orleans: American Printing Company, 1940.

Caughey, John W., *Bernardo de Galvez in Louisiana*. Berkeley, California: University of California, 1939.

Chambon, C. M., *In and Around the Old St. Louis Cathedral of New Orleans*. New Orleans: Philippe's Printery, 1908.

Desdunes, Rodolphe L., *Nos Hommes et Nôtre Histoire, Notices biographiques accompagnées de reflexions et de souvenirs personnels*. Montreal, Canada: Arbour et Dupont, 1911.

Durham, John P. and Ramond, John S. (editors), *Baptist Builders in Louisiana*. Shreveport, Louisiana: Art Craft Press, 1934.

Franklin, John H., *The Free Negro in North Carolina*. Chapel Hill, North Carolina: The University of North Carolina Press, 1943.

Frazier, E. Franklin, *The Free Negro Family A Study of Family Origins before the Civil War*. Nashville, Tennessee: Fisk University Press, 1932.

Hicks, William, *History of Louisiana Negro Baptists from 1804 to 1914*. Nashville, Tennessee: Baptist Publishing Board, n.d.

Paxton, Rev. William E., *A History of the Baptists of Louisiana from the Earliest Times to the Present*. St. Louis: C. R. Barnes Company, 1888.

Roussève, Charles B., *The Negro in Louisiana Aspects of His History and His Literature*. New Orleans: The Xavier University Press, 1937.

Russell, John H., *The Free Negro in Virginia, 1619–1865*. Baltimore, Maryland: The Johns Hopkins Press, 1913.

Shugg, Roger W., *Origins of Class Struggle in Louisiana A Social History of White Farmers and Laborers during Slavery and After, 1840–1875*. Baton Rouge: Louisiana State University Press, 1939.

Treudley, Mary, *The United States and Santo Domingo, 1789–1866*. Washington, D. C.: n.p., 1918.

Wright, James M., *The Free Negro in Maryland, 1634–1860*. New York: Columbia University Press, 1921.

GENERAL WORKS:

Eaton, Clement, *A History of the Old South*. New York: The Macmillan Company, 1949.

Ficklen, John R., *History and Civil Government of Louisiana*. Chicago: Werner School Book Company, 1901.

Fortier, Alcée, *A History of Louisiana*, 4 vols. New York: Manzi, Joyant and Company, 1904.

Gayarré, Charles E., *History of Louisiana*, 4 vols. New Orleans: F. F. Hansell and Brothers, 1903.

King, Grace, *New Orleans, the Place and the People*. New York: The Macmillan Company, 1915.

Phelps, Albert, *Louisiana, A Record of Expansion*. New York: Houghton, Mifflin and Company, 1905.

Phillips, Ulrich B., *American Negro Slavery A Survey of the Supply, Employment and Control of Negro Labor as Determined by the Plantation Regime.* New York: D. Appleton and Company, 1928.

Rightor, Henry, *Standard History of New Orleans, Louisiana.* Chicago, Illinois: Lewis Publishing Company, 1900.

Sitterson, J. Carlyle, *Sugar Country The Cane Sugar Industry in the South, 1753–1950.* Lexington, Kentucky: The University of Kentucky Press, 1953.

THESES AND DISSERTATIONS

Borgia, Sister Mary Frances, A History of the Congregation of the Sisters of the Holy Family of New Orleans. B.A. Thesis, Xavier University of New Orleans, Typescript in University Library, 1931.

Everett, Donald E., The Free Persons of Color in New Orleans, 1803–1865. Ph.D. Dissertation, Tulane University, Typescript in Howard-Tilton Memorial Library, 1952.

McGowan, Emma, Free People of Color in New Orleans. M.A. Thesis, Tulane University, Typescript in Howard-Tilton Memorial Library, 1939.

Index